The Emergence of Modern Lithuania

STUDIES OF THE RUSSIAN INSTITUTE

COLUMBIA UNIVERSITY

ALFRED ERICH SENN

The Emergence of
Modern Lithuania

1959

Columbia University Press
Morningside Heights   New York

The transliteration system for Russian words and names used in this work is based on the Library of Congress system with some modifications. Polish and Lithuanian personal names and words have been left in their original form.

In many cases the names of cities are a matter of dispute, and a great deal of significance is attached to whether a writer says "Wilno" or "Vilnius." In order to avoid this problem, I have used the forms of geographic names to be found in the *Columbia Lippincott Gazetteer of the World.*

Copyright © 1959 Columbia University Press, New York

Published in Great Britain, Canada, India, and Pakistan
by the Oxford University Press
London, Toronto, Bombay, and Karachi

Library of Congress Catalog Card Number: 59-6606
Manufactured in the United States of America

The Russian Institute of Columbia University

THE RUSSIAN INSTITUTE was established by Columbia University in 1946 to serve two major objectives: the training of a limited number of well qualified Americans for scholarly and professional careers in the field of Russian studies, and the development of research in the social sciences and the humanities as they relate to Russia and the Soviet Union. The research program of the Russian Institute is conducted through the efforts of its faculty members, of scholars invited to participate as Senior Fellows in its program, and of candidates for the Certificate of the Institute and for the degree of Doctor of Philosophy. Some of the results of the research program are presented in the Studies of the Russian Institute of Columbia University. The faculty of the Institute, without necessarily agreeing with the conclusions reached in the Studies, believe that their publication advances the difficult task of promoting systematic research on Russia and the Soviet Union and public understanding of the problems involved.

The faculty of the Russian Institute are grateful to the Rockefeller Foundation for the financial assistance which it has given to the program of research and publication.

Studies of the Russian Institute

To my Parents

Preface

LITHUANIA as a national state arose out of the turmoil following the collapse of the Russian Empire in 1917. Although the Russian revolutions of 1917 and their aftermath have been subjected to a great deal of detailed investigation, there still remains much to be learned about the specific reasons for the failure or success of the attempts by the various border nationalities to form their own independent states. The case of each nationality must be considered individually, for each case had its own particular circumstances.

In November, 1918, Lithuania was a state only on paper. It had no administration or army, and even the existence of a Lithuanian nation was disputed. By 1920 the Lithuanian national community was generally recognized as a reality, and although the country's frontiers were not yet settled, Lithuania had a duly elected government which had received at least *de facto* recognition from all the major countries of the world but the United States. The story of how Lithuania became a state is the one this study attempts to tell.

It is a somewhat audacious undertaking to try to reconstruct an era of which one was not a part, but which is still remembered well by many. Therefore it is my pleasant duty here to express my indebtedness and thanks to the many persons who have helped me in one way or another in preparing this study: Professor Philip E. Mosely, my guide throughout my graduate studies, Professor Oscar Halecki, Professor Charles E. Seymour, Professor Otakar Odlozilik, Professor Mykolas Biržiška, Professor Juozas Kaminskas, Dr. Julius J. Bielskis, Consul Jonas Budrys, Mr. Anicetas Simutis, Dr. Vincas Maciunas, Dr. Kostas

Preface

Ostrauskas, and Mr. Witold Sworakowski. I am especially indebted to my father, Professor Alfred Senn, for sharing with me
his vast knowledge of Lithuanian affairs. I would also like to
thank the staffs of the University of Pennsylvania Library,
Philadelphia; the Hoover Library on War, Revolution, and
Peace, Stanford, California; the University of Warsaw Library,
Warsaw; Biblioteka Narodowa, Warsaw; Bibliothèque Nationale, Paris; the British Museum, London; the National Archives, Washington, D. C.; the New York Public Library; the
Philadelphia Public Library; the Columbia University Library,
New York; Yale University Library, New Haven, Connecticut;
the University of Illinois Library, Champaign; and the maga-
zine *Lithuanian Days*, Los Angeles. This study was completed under a fellowship granted by the Ford Foundation.

The conclusions, opinions, and other statements in this study,
unless otherwise noted, are my own and are not necessarily those
of any of the persons named above.

In conclusion, I would also like to express my gratitude to the
Nida Press, London, for permission to translate at length pass-
ages from their collection *Pirmasis nepriklausomos Lietuvos dešimtmetis.*

ALFRED ERICH SENN

Rutgers University
Newark, New Jersey
October, 1958

Contents

The Emergence of Modern Lithuania

I

The Development of Lithuanian Nationalism

As THE clocks in Vilna struck midnight on November 2, 1918, the Lithuanian Taryba completed the third and final reading of the Provisional Constitution of Lithuania. The preamble proclaimed:

Until the establishment by the Constituent Assembly of a permanent government and of a Constitution for the Lithuanian State, the Lithuanian State Council, in its capacity as the supreme power of the Lithuanian State (*summa potestas*), establishes its government on the basis of the following provisional laws.[1]

Now the Provisional Government of Lithuania, the Taryba—its full title was Lietuvos Valstybės Taryba, or Lithuanian State Council—based its claims to sovereignty on the declaration of independence which it had issued on December 11, 1917, and on the recognition of that declaration by the German government on March 23, 1918.[2] Its mandate, however, was not generally recognized, and not the least of the reasons for this lay in the character of the Taryba itself. Organized under the watchful eye of the German occupation authorities in September, 1917, the Taryba had found its every move severely restricted, and even in November, 1918, it had neither an administration nor an army. In fact, until about two weeks before the meeting of November 2, the Germans had refused to recognize its right to any independent political action and had even opposed its assumption of the title "State Council."

In promulgating the constitution of November 2, the Taryba assumed the role of governing organ of the nascent Lithuanian

[1] Klimas, *L'état lituanien*, p. 250. See also M. Yčas, "Lietuvos vyriausybės sudarymo etapai," in *Pirmasis dešimtmetis*, I, 80.

[2] Smetona at the Lausanne Lithuanian Conference, September 9, 1918. Stenograms of the conference (mimeographed), Šaulys Archives, f. 30.

national state. Criticized by some as a German puppet, by others as ungrateful to its German "benefactors," the Taryba has also had its defenders, who praise it for its seizure of the right moment to realize Lithuanian national ambitions. Actually the members of the Taryba simply followed the traditional Lithuanian course through the troubled waters of Eastern European political and national conflicts. But to gain an understanding of the problems the Lithuanians faced in 1918, we must first examine the previous development of the Lithuanian national movement and discover how the Taryba came to lead that movement.

THE ROOTS OF LITHUANIAN NATIONALISM

Because of the Germans' favorable policy toward the Lithuanians during the First World War, the charge has been made that the Lithuanian nationality was "invented in Berlin in 1916."[3] This assertion is unfounded, but it does point to an element of great importance in the development of the Lithuanian national consciousness, namely, the environment in which it developed— the mutual rivalries and antagonisms between the Germans, the Russians, and the Poles. Based mainly on a distinct language, Lithuanian nationalism is not open to the charge of being a creation out of whole cloth, but its character and the manner of its growth unquestionably were determined not only by internal factors, but also by the role which it assumed or which was bestowed upon it in the interplay of the rival nationalisms in the Baltic area.

At the beginning of the twentieth century, there was no political entity bearing the name Lithuania. The area inhabited by the Lithuanian nation was divided between the German and the Russian empires. The main body of Lithuanians, numbering some 2 to 2½ million, lived within the borders of the Russian Empire, comprising a majority in the guberniyas of Kaunas and

_____

[3] Johannet, *Le principe des nationalités*, p. xlvii. A writer in *Le Temps* (February 1, 1919) asserted, "It has been proven that Lithuanian separatism has been artificially created by the Germans."

Suwalki, and a significant minority in the guberniyas of Vilna and Courland. These territories, making up so-called "Lithuania Major," were under three different regional administrations within the Empire; Vilna and Kaunas were part of the Northwest Territory, Courland was one of the Baltic Provinces, and Suwalki was included in the Polish Kingdom (created by the Congress of Vienna in 1815). So far as the Russian government was concerned, "Lithuania" did not exist. "Lithuania Minor" refers to that part of East Prussia inhabited by about 200,000 Lithuanians. The "two Lithuanias" had been separated for centuries. The Prussian Lithuanians had been historically linked with the Germans and were Protestant, whereas the Russian

Lithuanians had been historically linked with the Poles and were Roman Catholic. Nevertheless there was a sense of kinship between the two groups, which cooperated extensively in the development of a national culture. An important role in Lithuanian national life was also played by the emigration, estimated at anywhere between 800,000 and 2,000,000, which had been directed mainly to the United States.

Lithuania Major. The center of the Lithuanian national movement was naturally in Russian Lithuania, where the majority of the Lithuanians lived. But here the historical spread of Polish culture into Lithuania presented a major block to the development of a Lithuanian national consciousness. In the course of the union between Lithuania and Poland from 1386 to 1795, the upper classes in Lithuania, having largely adopted Polish culture and the Polish language, had abandoned their role as leaders of the Lithuanian community and now considered themselves part of a greater Polish cultural area. Hence their loyalty was to the Polish, rather than to the Lithuanian, national idea.

Although Lithuanian national feeling grew to significant strength only in the latter part of the nineteenth century, there were earnests of the Lithuanian national idea in the first half of the century, largely among the lesser gentry in Samogitia.[4] This stemmed directly from the influence of the German Romantics, whose philological interests gave Lithuanian, hitherto a despised peasant dialect, new stature as an ancient and honorable language, and from the reaction to the intense Polish nationalism which was manifested at the University of Vilna (closed by the Russian authorities after the rising of 1831).[5] Polish nationalism in Lithuania was also a direct stimulant to its Lithuanian counterpart through its glorification of earlier Lithuanian history, even though writers, such as Adam Mickiewicz, regarded Lithuania as Polish.[6] The stratification of the rival national ideas along lines of social cleavage served to intensify the conflict be-

---

[4] See Alseika, *Lietuvių tautinė idėja*, pp. 28-32.

[5] See Römer'is, *Litwa*, p. 56; Vladimirovas *et al.*, *Vilniaus Universitetas*, pp. 43 ff.

[6] Maciunas, "Adam Mickiewicz in Lithuanian Literature," in Lednicki (ed.), *Adam Mickiewicz*, pp. 383-97.

tween the two, a fact reflected, perhaps to an exaggerated extent, in the growing Lithuanian literature.[7]

The Lithuanian national movement received great impetus from the emancipation of the Russian peasantry in 1861 and from the anti-Polish policies of the tsarist government after the Polish and Lithuanian insurrection of 1863. That insurrection "marked the last time that Lithuanians fought under Polish leadership against the Russian world and for the reestablishment of a united Polish-Lithuanian political structure."[8] With the rapid development of Lithuanian nationalism in the years after the emancipation, the Lithuanians turned away from their earlier ties with Poland and sought to establish their separate identity. At the same time, the Russians followed a policy of "divide and conquer," seeking to prevent what might be called a natural alliance between the Poles and the Lithuanians against the culturally alien Russian rule by playing upon the differences between the two competing nationalisms. Although the Russian regime under Mikhail N. Muraviev and his successors was oppressive toward the Lithuanians, it indirectly gave aid to the national movement through its policy of encouraging the Lithuanians to set themselves apart from all things Polish.[9]

Russian policy after 1863 was aimed first of all at weakening the Polish landlords. Thus it gave the Lithuanian and Polish peasants much better terms on which to purchase land from the lords' estates than were given to the peasants elsewhere in Russia.[10] In an effort to break down the cultural bonds between the Poles and the Lithuanians, the Russians sought to convert the Lithuanians to the use of the Cyrillic alphabet by banning

---

[7] See S. R. Steinmetz, *De Nationaliteiten in Europa* (Amsterdam, 1920), p. 360.

[8] Hellmann, "Die litauische Nationalbewegung," *Zeitschrift für Ostforschung*, II (1953), 78.

[9] Some Lithuanian writers argue that the Russian oppression aided the process of Polonization of Lithuania. See Alseika, *Lietuvių tautinė idėja*, pp. 33 ff. Although the oppression by the Russians may have forced some Lithuanians to unite more closely with the Poles, the economic favors granted the peasantry were probably more important in the long run in encouraging Lithuanian nationalism.

[10] See Robinson, *Rural Russia*, pp. 85 ff.; Harrison, *Lithuania*, pp. 55-61; Chase, *Lithuania*, pp. 226-35. The Russians later expected loyalty from the Lithuanians in return for this "aid." See Miliukov, *Natsional'nyi vopros*, p. 156.

the printing of Lithuanian works in Latin characters. This aim
was not realized, and the measure amounted to a prohibition of
Lithuanian printing in Russia. However, publications in Lithuanian produced at Tilsit in East Prussia, were smuggled regularly into Russian Lithuania. It was during this period of the press
ban that the modern orthography, based on the Czech alphabet,
was introduced, replacing the old style which had been based on
Polish spellings.[11]

Their language was one of the two major factors in establishing
the national identity of the Lithuanians, while religion was the
other. But neither of these two is a definitive criterion for Lithuanian nationality. Indeed there is no definitive criterion. The
religion of the majority of the Russian Lithuanians, Roman
Catholicism, was neither an inclusive nor an exclusive characteristic of Lithuanian nationals. The Poles were also Catholic, and
in fact, religion was the closest bond between the two nations.
The Poles claimed credit for the Christianization of Lithuania, a
condition of the marriage contract of Krevo in 1385 between the
Lithuanian Grand Duke Jagiełło (Lith. Jogaila) and the Polish
Queen Jadwiga. In the nineteenth century many Lithuanians
began to criticize the historic religious ties as having been abused
by the Poles to promote their own selfish interests in Lithuania,
and some efforts were made to persuade Rome to grant the
Lithuanians a separate national ecclesiastical organization.[12]
But not all the Lithuanian national leaders were Catholic. Martynas Yčas was a Calvinist, the Prussian Lithuanians, such as
W. Gaigalat, were Lutherans, and, of course, the socialists were
anticlerical and even militantly atheistic.

Community of language is the most important factor in
Lithuanian nationalism, although to many nationalists Lithuanian was a second language, with Polish the real "mother
tongue." Language, the original objective difference between the

---

[11] The Prussian Lithuanians had used German script. For an account of the
development of the literary language, see Alfred Senn, "Standard Lithuanian in the
Making," *The Slavonic and East European Review*, XXII (1944), 102-16. On the
Russian school system, see Matušas, *Lietuvių rusinimas*.

[12] See Römer'is, *Litwa*, p. 15; Propolanis, *Polskie Apostolstwo*.

two nationalities, became the rallying point for the national idea. Krėvė, perhaps Lithuania's greatest literary figure, had the bard Dundys declaim in the drama *Šarūnas* (1911):

> Let the warriors use their swords. We, brothers, will go forth into the wide world on narrow paths, on broad boulevards, we will go from border to border, wherever Lithuanians live, and we will proclaim: one sun in the sky, one fatherland on earth, one ruler for all the land in which the holy language of our fathers is heard![13]

Language was also the connecting link between the Russian and the Prussian Lithuanians. But that it alone was not enough as a basis for a common culture is shown by the troubles the young Lithuanian state experienced in the 1920s trying to assimilate the Protestant Memellanders.[14]

The problems involved in using language as a criterion of nationality are to be seen in the attitude of the Lithuanians toward the Polonized upper class. The Lithuanian writings on this question range from condemnations of the nobility for its linguistic apostasy to pleas for its return to the fold. Lazdynų Pelėda, in her short story *A Sad Incident* (*Nesmagus atsitikimas*, 1911), told of a Polonized Lithuanian, who, having died, discovers that all souls in heaven are grouped by language. He is rejected by the Poles for his bad grammar and in turn refuses to join the Lithuanians, whom he considers inferior. Man's mission being the glorification of God, this unfortunate soul is condemned for his renunciation of "your father, your mother, your brothers, love of your country, and the dearest gift of the Holy Ghost to every honorable man—your native language."[15] Lithuanian writers generally tended to consider language as being something innate, and so continually exhorted the Polonized elements of the population to return to "the language of your blood."[16]

In fact, there could really be no objective criteria for determining whether a bilingual person was a Lithuanian or a Pole.

---

[13] Vincas Krėvė-Mickevičius, *Raštai* (Works) (Kaunas, 1923), V, 278.

[14] See Markwardt, "Der Vielvölkerstaat," in *Litauen und seine Deutschen*, pp. 49-72.

[15] Lazdynų Pelėda, *Raštai* (Works) (Kaunas, 1922), II, 182.

[16] See Chase, *Lithuania*, p. 252.

In the final accounting, this was to be decided by the personal inclinations of the individual and by nothing else. Thus we find a case such as that of the Narutavičius (Lithuanian form) or Narutowicz (Polish form) brothers, one of whom was a member of the Lithuanian Taryba while the other later became president of Poland.

With the emancipation of the serfs of the Russian Empire in 1861, the guiding spirit of the Lithuanian national awakening, the new intelligentsia, came largely from among the peasants. The center of the movement shifted southward across the Neman River into Suwalki *guberniya*, and the new leaders, such as Dr. Jonas Basanavičius and Vincas Kudirka, are somewhat humorously referred to by the linguistically hybrid term "Zanemunčikai" (Transnemanites).

Most well-to-do peasants felt that the only fit occupations for their sons were farming and the priesthood. For prestige, and also for economic reasons— such as providing for old age—every peasant who could possibly do so tried to educate one son for the clergy. This benefited the Lithuanian national movement in two ways: the priests themselves made great contributions to the formation of a national intelligentsia, and they also aided in educating relatives who might otherwise have been denied the opportunity. Perhaps through the wisdom of experience, the priests were not very demanding in prescribing the course of study for their protégés, with the result that a great many radicals were put through school by members of the clergy. The clergy cannot, of course, be regarded as a national unit, for in it, too, the national question caused divisions. Some Polish writers have considered the Lithuanian priests the backbone of anti-Polish feeling in Lithuania.[17] But some Lithuanian writers have attacked the clergy as the stronghold of Polonism in Lithuania.[18] Nevertheless, those priests who regarded themselves as Lithuanians, such as Father Juozas Tumas-Vaižgantas, were fervent nationalists, and the persecution of the Catholic religion by the

---

[17] See Wasilewski, *Litwa i Białoruś*, pp. 205-6.
[18] See Bagdonas, *Iš mūsų kovų ir žygių*, p. 8.

Russian government united the priests with the liberals and even the anticlerical radicals in their opposition to the tsarist regime.

The importance of the clergy was heightened by the fact that they were the only segment of the national intelligentsia which had some assurance of being allowed to remain in Lithuania. Many intellectuals in secular pursuits were sent to other parts of Russia, where "they passed away without being of any use to their nation."[19] After 1905, however, the local Russian authorities were much more sympathetic toward Lithuanian aspirations, finding them increasingly useful against the Poles, and they made special efforts to provide jobs for Lithuanians in Vilna and Kaunas guberniyas.

As early as April, 1904, the Russian government, at the urging of the Governor General of Vilna, Prince Sviatopolk-Mirskii, eased its Russification campaign and removed the ban on the use of the Latin alphabet in Lithuania. Actually Lithuanian publications had already been pouring into Russian Lithuania in great numbers from Tilsit and from the United States as contraband. In the period from 1900 to 1902, over 56,000 copies of various Lithuanian books and pamphlets were confiscated by the Russian police at the border. The penalty for smuggling was exile to Siberia, and the smugglers, *knygnešiai* (book carriers), became great national heroes.[20]

Despite this relaxation, the Lithuanians took an active part in the Revolution of 1905 in Russia. They engaged in widespread rioting, both for political or economic reasons, and just for the sake of rioting, at the instigation of the so-called *giltininkai* (death gangs).[21]

Much more important for the Lithuanians than the violence was the peaceful political movement, culminating in the Grand Vilna Congress, held in December, 1905. This meeting, the only national congress held in Russia in that year, was attended by

---

[19] Biržiška, *Lietuvių tautos kelias*, I, 115.
[20] See Šapoka (ed.), *Lietuvos istorija*, p. 513.
[21] On the events of 1905 in Lithuania, see Römer'is, *Litwa*, pp. 339-436.

over two thousand Lithuanians from all parts of Russia and from abroad. The congress affirmed its support for a manifesto which had been issued by Lithuanian leaders in Vilna in October, 1905, demanding "autonomy for Lithuania with a Diet in Vilna, elected by general, equal, direct, and secret ballot, without racial, national, or religious discrimination."[22]

To realize these demands, the congress called on the people not to pay taxes, to fight the liquor monopoly, and to boycott Russian institutions. The immediate result of these demands was action by the Governor General of Vilna, Freze, who allowed Lithuanian to be taught in the elementary schools and granted other rights. (But the reforms were limited, as is shown by the biting speeches of Antanas Povylius and Andrius Bulata in the Russian Duma on May 15, 1907, calling for freedom of national education and defending private teaching.[23]) The Lithuanians of Suwalki demanded that their province be joined to the other Lithuanian guberniyas, and they refused to pay taxes. The Russian authorities imposed martial law, and it took three days to restore order in the region.[24] Freze's first concessions were followed shortly by repressions, and, as one writer stated in 1910, "It may be said that our revolutionary period came to an end in 1907."[25]

After 1905 the Lithuanian leaders worked strictly within the officially allowed limits of the Russian political system. Deputies were dutifully elected to the newly established Russian parliament, the State Duma, and sent to St. Petersburg. In order to insure the election of their own candidates, the Lithuanians in Kaunas made a deal with the Jews, whereby, in return for Jewish backing of Lithuanian candidates, the Lithuanians would support one Jewish candidate. There were seven Lithuanian deputies each in the First and Second Dumas, and after Stolypin's re-

---

[22] Quoted in *ibid.*, p. 393.
[23] *Gosudarstvennaia Duma* (1907), Vol. II, 15/v—II, cols. 554-62.
[24] Šapoka (ed.), *Lietuvos istorija*, pp. 517-18.
[25] Šešėis (pseud. of Mykolas Biržiška), " 'Pirmeivių' darbas ir vis. demokratai," (The Social Democrats and the Work of the "Progressives"), *Visuomenė* (Society), I (1910), 113.

vision of the electoral law in 1907, four each in the Third and Fourth, all coming from Suwalki and Kaunas guberniyas.

The Lithuanian political leaders at the turn of the century have been justly described as "generals without armies."[26] The Lithuanian deputies to the Duma joined parties there according to their personal inclinations, and not through direct connections between their local political groups and the parties in the capital.[27] Individually the Lithuanians had some success. Andrius Bulata was the chairman of the Bureau of the Trudoviki in the Third Duma, while Martynas Yčas became a high-ranking Kadet in the Fourth Duma and served as Vice Minister of Education in the L'vov cabinet of March, 1917. But the deputies were able to accomplish little for Lithuanian national interests. Yčas complained that in the Fourth Duma he found that, to the Kadets, the "national question" still meant only the Poles and the Jews.[28] The Lithuanian deputies remained aloof from the bloc of nationalities for fear of Polish domination and limited themselves to demanding certain national rights in Vilna and Kaunas, and protection of Lithuanians in Suwalki against Polish encroachments.

In Lithuania itself after 1905 the Lithuanians were making great advances culturally, although their political rights were limited. Local self-government in the form of zemstvos was still denied them by the central government "lest with the economic preponderance in the region of the Polish element, the zemstvos fall completely into the hands of the Poles and serve as a strong weapon for the Polonization of the Russian population."[29] In cultural affairs, however, the Lithuanians enjoyed the benevolent patronage of local Russian officials who had a strong anti-Polish orientation.

The Lithuanians organized a number of societies, one of the most important of which was the Lietuvių Mokslo Draugija

[26] Šapoka (ed.), *Lietuvos istorija*, p. 519.

[27] See Martynas Yčas's account of how he joined the Kadets in his *Atsiminimai*, I, 61. [28] *Ibid.*, I, 165.

[29] *Natsionalisty v 3-ei Gosudarstvennoi Dume* (The Nationalists in the Third State Duma) (St. Petersburg, 1912), pp. 96-97.

(Lithuanian Scientific Society), founded by Dr. Basanavičius in 1907 at Vilna. Its aim was to collect material on all phases of Lithuanian history, both to preserve the material and to publicize it.[30] The first Lithuanian consumer cooperative was formed in 1900; by 1910 there were about 120; and as of January 1, 1915, there were 161.[31]

The first nationally minded Lithuanian newspaper, *Aušra* (Dawn), was founded at Tilsit in 1883, under the editorship of Dr. Basanavičius, who has been called the "patriarch of the Lithuanian national renaissance."[32] *Aušra* fell by the wayside in 1886, and in 1889 *Varpas* (Bell) began publication as a channel for more radical views. Both newspapers left their mark in Lithuanian literature: "*Aušra* was a stimulus to romanticism, while *Varpas* brought out writers of the realistic school."[33]

In the 1890s and the early years of the twentieth century, a number of other newspapers were founded which served as organs of embryonic parties. *Tėvynės Sargas* (Guardian of the Fatherland) was Catholic and conservative; *Darbininkų Balsas* (Workers' Voice) was Social Democratic and internationalist, although it had a strong admixture of nationalist sentiments; and *Lietuvių Ukininkas* (The Lithuanian Farmer) represented the Liaudininkai (Populists), the Lithuanian version of the Russian *narodniki*. The connection between these newspapers and the parties of 1918 and 1920 is to be found in the individuals behind the publications: Tumas-Vaižgantas with *Tėvynės Sargas;* Jurgis Šaulys and Mykolas Sleževičius with *Lietuvių Ukininkas;* Steponas Kairys, Mykolas Biržiška, Vincas Mickevičius-Kapsukas, and even Felix Dzerzhinskii with *Darbininkų Balsas.*[34]

[30] The Lithuanian societies found themselves in lively competition with corresponding Polish groups. See Puzinas, *Vorgeschichtsforschung*, pp. 93-98.

[31] Viscont, *La Lituanie et la guerre*, p. 98. See also Simutis, *Economic Reconstruction of Lithuania*, pp. 32-33.

[32] On the background of the publication of *Aušra*, see Römer'is, *Litwa*, pp. 87-88. Basanavičius's role in the Lithuanian national movement has now been recognized by the Communists; in Varna, Bulgaria, where Basanavičius lived for a while in exile, there is a street bearing his name.

[33] Vaičiulaitis, *Lithuanian Literature*, p. 28.

[34] For accounts of the activities and politics of the newspapers, see Hellmann, "Die litauische Nationalbewegung," *Zeitschrift für Ostforschung*, II (1953), 66 ff.; Römer'is *Litwa*, pp. 156 ff.

In general, from 1905 to the outbreak of the First World War, the Lithuanians followed a course of cooperation with the Russian government. The use of violence to gain political ends fell into disfavor as a result of the repressions after 1905. In 1907, Antanas Smetona wrote, "Without culture not even a strike will be of any use. Blow on the thermometer all you want, but you will not heat a cold house. The inflated mercury will show an untrue measure of warmth."[35] The Lithuanians did not abandon the hope of eventual independence, but they did realize their own weaknesses and now were concentrating on strengthening the national movement.

In 1909 one Russian observer came to the conclusion that the program of the Lithuanian nationalists was not a threat to the unity of Russia. The Russian liberals, he continued, could take the movement under their wing simply by rejecting the policy of Russification, which really only served to arouse separatist sentiments.[36] There is much truth in this appraisal. The immediate goal of the Russian Lithuanians after 1905 was autonomy; the idea of independence was a distant dream. It was not until after the March Revolution in 1917 that the program was altered.

Lithuania Minor. The history of Lithuania Minor followed a completely different course from that of Lithuania Major. The line of separation between the two had been set up by the Treaty of Melno in 1422 between the Teutonic Knights and the Grand Duchy of Lithuania, after the famous battle of Tannenberg in 1410 had allowed Vytautas to recapture Samogitia for the grand duchy.[37] The division made at this time stood until 1919, except for the brief period from 1795 to 1807, when Prussia also held Suwalki as a result of the third partition of the Polish-Lithuanian

[35] Antanas Smetona, *Vienybės gairėmis* (For Unity) (Kaunas, 1930), p. 20.

[36] A. L. Pogodin, "Litovskii vopros v nastoiashchee vremia" (The Lithuanian Question at the Present Time), *Russkaia Mysl'* (Russian Thought), December, 1909, pp. 86-87.

[37] In a letter to Emperor Sigismund in 1420, Vytautas justified the conquest of Samogitia on the grounds that the population was Lithuanian. *Codex epistolaris Vitoldi Magni Ducis Lithuaniae*, edited by Antoni Prochaska (Cracow, 1882), p. 467.

state.[38] While Lithuanian authors usually claim that Lithuanians inhabited East Prussia before the establishment of the rule of the Teutonic Knights, there is evidence that Lithuanian settlement grew there only after 1422 as a result of the colonization policy of the Knights, who invited settlers from Lithuania.[39]

In the sixteenth century the "two Lithuanias" were further isolated from each other by the Reformation, when the Prussian Duke Albrecht adopted Lutheranism in 1525. Yet the Reformation also aided the development of the Lithuanian national consciousness by making Lithuanian a written language. Both Protestant and Catholic Reformers sought to reach the peasant in his own tongue.[40] In order to produce loyal leadership for the Prussian Lithuanians, the Prussian duke established a program of Lithuanian studies at Königsberg, even inviting students from the Lithuanian grand duchy.

A third major event in the history of Lithuania Minor was the plague of 1708-11, the same plague that crippled Charles XII before Poltava. Both Lithuania Major and Lithuania Minor suffered tremendously,[41] but it was in Prussia that the consequences were eventually more important for the Lithuanian national movement. King Frederick William I sought to make good the losses in Lithuania Minor by colonizing Germans and Swiss in the area. One result was a great improvement in agricultural methods; another, more important here, was a reduction in the proportion of Lithuanians in the population.

In the latter part of the nineteenth century, under Bismarck, there was a Germanization campaign, just as there was a Russi-

[38] In 1807, Napoleon made Suwalki part of the Duchy of Warsaw, and it was through this move that Suwalki was separated administratively from the rest of the Lithuanian territories in the Russian Empire.

[39] See Gertrud Mortensen, *Beiträge zu den Nationalitäten- und Siedlungsverhältnissen in Preussisch-Litauen* (Berlin, 1927); Wielhorski, "Warunki rozwoju świadomości narodowej Litwinów," in *Pamiętnik VI Powszechnego Zjazdu Historyków Polskich*, p. 127.

[40] See the fiery call by Canon Daukša in 1599 for wider use of the Lithuanian language in the introduction (written in Polish) to his *Postilla*; reprinted as *Daukšos Postilė* (Kaunas, 1926).

[41] See the account in J. Yčas, "Mažosios Lietuvos praeitis," in *Kovo 20 diena*, p. 52; Wilhelm Sahm, *Geschichte der Pest in Preussen* (Leipzig, 1908).

fication campaign to the East.[42] But the German manner was not so oppressive as the Russian. Publication was allowed, and, as has been noted, it was in Tilsit that most of the materials were published for smuggling into Russia. The importance of this freedom diminished after the raising of the press ban in Russia in 1904, but the presses in East Prussia continued to be used to print publications for distribution in Russian Lithuania.

Although the Prussian Lithuanians showed a definite national consciousness before 1914, it is doubtful whether, as a group, they harbored any political ambitions. The Russian Lithuanians viewed them as something like little brothers and hoped somehow to bring about unification with them. The Prussian Lithuanian leaders did support the autonomist ideas of their conationals across the border, but there was no appreciable movement for separation from East Prussia or even for autonomy.[43] Whether this was caused by genuine satisfaction with their lot in the Prussian state or just from weakness of national consciousness is not clear.

The Emigration. In the nineteenth and twentieth centuries, the emigration also played a very important role in Lithuanian national history. Although there had been some emigration for several centuries, it was only after the emancipation of the peasants in Russia, and especially after 1867-68, that the flow reached sizable proportions. Most of the emigrants were landless or small-holding peasants, who left for political or criminal reasons—often to escape military duty—or just to start life anew. Many went to other parts of Russia—Siberia, Latvia, the U-kraine. Settlements were also to be found in England, Scotland, Canada, and even Africa and Australia. But by far the major part, and politically the most important part, went to the United States.[44]

[42] See Šapoka (ed.), *Lietuvos istorija*, pp. 616-20.

[43] See Römer'is, *Litwa*, p. 87; F. A. Golder, Lithuania (House Inquiry Document No. 185, 1918, United States, National Archives), Appendix, pp. 53-54.

[44] Accounts of the various settlements can be found in the articles on the respective countries in *Lietuvių Enciklopedia* (Lithuanian Encyclopedia) (Boston, 1953-58). See also Šapoka (ed.), *Lietuvos istorija*, pp. 633 ff.

The new settlers in America each had to have thirty to fifty dollars to prove to the United States immigration officials that they could support themselves at the start, but they rarely had more than that minimum. Because of the industrial boom in the United States in the latter part of the nineteenth century, many of the immigrants found their greatest opportunities in the coal-mining regions, especially in Pennsylvania. Many others settled in such cities as New York, Boston, and Chicago. Although some went into business for themselves, setting up stores and even a few banks, most worked as hired labor. There was no appreciable tendency to buy land—the early arrivals seemed to have a definite hope of some day returning to Lithuania.[45]

The two leading figures in the early emigration to America were Father Aleksandras Burba and Jonas Šliupas. Although they at first cooperated, Šliupas's anti-Catholic attitude soon brought about conflict, and from these two sources came the Catholic and the nationalist, liberal (Tautininkai) trends in American Lithuanian politics. When Pijus Grigaitis arrived in the United States in 1911, the Lithuanian Socialists began to organize around his newspaper, *Naujienos* (News), in Chicago. In all, by 1914 there were about thirty different major organizations of Lithuanians in America. Their contributions to the national movement up to that time were mainly in the cultural field, keeping alive the idea of a Lithuanian nationality throughout the period of the persecutions in Lithuania. No political aims can be attributed to them as a national group.

LITHUANIAN NATIONALISM ON THE EVE OF THE FIRST WORLD WAR

From these various strands a definite Lithuanian national consciousness had taken shape by the eve of the First World War, although its political ambitions were still uncertain. It was strongest among the Russian Lithuanians and the Lithuanians

[45] For accounts of the American Lithuanians, see Šapoka (ed.), *Lietuvos istorija*, pp. 637 ff.; Bartuška, *Lituaniens d'Amérique;* Biržiška, "Amerikos lietuviai," in *Lietuviškoji Enciklopedia*, Vol. I, cols. 405-84; A. Kučas, "Jungtinių Amerikos Valstybių lietuviai," in *Lietuvių Enciklopedia*, X, 36-71.

in America. Its strength in East Prussia was doubtful. But despite
the fact that there was a strong national consciousness, the Lithuanians found it difficult to make their case clear to other
peoples. The grand duchy, although its leaders were Lithuanians
who spoke Lithuanian, had a Slavic majority in its population
and had even used a Slavic language akin to Belorussian as its
official tongue. Furthermore, the union with the Poles and the
consequent spread of Polish culture throughout the grand duchy
—in 1697 Polish was made the official language—made the
historical argument even weaker: "Thus there are not one or two
but four interpretations of Lithuanian history, the Polish,
Lithuanian, White Russian, and Great Russian, all four of which
can be used for the assertion of claims at the present day."[46]

The problem facing the Lithuanians in seeking recognition as
a distinct nationality can be seen in the various commentaries
made about them at this time. Arnold J. Toynbee called them
"the most backward race in Europe." Leon Dominian believed
them to be Lutherans. Nevin Winter called them "undoubtedly
Slavonic" and "divided between the Lutheran and the Orthodox
faiths." Peter Kroptkin, in an article in the *Encyclopaedia Britannica*, denied them their name, calling them just "Zhmudi" (i.e.,
Samogitians), reserving "Lithuanian" for the Slavs, although E.
Volter—a Latvian—in the Russian Brokhaus-Efron encyclopedia made a clear distinction between Lithuanians and Slavs.[47]

The task of gaining recognition was complicated by the opposition of the Poles. The idea that Lithuania was as Polish as
Warsaw had been current long before the Lithuanian movement
gained any momentum. This image proved very hard to dis-
lodge, and since frustration breeds violence, the new Lithuanian

[46] Kolarz, *Myths and Realities*, p. 111. On Lithuania before the union of 1386,
see Henryk Paszkiewicz, *The Origins of Modern Russia* (London, 1955), pp. 187-232.

[47] Arnold J. Toynbee, *Nationality and the War* (London, 1915), p. 285; Leon
Dominian, *The Frontiers of Language and Nationality in Europe* (New York, 1917),
p. 105; Nevin O. Winter, *The Russian Empire of To-Day and Yesterday* (Boston, 1913),
p. 204; *Encyclopaedia Britannica* (11th ed., 1911), XVI, 790; *Entsiklopedicheskii slovar'*
(Encyclopedia) (F. A. Brockhaus and I. A. Efron), Vol. XVII-A (St. Petersburg,
1896), cols. 827-30. See also Inorodetz (pseud. of Juozas Gabrys), *La Russie*, p. 106;
Moriez, *La question polonaise*, p. 229.

nationalism, stimulated by Polish opposition to its "separatism," soon acquired an aggressive character. As a result, Polish writers tend to criticize the Lithuanians for breaking the "solid front" against the Russians and to picture Lithuanian nationalism as being inherently aggressive.[48]

The Lithuanians were further handicapped by a lack of economic unity. Although Vilna was a large city (population 200,000), it was not the economic focal point that might have been expected. With the exception of some heavy industry in Grodno, industry in historic Lithuania was based entirely on the processing of local products such as timber, hides, and flax. The Neman River, the basin of which covers two thirds of present-day Lithuania, flowed to the sea through Prussian territory, and Memel (now Klaipeda), which controlled the outlet to the Baltic Sea, was a Prussian port. There was no great transit trade as in Latvia or Estonia. Furthermore, economic development had been deliberately hamstrung by the Russian government since Lithuania was on the Prussian border.[49]

THE LITHUANIAN QUESTION DURING THE FIRST WORLD WAR

When war broke out on August 1, 1914, the Lithuanians in Russia quickly rallied behind the tsarist government, hoping now to realize some of their political ambitions. The Lithuanian leaders in Vilna drew up a declaration which Yčas presented to the government in St. Petersburg. The declaration affirmed the loyalty of the Lithuanians and expressed the hope that Russia would now unify Lithuania Major and Lithuania Minor "not to absorb them but to make them a state in a powerful federation of nations."[50] The reaction of the Russian Prime Minister, Goremykin, dashed cold water on the ardor of the Lithuanians. After listening to Yčas read the declaration, he exclaimed, "Such nonsense! What are you really asking for?" After Yčas had pain-

---

[48] See Gorzuchowski, *Les rapports politiques*, p. 52. The Poles called Lithuanian nationalism *lituomania* and Lithuanian nationalists *lituomanes*.

[49] See Great Britain, Foreign Office, *Russian Poland, Lithuania and White Russia*, pp. 108-9.

[50] Text in Viscont, *La Lituanie et la guerre*, pp. 175-77.

fully explained that it was simply a declaration and not a petition, Goremykin thanked him, and there the matter ended.[51] Yčas read another declaration of Lithuanian loyalty in the Duma on July 26/August 8:

The Lithuanian people, on whose land have been struck the first blows, who are forced to stand in the front line, enter upon this war as on a crusade; they put aside all their resentments, hoping to see Russia free and happy after this war, and they hope that the Lithuanians, now split in two, after the smashing of the German forces, will be united under a single Russian banner.[52]

The Russian government offered the Lithuanians no sign that their hope would be fulfilled.

The Lithuanians organized several committees to handle the new problems now arising. The Lithuanian Center was set up in Vilna in August, 1914, with the participation of all political parties except the Social Democrats. The Petrograd Lithuanian Committee was immediately formed by the Center to work for Lithuanian interests in the capital. When the Germans overran Lithuania in 1915, many members of the Center remained in Vilna, and the Petrograd committee, headed by Yčas, became the chief Lithuanian group within the confines of Russia. Smetona became chairman of the Center, which was now joined by representatives from the Social Democrats.

Yčas continued his efforts in behalf of autonomy right up to the Russian Revolution of March, 1917. He claimed in his memoirs that the Kadets would have debated the issue in 1917 but for the March Revolution.[53] However, a contemporary account contradicts this statement, saying,

The Kadets in this connection have asserted that the autonomy of Lithuania is not a part of the program and that neither the Duma faction nor the Central Committee has a right to change the party program.[54]

The problems of war failed to heal the old political breaches in the national ranks. When Father Tumas called national in-

---

[51] Yčas, *Atsiminimai*, I, 230-31.
[52] *Gosudarstvennaia Duma* (July 28, 1914), p. 23.   [53] *Atsiminimai*, I, 68.
[54] *Utro Rossii* (The Morning of Russia), February 9, 1917.

dependence the first task of the people, the leftist newspaper
Lietuvos Žinios (News of Lithuania) took him severely to task,
commenting sarcastically,

To the Lithuanians the class struggle is just a fabrication by the
"cicilikai" [Socialists] and a thing, no doubt, entirely unnecessary. . . .
And this demagogy—pardon me, democrat-ism (for Father Tumas is
a democrat)—must be upheld by all means.[55]

Yet despite these efforts to be internationalist, the Lithuanian
left was opposed to the Poles on the national question, feeling
that in Lithuania—including therein Suwalki and Vilna—the
Lithuanians should have the leading role and that it was up to
the Poles to cooperate with them.[56]

Shortly after the outbreak of war, Grand Duke Nikolai
Nikolaevich of Russia promised autonomy to the Poles. The
Lithuanians viewed this move with suspicion, fearing the restoration of the boundaries of 1772. But as the war went on, this
problem faded into the background as more threatening situa-
tions arose. Since they were Roman Catholics, Lithuanians were
being registered in the Russian army as Poles. The Lithuanians
complained that the Poles were encouraging this practice: "The
Poles, it seems, cannot bring themselves to shake off the idea
that a Catholic is ipso facto a Pole."[57] Moreover, the Lithuanian
refugees from Suwalki were unable to get their demands for
another Lithuanian Catholic Church in Vilna fulfilled—there
was just one—because of Polish opposition.[58] As a corrective
measure one writer suggested a letter-writing campaign directed
to Russian newspapers in order to make the "national aims"
known:

That the Russians know too little about us is the fault of the Lithuanians
themselves: why don't they write about themselves to Russian newspapers? It would be worth while to choose small organizations whose
task it would be to inform the Russian public about Lithuanian affairs.

[55] *Lietuvos Žinios*, No. 75 (July 3, 1915).
[56] *Ibid.*, No. 183 (November 23, 1914).
[57] *Ibid.*, No. 186 (November 30, 1914). For an example of this attitude, see
Alexander Syski, *The United States of Poland* (Boston, 1919), p. 19.
[58] *Lietuvos Žinios*, No. 39 (April 8, 1915).

The Poles do this, and so the Russians know about them. The Lithuanians remain silent, and so the Russians know little about them.[59]

The fortunes of war brought a new participant into the conflict between the Poles and the Lithuanians, as the Germans occupied Vilna in the late summer of 1915. The Germans silenced the local press, replacing it with an innocuous set of official newspapers which never discussed controversial topics. The occupation authorities seemingly made a concession to the Lithuanians by organizing a separate administration for Lithuania, but their motives were undoubtedly more anti-Polish than pro-Lithuanian.[60] The Lithuanian Military District comprised all Suwalki, all Kaunas, and western Vilna, including the city of Vilna. There was some demand from the Poles to unite Lithuania with the state of Poland which had been proclaimed in November, 1916, by the Germans, but it was disregarded by the German High Command, which postponed decision on the boundaries of the Polish state and promised nothing.[61]

The Germans had apparently entered Lithuania with little understanding of the national problem there, but they quickly saw the davantages to be gained by playing upon the existing rivalries. In general, the Germans favored the Lithuanians, although there were some misgivings in German circles over the realism of this policy after the census of 1916 had evidenced a much greater Polish element than had been hitherto believed to exist in Lithuania.[62] The German administration in any case was not an altruistic one, and the Lithuanians realized this fact. The administration was geared to the needs of the German war machine, not to the needs of the population.

The Lithuanians writing for German readers stressed the antagonism between the Poles and the Lithuanians, urging ex-

[59] *Ibid.*, No. 25 (March 1, 1915).

[60] See Colliander, *Litauen und Deutschland*, pp. 22-26; New York *Times*, August 13, 1916.

[61] Ludendorff, *The General Staff*, II, 382.

[62] See Great Britain, Foreign Office, *Russian Poland, Lithuania and White Russia*, p. 62. General Hoffmann thought the Lithuanians were as capable of governing themselves as "my little daughter Ilse is of educating herself." See Ivinskis, "*Lietuvos padètis*," *Židinys*, XXVII (1938), 629.

ploitation of the rivalry as a solution to the problem of Germany's eastern frontier: "The rule should be: Lithuania to the Lithuanians and Poland to the Poles. The Lithuanians as a people have not the slightest thing in common with the Poles."[63] They called for independence for Lithuania, in which case Lithuania would serve as a balance to an independent Poland. Care was taken not to antagonize the Germans by advocating separatism from the German Empire. Gaigalat reassured his readers, "The fear that the Prussian Lithuanians would want to join such a Lithuanian state is completely unfounded."[64]

These appeals brought little immediate result. In the first years of the war, the Germans, like the Russians, were not ready to offer any direct support to the Lithuanian nationalists. The war, however, had nevertheless, opened up great possibilities for political changes in Lithuania, and the Lithuanians of the emigration were not slow to realize this.

In America, in September, 1914, the Lithuanian Catholic organizations held a congress in Chicago, while the Tautininkai and the Socialists met in Brooklyn in October. The Catholics called for Lithuanian autonomy within Russia, annexation of East Prussia, and federation with Latvia. They maintained that Lithuania should be represented at the peace conference, and they named Juozas Gabrys their representative to the conference. Gabrys was also empowered to organize a Lithuanian Information Bureau in Paris, which was moved to Geneva in 1915. A fund was set up to aid Lithuanian war-sufferers, and plans were started for the formation of a national council, finally organized in 1916 (Lietuvių Tautos Taryba).

At the meeting in Brooklyn the Socialists rejected a resolution offered by the Tautininkai which would have called for autonomy, and no political recommendations were made. But this conference, too, set up a fund for war-sufferers. Later the Tautininkai withdrew to organize their own fund, and in 1917 they also

[63] Gaigalat, *Litauen*, pp. 124-35.
[64] Gaigalat, *Die litauisch-baltische Frage*, p. 22. Gaigalat was a member of the Prussian Landtag. For the reactions of one Lithuanian nationalist to this stand, see Bartuška, *Kryžiaus keliais*, p. 46.

organized their own national council (Amerikos Lietuvių Tautinė Taryba). Only in the spring of 1918 were the Tautininkai and the Catholics able to come together with the organization of the Lithuanian Executive Committee, which was made up of representatives from both councils. The Socialists continued to remain aloof.[65]

From 1914 to 1917 the center of the Lithuanian national movement was located in Western Europe. There were no large Lithuanian colonies in that area, but the students and the intellectuals, especially in Switzerland, more than made up with their zeal for their lack in numbers. By far the most outstanding figure was Juozas Gabrys. He had been the secretary of the Grand Congress of Vilna in 1905, and after the failure of the revolution, he had gone to Paris to study. There he began to work with other nationalities, in the belief that the greatest progress could be made through this sort of cooperation.[66] A man of strong will, tremendous self-confidence, and great ambition, he was the first Lithuanian to become internationally known as a leader of the national movement. His personal problems and his bitter disputes with other Lithuanians, together with the open expression of his disappointment in the events after the war, have made an accurate evaluation of his work extremely difficult.

During the war Gabrys worked in Lausanne, maintaining close touch with both German and Allied officials. At the same time he played a leading role in the intermittent Lithuanian conferences in Switzerland. These conferences were attended by delegates from the American Lithuanians, by Lithuanian leaders in Western Europe, and even by representatives from German-occupied Lithuania. It was such a conference, held at Bern in March, 1916, which first called for a Lithuanian state independent of ties to any other nation.[67] After this meeting the emigration stood firmly for independence.

[65] See Biržiška, "Amerikos lietuviai," in *Lietuviškoji Enciklopedia*, Vol. I, cols· 468-78; Jurgela, Lithuania and the United States (MS), p. 93.

[66] See Miliukov, *Natsional'nyi vopros*, p. 177.

[67] See Graham, *New Governments of Eastern Europe*, p. 360.

The writers of the emigration in Western Europe and the United States who sought to reach the public in the Entente countries and in America were not so agressive in tone as those in Lithuania who were addressing the Germans. The fundamental position of the emigrants was that each nation should be allowed to develop freely in its own fashion, and that the Poles, intentionally or not, represented a danger to the Lithuanians. In general they regarded nationality as a matter of choice, and thus viewed the Polonized nobility as Poles. Naturally there were some who tended toward the idea of a "national blood," but the majority of these writers advocated only mildly an effort to show the nobility the error of their ways and, failing in this, were willing to dismiss them as lost souls.[68]

The February/March Revolution in Russia brought the Lithuanian problem to a head. The Germans had already proclaimed a Polish state, and there was some speculation that the proclamation of a Lithuanian state would follow shortly, although there was little evidence to support this notion. After the revolution the Petrograd Lithuanians set to work with redoubled fervor. In early February the Lithuanian National Council had been formed, made up of fourteen former deputies in the Duma. In May a congress of refugees from German-occupied Lithuania, meeting in Petrograd, took a stand in favor of independence over the opposition of the Socialist delegates, who argued that independence under existing conditions could only mean subjugation by the Germans, who were then still in Lithuania. They challenged the right of a congress of refugees to pass on this issue, and they also contended hotly that it would be advantageous for Lithuania to remain in a democratic Russia, thus convincing the Russian Provisional Government that independence was the demand of only the extreme right among the Lithuanians and that the "democratic" elements in Lithuania all preferred to remain part of Russia.[69] Accordingly, the Pro-

[68] See John Szlupas (Jonas Šliupas), *Lithuania in Retrospect and Prospect* (New York, 1915), pp. 96-97.
[69] *Lietuvių Balsas* (The Lithuanian Voice) (Petrograd), No. 46 (June 29, 1917).

visional Government postponed any consideration of Lithuanian national demands.[70]

The new look in Russia, combined with the apparent failure of their Polish policy, brought the Germans to another stage in their Lithuanian policy. German policy was being formulated through a tug of war between the German High Command and the Reichstag majority, which was soon to issue its famous *Friedenserklärung*.[71] Under pressure to make concessions to the populations in the occupied territories, the High Command planned to choose a *Vertrauensrat* for Lithuania which would have advisory functions. The Lithuanians opposed this move, demanding the right to elect their own council and to have an active voice in their own affairs.

The Germans finally yielded, and in September, 1917, a conference of Lithuanians met at Vilna. Much ink has been spilled condemning or explaining this act of "collaboration," but in view of the Lithuanians' desire for recognition of their national movement, there could be little question as to the course for them to choose. Some writers have pointed to the hopelessness of independent action for the Lithuanians in this position and so have considered the Taryba, which was elected by the conference, practically a German puppet.[72] But the fact remains that the Germans were the only hope the Lithuanians had for immediate, albeit not disinterested, aid. The Russians had refused to listen to Lithuanian demands, and the Lithuanians could hardly look to the Entente for aid to a national movement which was opposed by Russia, a member of the Entente. To turn to the Poles was out of the question. Moreover, the Lithuanians realized that they could not achieve independence alone. Their demands were known to all; they could only look for the best offer now.[73]

[70] On Lithuanian activities in Russia at this time, see M. Yčas, "Rusijos lietuvių pastangos," in *Pirmasis dešimtmetis*, I, 33-49; Rauch, *Russland*, pp. 204-10.

[71] See Ludendorff, *Ludendorff's Own Story*, II, 154-55.

[72] See Moriez, *La question polonaise*, chapter XV, "La Lithuanie, colonie allemande."

[73] On the problem of the alternatives in seeking outside aid, see Ivinskis, "Lietuvos padėtis," *Židinys*, XXVII (1938), 619-21.

The members of the Vilna conference, contrary to the belief of
many, were not chosen by the Germans. Some delegates, to be
sure, were named by the Germans, but the great majority were
chosen by the Lithuanian leaders in Vilna, and they made a
serious effort to select a representative assembly. The conference
was divided by political factions, but these were not so sharply
antagonistic as they had been in the Petrograd congress of May,
1917. The conference finally resolved that Lithuania should become independent and appealed for German aid toward this
end. It elected a council, the Taryba, which was to execute the
decisions of the conference. The left was at first dissatisfied with
the results of the election, and in order to placate it, two priests
withdrew in favor of J. Vileišis and S. Narutavičius, both Socialists, thus giving the left four of the twenty seats filled.[74] Six additional seats were reserved for the other nationalities in Lithuania—Jews, Belorussians, and Poles, but these refused to take part,
their national aspirations having other targets at that time.[75]

Antanas Smetona was elected chairman of the Taryba. Later a
dictator of Lithuania, at this time he was well known as a publi-
cist. He had a keen mind and was very capable in discerning
problems and planning tasks, but he was always hesitant to act
himself. Already, there were stories that he was dominated by
his wife, an intelligent and ambitious woman.[76]

Despite criticisms leveled at it, the Taryba gained recognition
from several Lithuanian conferences abroad. In October, 1917,
a conference held at Stockholm recognized the Taryba as the
supreme organ in the movement for independence, and a conference at Bern in November of the same year followed its example. In November, too, the Bolsheviks seized power in Russia,
and they forced the disbanding of the Lithuanian council in

[74] *Ibid.*, pp. 622-23. There were no real party factions as such in the Taryba,
just a general left and right. See Römer'is, *Litewskie stronnictwa polityczne*, p. 37.

[75] The Lithuanians had decided to limit participation in the Vilna conference
to Lithuanians alone because they wanted to settle their own problems first, and
then, as a unit, they could treat with the other nationalities. Klimas, "Lietuvos
valstybės kurimasis," in *Pirmasis dešimtmetis*, I, 14-16.

[76] See *Rigaer Zeitung*, June 26, 1919.

Petrograd. Some of the Lithuanian leaders reorganized at Voronezh as the Supreme Lithuanian Council in Russia, and this group recognized the Taryba in December, 1917.[77]

The Lithuanians had now turned away from their former program of autonomy within the Russian Empire. The intervention of the Germans had opened up the possibility of their gaining independence of Russia. But as matters stood in the fall of 1917, independence of Russia almost certainly meant subordination to Germany. The Lithuanians must have realized this, but apparently they felt that more was to be gained by cooperation with the Germans than by waiting for the Russians to act. The Russians had ignored them; the Germans at least offered recognition. The Germans appeared to be the masters in Eastern Europe, and the Lithuanians hoped to make their peace with them on the best terms possible.

[77] Graham, *New Governments of Eastern Europe*, p. 365.

II
"A Permanent and Firm Alliance"
SEPTEMBER, 1917–NOVEMBER, 1918

THE LITHUANIANS soon discovered that the Germans intended to keep as tight a rein as possible on the Taryba. The Taryba was not permitted to organize any sort of administration, and the Germans sought to use it as the *Vertrauensrat* they had originally wanted, demanding obedience "mit Rat und Tat." As one of its members, Justinas Staugaitis, characterized it. "The work [of the Taryba] was in effect limited to protests and written complaints about occupation organs which were hurting the people."

From the beginning the German occupation authorities exerted pressure on the Taryba to declare itself for union with the German Empire, warning that an independent Lithuania, adrift in Eastern Europe, would be a helpless prey to Russian and Polish intrigues.[2] Although the Catholic Zentrum in the Reichstag favored a liberalization of the policy of the military toward the nationalities of Eastern Europe, there was little restraint from Berlin on the army leaders in Lithuania since most Germans still doubted the strength of the Lithuanian national movement.[3]

Meanwhile the picture in Russia was again changing. On November 7 the Bolsheviks seized power in Petrograd. Although willing enough while an opposition party to exploit the national antagonisms within Russia, the Bolsheviks now sought to restrain those same national passions which had contributed to their own rise to power. As a step toward pacification, on November 15 they issued their famous Declaration of the Rights of the Peoples

[1] Ivinskis, "Lietuvos padėtis," *Židinys*, XXVII (1938), 632.
[2] Ludendorff, *Ludendorff's Own Story*, II, 156.
[3] See Ivinskis, "Lietuvos padėtis," *Židinys*, XXVII (1938), 629-30.

of Russia, a decree aimed at showing the nationalities which planned to form their own states that the Bolsheviks really were in sympathy with their grievances and would do nothing to suppress their rights. The declaration even stated that the Council of People's Commissars recognized the "right of the peoples of Russia to free self-determination even to the point of separation and the formation of an independent state."[4] At the same time, however, the Bolsheviks gave notice that they had no intention of denying themselves any role in determining the future of the various nationalities. Although Stalin, then the Commissar of Nationalities of the RSFSR, declared that "no one has the right to interfere by force in the internal life of nations and by force 'to correct their errors,'"[5] the Communists reserved for themselves "the freedom of agitation for or against separation, depending on the interests of the proletariat and on the interests of the proletarian revolution."[6]

In the case of Lithuania, the Bolsheviks made their stand clear almost immediately. Within the People's Commissariat of Nationalities, they established a Commissariat of Lithuanian Affairs, headed by Vincas Mickevičius-Kapsukas, a former member of the Lithuanian Social Democratic Party, which was to work among the Lithuanian refugees in Russia "regarding as one of its chief tasks the strengthening of Soviet authority in Russia and the spreading of the ideas of this authority among the wide masses of Lithuanian refugees."[7] In the fulfillment of its task the commissariat suppressed the nationalist Lithuanian National Council, organized in Petrograd in February, 1917, and prepared to take over the facilities of various Lithuanian

[4] James H. Meisel and Edward S. Kozera (eds.), *Materials for the Study of the Soviet System* (2d ed.; Ann Arbor, Mich., 1953), p. 26.

[5] Stalin, *Sochineniia*, III, 209.

[6] *Ibid.*, III, 52. See the account of the formulation of the Bolsheviks' national policy in Carr, *The Bolshevik Revolution*, I, 253 ff. Cf. Mickevičius-Kapsukas, "Bor'ba za sovetskuiu vlast', *Proletarskaia Revoliutsiia*, No. 108 (1931), p. 73.

[7] Pesikina, *Narodnyi Komissariat po Delam Natsional'nostei*, p. 55. See also Carr, *The Bolshevik Revolution*, I, 276-77. Kapsukas estimated that the Lithuanian refugees in Russia made up one third of the adult population of Lithuania. See his "Litovtsy za 5 let," *Zhizn' natsional'nostei*, No. 1 (1923), p. 225.

refugee organizations.[8] Within the Bolshevik Party organization, the Lithuanian members were organized in special sections, coordinated by a central bureau attached to the Central Committee of the Russian Social Democratic Labor Party (Bolshevik) (RSDLP[b]).[9] These moves were clear evidence that the Bolsheviks had little intention of recognizing the Taryba as the legitimate representative of the Lithuanian people.

One of the first official moves of the Bolshevik government in November, 1917, was to issue a manifesto calling for a general end to the three-year-old war. When this effort met with no response from the Allied and Associated Powers, the Bolsheviks arranged for the opening of bilateral talks with the Germans at Brest-Litovsk.[10] Among the major issues to be decided in these talks was the fate of the territories of Russia occupied by the German army, including Lithuania.

The members of the Taryba hoped to exploit the negotiations at Brest-Litovsk in order to gain a little more freedom than the Germans had so far been willing to offer them. They saw that they could not avoid declaring themselves in favor of close ties with Germany, but by December 7 they had agreed on a draft declaration of independence which went to the extent of planning an independent administration. On December 10 a delegation from the Taryba consulted with the German military authorities in Kaunas regarding the declaration, but the Germans, now confident of a quick and victorious peace at Brest-Litovsk, rejected the Lithuanian draft and substituted for it one of their own. On December 11 the Taryba discussed the German draft and after heated debate accepted it. The final version proclaimed the "reconstitution of the independent Lithuanian state" with Vilna as its capital, at the same time requesting the aid and

---

[8] *Darbo Balsas*, No. 9 (February 18, 1918); *Lietuvių Balsas*, No. 2 (January 5, 1918). The refugee groups in Petrograd were suppressed in December, 1918. Kapsukas, however, allowed the Voronezh group to continue its work. See *Darbo Balsas*, No. 30 (August 7, 1918). See also *Lietuvos TSR istorijos šaltiniai*, III, 29-31.

[9] *Bor'ba litovskogo naroda*, pp. 26-27.

[10] See George F. Kennan, *Russia Leaves the War* (Princeton, N. J., 1956), pp. 74 ff., 104.

protection of the German Empire in a "permanent and firm alliance."[11] That the Germans intended the declaration to leave the way open for the attachment of Lithuania to the German Empire was an open secret.

The declaration of December 11 failed of its immediate purpose for the Lithuanians, since they were not able to persuade the Germans to invite a Lithuanian representative to the peace talks. There were two Lithuanians present at Brest-Litovsk, but neither was there as a representative of the Taryba. The Supreme Lithuanian Council in Russia, organized in Voronezh after the suppression of the Lithuanian National Council in Petrograd, had named its own representatives to the talks, and these men went to Petrograd where they asked Trotsky to accept them as part of his delegation. Trotsky refused and instead sent Kapsukas to Brest. Unable to reach the talks through the German or the Bolshevik delegations, the Lithuanian nationalists found entry through another door. One of the men named by the Voronezh council, Augustinas Voldemaras, made his way to the Ukraine, where he succeeded in getting himself named "Lithuanian advisor" to the Ukrainian delegation to the peace talks.[12]

Although they refused to take official recognition of the Taryba's declaration of December 11, the Germans at Brest-Litovsk demanded that the Russians recognize

the decisions expressing the will of the people demanding full State independence and separation from the Russian Empire for Poland, Lithuania, Courland, and portions of Estonia and Livonia.[13]

Trotsky rejected this demand, maintaining,

Our standpoint is that only such a manifestation of will can be regarded as *de facto* the expression of the will of the people as results

---

[11] For an account of the discussions leading up to the declaration, see Ivinskis, "Lietuvos padėtis," *Židinys*, XXVII (1938), 632-33. Text in Klimas, *L'état lituanien*, p. 142.

[12] See Būtėnas and Mackevičius, "Gyvenimas ir darbai," in *Mykolas Sleževičius*, p. 73; Bartuška, *Kryžiaus keliais*, p. 211; Pesikina, *Narodnyi Komissariat po Delam Natsional'nostei*, p. 57; *Prof. Augustinas Voldemaras*, by "J. Gs." (Plunge, 1930), pp. 25-27.

[13] *Proceedings of the Brest-Litovsk Peace Conference*, p. 44.

from a free vote taken in the districts in question with complete absence of foreign troops.[14]

Kapsukas too spoke out against the Taryba's separatism, declaring that the "decisive word on the fate of Lithuania" belonged not to "those bourgeois groups who earlier supported tsarism," but rather to the "democratic population of Lithuania, first of all to the workers and poor peasants of Lithuania, regardless of nationality."[15]

In Vilna, though disappointed by the refusal of the Germans to act on the declaration of December 11, the Taryba yet continued to press for some action from them. In January it declared that only a constituent assembly could decide the form of the Lithuanian state, a move which apparently sought to avoid the pressure from the Germans for a direct agreement on union.[16] On January 27 the Taryba received notice from the Germans that recognition would soon be forthcoming but that no date could be specified.[17] This proved unsatisfactory for the Lithuanians, and on February 16, the Taryba issued another declaration of independence. The new declaration, actually just an edited version of the earlier one, omitted the provision calling for close ties with the German Empire.[18]

The Germans were angered by this move. In a letter dated February 21, Count Hertling, the German Chancellor, stated,

The Imperial Government was prepared to recognize Lithuania as an independent state on the basis of the resolution of the Taryba of December 10 [*sic*], 1917, and to guarantee to it the protection and the help of the German Empire for the building of the new state. By the resolution of February 16, 1918, the Taryba has made void the basis for this measure by the Imperial Government.[19]

[14] *Ibid.*, p. 45. See also p. 63.
[15] Text of speech, given on February 10, 1918, in *Lietuvos TSR istorijos šaltiniai,* III, 35-38.
[16] Text in Klimas, *L'état lituanien*, p. 144.   [17] *Ibid.*, p. 146.
[18] Text in *ibid.*, p. 147. The Socialists, who advocated a more aggressive policy even before the declaration of December 11, left the Taryba in January in protest against what they considered too timid a policy. They returned on February 16 and signed the new declaration. This declaration of February 16 has come to be regarded by Lithuanians as marking the birth of the independent state of Lithuania.
[19] Text in *ibid.*, pp. 147-48. See also pp. xxv ff.

In answer the Lithuanians protested that the new resolution was not meant to abrogate the old one, that the new one was in no way contradictory to the old one, and that the foundation laid by the old one for future German-Lithuanian relations had not been destroyed.

All this while the Bolsheviks had continued their stalling tactics at Brest-Litovsk. In late February the Germans resumed military operations. Unable to offer any defense, the Bolsheviks agreed to terms for peace and signed a treaty on March 3, yielding all claims to sovereignty to Lithuania and the other territories held by the Germans, and foreswearing any interference in the internal affairs of those territories.[20]

On March 23 the German government formally recognized Lithuania's independence on the basis of the declaration of December 11. That the recognition was not unconditional may be seen from the full text of the recognition as given by Emperor Wilhelm II on May 4, 1918:

We proceed from the assumption that the agreements to be concluded between Germany and Lithuania will take the interests of the German Empire into account equally with those of the Lithuanians, and that Lithuania will participate in the war burdens of Germany, which were incurred also in her liberation.[21]

The immediate Lithuanian reaction to the news of the recognition was naturally jubilation, and the Lithuanians did not at first pause to look the gift horse in the mouth. Statements such as the toast by Smetona, the president of the Taryba, "Ein dreifaches Hoch an unseren lieben Kaiser,"[22] were typical, but they provided more fuel for those who viewed the Taryba as a German puppet.

Though the independence of Lithuania was now officially recognized, the problem of the form the country's government was to take remained unresolved. In direct contravention of the terms of the Treaty of Brest-Litovsk, the Bolsheviks continued

---

[20] *Texts of the Russian "Peace,"* pp. 15-16.
[21] Klimas, *L'état lituanien*, p. 151.
[22] *Das neue Litauen*, No. 10 (April 1, 1918).

and, as the opportunity presented itself, even increased their efforts to intervene in Lithuanian affairs. Lithuanian units of the Russian army which were trying to go home were demobilized and disarmed by the Bolsheviks, who in turn set about organizing their own Lithuanian units.[23] The Voronezh council, which had announced its recognition of the Taryba, was suppressed in March, and the presses of the council were taken over by the Commissariat of Lithuanian Affairs.[24] In April the Commissariat of Nationalities of the RSFSR ordered its divisions to infiltrate the German-occupied territories of the Russian Empire, and accordingly the Commissariat of Lithuanian Affairs began training special agents.[25]   It would seem, however, that the Commissariat of Lithuanian Affairs limited its activity to the territory held by the Bolsheviks before the German offensive in February, 1918, and that it was the duty of the Communist Party to carry on the work in Lithuania itself.[26]

In April the first Bolsheviks from Moscow, sent by the Central Bureau of the Lithuanian sections of the Central Committee of the Russian Communist Party, arrived in Vilna. There they found the Social Democrats split over the issue of the membership of Mykolas Biržiška and Steponas Kairys in the Taryba. A secret conference of Social Democrats in Vilna in March, 1918, had been marked by an unsuccessful effort on the part of the extreme left to censure the two men for their participation in the work of the Taryba.[27] The newly arrived Bolsheviks began immediately to organize a Communist organization in Lithuania, and in July a conference of Communist sympathizers in Vilna

[23] Pesikina, *Narodnyi Komissariat po Delam Natsional'nostei*, pp. 81-82; Mickevičius-Kapsukas, "Litovtsy za 5 let," *Zhizn' natsional'nostei*, No. 1 (1923), p. 225; Andreev, *Bor'ba litovskogo naroda*, pp. 33-34.

[24] The Bolsheviks got 90,000 rubles, 60 books, 320 puds of type, two large presses, and one small press. See *Darbo Balsas*, No. 30 (August 7, 1918).

[25] Pesikina, *Narodnyi Komissariat po Delam Natsional'nostei*, p. 85.

[26] In May, 1918, a report on the activities of the commissariat listed Pskov, Mogilev, Polotsk, and Minsk as sites of the activity of the commissariat. *Ibid.*, p. 85. Cf. Andreev, *Bor'ba litovskogo naroda*, pp. 27, 30.

[27] See Mickevičius-Kapsukas, "Istoki i zarozhdenie," *Proletarskaia Revoliutsiia*, No. 84 (1929) p. 170. But cf. Girinis, "Kanun i sumerki," *Proletarskaia Revoliutsiia*, No. 8 (1922), p. 76.

laid the foundations of The Social Democratic Workers' Party of Lithuania and Belorussia.[28] The word "Communist" was not used at first for fear of frightening off prospective converts,[29] but on August 14 the Central Committee of the new party, meeting in Vilna, changed the name to the Communist Party of Lithuania and Belorussia.[30]

The Russian Bolsheviks were becoming increasingly aware of the strength of the various national movements in the border areas, and they took every opportunity to assure the nationalities that their desires and needs would be best met under the Communist system. From their examination of the archives of the tsarist and provisional governments, they came to the conclusion that much of the trouble with national separatism had arisen from the refusal of the Russian government to consider the demands of the nationalities.[31] Accordingly, the Bolsheviks seized every opportunity to assure the nationalities of their respect. The constitution of the RSFSR, adopted in July, 1918, carried a provision allowing regions "with special usages and national characteristics of their own" to join the RSFSR "on a federal basis."[32]

Meanwhile, despite the German recognition, German soldiers remained in Lithuania as conquerors, and requisitions continued unrestrained. The protests of the Taryba were all in vain, and the Bolsheviks found the *Räuberbande* a vulnerable target for the propaganda being smuggled in from Russia.[33] The German military authorities in Lithuania openly favored union of that country with Prussia. A petition was being circulated asking the

[28] Andreev credits Eidukevičius with this move (*Bor'ba litovskogo naroda*, pp. 27-28). Kapsukas, on the other hand, credits Comrade Anna Drobovich ("Istoki i zarozhdenie," *Proletarskaia Revoliutsiia*, No. 84 [1929], p. 173). Cf. Girinis, "Kanun i sumerki," *Proletarskaia Revoliutsiia*, No. 8 (1922), p. 76.

[29] Kapsukas considered this move a grave mistake. See his "Istoki i zarozhdenie," *Proletarskaia Revoliutsiia*, No. 84 (1929), pp. 173-74.

[30] Andreev, *Bor'ba litovskogo naroda*, pp. 28-29.

[31] See the account of the Lithuanian situation in *Pravda*, No. 225 (December 29, 1917/January 11, 1918).

[32] James H. Meisel and Edward S. Kozera, (eds.), *Materials for the Study of the Soviet System* (2d ed.; Ann Arbor, Mich., 1953), p. 80.

[33] Colliander, *Litauen und Deutschland*, pp. 206-7.

Kaiser "to place our country also under Your Majesty's glorious scepter and to deign most graciously to take the Grand Ducal crown for yourself and for your Imperial and Royal Majesty's successor."[34] The election of the Kaiser's son Joachim as grand duke was an alternative to a personal union with Prussia through Wilhelm. Furthermore, the German High Command made a point of warning the Lithuanians that any Catholic ruling house in Lithuania would probably be dominated by the Poles.[35] Meanwhile, Saxony and Bavaria opposed such an expansion by Prussia, and Saxony put forth its own claim for the Lithuanian throne on behalf of Prince Frederick Christian, the second son of the king of Saxony. The Saxon ruling house was Catholic and had occupied the throne of the Polish-Lithuanian state from 1697 to 1763. Many other persons, both German and non-German, were also rumored to be possible candidates.[36]

The leading figure in Berlin espousing the Lithuanian cause was Matthias Erzberger, the leader of the Catholic Zentrum in the Reichstag. Since 1917, Erzberger had been working closely with the Lithuanians in Switzerland, and in answer to a Lithuanian inquiry he recommended the election of Wilhelm von Urach, Duke of Württemberg, who, Erzberger thought, would rule only in the best interests of the Lithuanians, since he was not in line to ascend the throne in Württemberg.[37] The duke was a Catholic, but he assured Erzberger that he had no intention of maintaining a Polish court.[38]

On June 4, 1918, the Taryba voted to ask Urach to become king of Lithuania. The military government opposed the move and created great difficulties for the Lithuanians in their attempt to send a delegation to Germany to see Urach. Nevertheless, the delegation finally succeeded in meeting him on July 1 in Freiburg im Breisgau, and Urach accepted the offer

[34] Erzberger, *Erlebnisse im Weltkrieg*, p. 191.
[35] Ludendorff, *Ludendorff's Own Story*, II, 156.
[36] Colliander, *Litauen und Deutschland*, pp. 186-87. The American Lithuanians favored a republic, perhaps federated with Latvia, and the Voronezh council had favored an independent republic.
[37] Erzberger, *Erlebnisse im Weltkrieg*, p. 186.   [38] *Ibid.*, p. 191.

of the throne.[39] His election was announced by the Taryba on July 13, and on August 12 a formal invitation was extended to him to take the Lithuanian crown as Mindaugas II.[40] In another move in July, the Taryba assumed the title of *State* Council.[41]

The left had not taken part in the negotiations with Urach, and when his election was carried by a vote of thirteen to seven, four members of the Taryba—Kairys, Biržiška, Vileišis, and Narutavičius—resigned in protest, maintaining that such an action should be the sole prerogative of the constituent assembly.[42] In their place the Taryba co-opted six new members, including Martynas Yčas and Augustinas Voldemaras.

The German authorities opposed both the election of Urach and the assumption of the title "State Council." They refused to recognize any official actions of the Taryba and even refused to accept communications under the letterhead "State Council."[43] The official newspaper of the Imperial Chancery, *Die norddeutsche allgemeine Zeitung*, stated on July 21, 1918:

The independence of Lithuania was recognized by Germany only on the condition that the agreements to be concluded, including, naturally, the formation of the state and the occupation of the throne, would comply with German interests. Hence it follows that all affairs can be handled validly only in close contact with the German government. Therefore the right cannot be said to have been given to Lithuania to make an independent decision in the question of the throne, and even less can the arbitrarily formed State Council be viewed as a legitimate representation of Lithuania. The report that the Duke of Urach has accepted the crown is consequently false.[44]

The Germans demanded that Smetona, the president of the Taryba and the editor of *Lietuvos Aidas* (Echo of Lithuania, a

[39] Offer and acceptance in Klimas, *L'état lituanien*, pp. 178-80.

[40] *Ibid.*, pp. 180-81. Mindaugas was a Lithuanian monarch of the thirteenth century who had received a crown from the Pope and from whom Urach was allegedly descended.

[41] *Ibid.*, p. 178.

[42] Professor Mykolas Biržiška very kindly set forth his views in this matter to the author in an interview in Los Angeles, California, on August 14, 1956.

[43] In his recent study, Andreev displays a complete ignorance of the entire affair, as well as of sources, by stating that Urach was Kaiser Wilhelm's son. See *Bor'ba litovskogo naroda*, p. 34.   [44] Klimas, *L'état lituanien*, p. 181.

newspaper published since the summer of 1917), print the above statement. Smetona refused, and the occupation authorities suppressed his newspaper.[45] Under this pressure the Taryba dropped its new title in its correspondence with the Germans, but it did not back down from its election of Urach.[46] As a consequence, relations with the German authorities remained very strained into the month of October.

The conventions envisaged by the declaration of December 11 and the election of a German king were very damaging marks on the Taryba's record in the opinion of the Entente and of Lithuanians in the West, but the Taryba had been anything but a docile puppet. There was just no indication that there would be anyone but the Germans to deal with in postwar Eastern Europe, and so the Lithuanians had made their peace with them early in the hopes of a good reward.

In September, 1918, a conference took place in Lausanne, Switzerland, which was to be of great importance for the future of Lithuania. Four members of the Taryba—Smetona, Yčas, Puryckis, and Voldemaras—came to meet with the Lithuanians in Switzerland, and a delegation from the American Lithuanians was also expected. A major dispute arose immediately between Voldemaras and Smetona on the one side and Gabrys on the other as to the competence of the conference and the sovereignty of the Taryba. The Taryba delegates rejected the idea that the conference had any authority over the Taryba, maintaining that it could only offer advice. Some of the other delegates expressed the opinion that under those conditions the conference was a waste of time. To Gabrys's direct question as to the bases of the Taryba's sovereignty, Smetona named the declaration of December 11 and the recognition of March 23.

The upshot of the conference was further fragmentation rather than coordination of the Lithuanian movement. The Taryba members refused to recognize the competence of the conference to dictate to the Taryba. They felt that the Germans

[45] *Ibid.*, pp. 182-83.
[46] See Römer'is, *Lietuvos konstitucinės teisės paskaitos*, I, 43-48.

were the sole major power to be considered in the foreseeable future, and they argued that the Taryba needed the prestige of being the sole representative of Lithuanian interests or else it would be unable to deal effectively with the Germans. The émigrés, on the other hand, claimed that the future lay with the Entente and that the Lithuanians should therefore avoid any sign of dependence on the Germans. The refusal of the Taryba to recognize an equal in the West or to merge itself into a larger council centered in the West might well be considered a major policy error in the light of the reputation which, deservedly or not, it had come to have among those Entente authorities who had taken note of its existence. The split between the Taryba and the Western Lithuanians was aired publicly in an exchange of letters in the Swiss newspaper *Der Bund*, and caused not a little confusion in Western circles in regard to the Lithuanian question.[47]

The sudden collapse of Germany in the fall of 1918 gave the Taryba its chance at last. On October 16 a Lithuanian delegation in Berlin asked the German Chancellor, Prince Max von Baden, whether "it is the understanding of the present government that Lithuania has been recognized by Germany as a free and independent state."[48] On October 20 the Chancellor replied that the Germans had recognized Lithuania's right to independence. He stated that the military government would now be converted into a civil one, which "will exercise the executive power only until the Lithuanian government, after the building up of its own resources, is in a position to assume power itself."[49] This was deemed unsatisfactory by the Lithuanians who wanted the Germans to leave as quickly as possible and wanted no such "regency,"[50] but the Germans could not withdraw without an

[47] See *Der Bund*, No. 418 (October 1, 1918), No. 455 (October 24, 1918); *Germania*, October 15, 1918. The stenograms of the conference can be found in the Šaulys Archives or in Bartuška, *Kryžiaus keliais*, pp. 203-28 (see also pp. 229 ff.). See also Gabrys, *Vers l'indépendance*, 220 ff.; Gabrys, *Kodel aš nerėmiau laikinosios Lietuvos valdžios*, pp. 24-27; Pakštas, "Lietuvių amerikiečių kovos," *Židinys*, XXVII (1938), 642; United States, *Foreign Relations: 1918, Russia*, II, 839.

[48] Klimas, *L'état lituanien*, p. 241.   [49] *Ibid.*, p. 242.

[50] See Juozas Puryckis's protest, dated October 25, in *ibid.*, p. 247.

organized replacement. Therefore the plan to replace the military authorities with civil authorities went ahead, while the Lithuanians proceeded to organize their own government.

There seems to have been no debate in the Taryba at this time as to whether it had the right to form a government in accordance with Prince Max's declaration of October 20.[51] The members of the Taryba claimed that the Vilna conference of September, 1917, had empowered the Taryba to run the affairs of Lithuania until a constituent assembly had met.[52] The calling of a constituent assembly was of course out of the question since there was no machinery available to carry out the necessary preparations and since conditions in the country were too disorderly. The Socialists favored the calling of a general conference, to be elected by the most suitable process possible, which would then either reorganize or enlarge the Taryba. One Socialist leader, Mykolas Sleževičius, writing from Moscow, suggested the calling of such an assembly which would then become the governing body of the country, supplanting the Taryba completely.[53]

The final decision, embodied in the constitution of November 2, was that the Taryba should become a legislative body, with a presidium of three men which would constitute the formal head of the state. A cabinet of ministers was to be responsible to the Taryba. The idea of holding a general conference was not abandoned, but convening it was postponed, and when it finally did meet in January, 1919, its competence was still not clear. The new constitution specifically reserved to the constituent assembly the right to decide the final form of the Lithuanian government and the relations of that government with other states, so in order to start with a clean slate, the Taryba annulled the election of Urach. Then the council set about organizing the first cabinet of ministers and establishing relations with foreign governments.

---

[51] See Šaulys, "Nepriklausomybės išvakarese," *Mūsų Kelias*, Vol. IV, February 26, 1948; Römer'is, *Lietuvos konstitucinės teisės paskaitos*, I, 50-54.

[52] Smetona to the Taryba, November 14, 1918, quoted in *Revue Baltique*, I (1919), 203.

[53] Sleževičius (Moscow) to Šaulys (Vilna), letter, October 7, 1918, Šaulys Archives, f. 75.

Delegates had already been sent abroad to contact the Western powers, Voldemaras going to Switzerland and Yčas to Sweden.

The Lithuanians still had a long road to travel before they could be considered truly independent. The Germans had a stranglehold on the economy, controlling transportation, currency, industry, and economic life in general.[54] The Lithuanians had neither their own administration nor their own army. They were at the same time dependent upon and exploited by the Germans.

The impending German defeat in the West was of great consequence to the Lithuanians since it would upset the balance in the East, which had been based on German military might. For a year the Lithuanians had worked within that balance in an effort to realize their dream of independence. Now that balance was to be destroyed without their having achieved their goal. Despite all the conflicts between the Germans and the Lithuanians during the occupation, the Germans had served as a buffer against the Poles and the Bolsheviks. With this protection weakened, the Taryba faced the prospect of direct competition, possibly even military conflict, for Lithuania with these neighbors.

The countryside was wracked by great unrest. Communist organizations were growing in many areas, and on September 15 representatives of a number of such local groups met in Pilviškiai, where, after attacking the Taryba as an "organ of German imperialism, created to hold the workers and poor peasants of Lithuania in slavery and darkness," they decided to adopt the program of the Russian Communist Party, to organize Communist cells, and to join the Communist Party which had been organized in Vilna in August.[55] On October 1-3 the first conference of the Communist Party of Lithuania and Belorussia

---

[54] The German ostmark was the currency of the land, and although the name was now officially changed to *auksinas,* the change was not even recorded on the face of the notes. A genuine national currency, the lit, did not come into existence in Lithuania until 1922. See Karys, *Nepriklausomos Lietuvos pinigai,* pp. 105-29.

[55] Mickevičius-Kapsukas, "Istoki i zarozhdenie," *Proletarskaia Revoliutsiia,* No. 84 (1929), pp. 176-77.

was held in Vilna, attended by 34 delegates representing 60 cells and 800 members.[56] Thus by the time of the German collapse, the Bolsheviks had already completed the basic steps of organizing a party through which they could act in Lithuania.

The Taryba found the Poles also to be competitors in the race to organize effective government in Lithuania. Themselves virtually assured of an independent state existence, the Poles were engaged in a furious campaign to include all Polish nationals in the new state and to make the new state as strong as possible. Looking back at the historic union of Poland and Lithuania, the Poles refused to believe that the Lithuanians really had little desire to renew that union, and they considered the Taryba's separatist sentiments as induced by the Germans. For the Lithuanians the conflict with the Poles was both an internal and an external problem. The presence of Polish elements within Lithuania was serious enough by itself, but since it made impossible the drawing of a frontier between the Poles and the Lithuanians acceptable to both sides, it produced among the Lithuanians suspicion and even hatred of all things Polish.

The conflict of interests between the Poles and the Lithuanians found its strongest expression in the "Vilna problem." According to the Russian census in 1897, the population of the city of Vilna was 40.3 percent Jewish and 30.9 percent Polish, while the population of Vilna guberniya as a whole was 56 percent Belorussian. The Lithuanians comprised 7 percent of the city, 35 percent of the district exclusive of the city and 17.5 percent of the guberniya as a whole.[57] The Lithuanians claimed the city as their historic capital, maintaining that Lithuania had kept a distinct, separate identity throughout the history of the Polish-Lithuanian commonwealth. When discussing statistics, the Lithuanians pointed to earlier, unofficial censuses of Vilna *guberniya*, made in the latter half of the nineteenth century, which showed a clear

[56] *Ibid.*, p. 177. At this time a separate organization for Belorussia was apparently not planned. See the resolution of the Belorussian Congress of Soviets, in *Pravda*, No. 25 (February 4, 1919).

[57] See Tsentral'nyi Statisticheskii Komitet, MVD, *Statisticheskii ezhegodnik Rossii, 1913 g.* (Statistical Yearbook of Russia, 1913) (St. Petersburg, 1914), pp. 63-65.

majority of Lithuanians among the population.[58] But besides being estimates, such figures pertain to a period when the Lithuanians themselves admit that national consciousness was still weak. Hence many a Pole might then still have considered himself a Lithuanian, in the territorial sense, without even being able to speak Lithuanian.

The Poles, on the other hand, claimed that the Polish constitution of May 3, 1791, had destroyed the old distinctions between the Polish and the Lithuanian administrations and that thenceforth, Vilna had been directly subordinate to Warsaw. Furthermore they considered Vilna the "second capital" of the old Polish state and claimed that it was clearly Polish in culture. They felt that their case had been proved by the German census of 1916 which reported that the population of the city was 50.1 percent Polish and only 2.6 percent Lithuanian, while in the district the population was 89.8 percent Polish and 4.3 percent Lithuanian.[59] Almost every Polish writer since then, favoring incorporation of Lithuania into Poland, has used those figures to back his claims. The Lithuanians, however, have disputed the validity of the figures, claiming that the census was conducted by Poznan Poles and that it was extremely biased.[60] Above and beyond these various statistics, one must remember that the war brought about a great displacement of population throughout the region. Therefore while it was difficult enough to estimate the make-up of the population of Vilna in 1918, there was no assurance that any such estimates would accurately reflect the normal composition of the city.

From this brief account, it is obvious that as regards just the ethnic composition of Vilna, the Polish claims were much stronger than the Lithuanian. The chief hope of the Lithuanians lay in gaining the support of the other two nationalities in the area, the Belorussians and the Jews. As of the end of October, 1918, the

---

[58] See K. Werbelis (pseud of P. Klimas), *Russisch-Litauen* (Halle, 1916), p. 70.

[59] See Wielhorski, *Polska a Litwa*, p. 16.

[60] Klimas, *L'état lituanien*, pp. 32 ff. See Lithuania, Delegation to Paris, *Composition*, Section V, Nos. 2-4; Great Britain, Foreign Office, *Russian Poland, Lithuania and White Russia*, pp. 108-9.

Lithuanians had failed to accomplish this. What could be done in the future remained to be seen.[61]

The Poles were torn between several different programs for Lithuania. These are generally categorized as either annexationist or federalist, but there were several variations within each category. Józef Piłsudski is generally associated with the federalist program, which favored some sort of union with a Lithuania framed in its historical boundaries, thus yielding Vilna in return for Lithuanian acceptance of federation. One such scheme, made public in the latter part of 1918, proposed the formation of an independent Lithuania made up of three cantons—Kaunas, Vilna, and Minsk. In view of the problems of foreign policy, that state was expected then to enter freely into union with Poland.[62] The hope for federation was one-sided, since the majority of the "Lithuanians" who favored it already considered themselves Poles.

The alternative to the federalist idea, the so-called "annexationist" program, found its leading advocate in Roman Dmowski, and the majority of the politically conscious Poles in Vilna seem to have belonged to his National Democratic Party.[63] Dmowski urged the direct attachment to Poland of all the territories inhabited by a significant Polish population, with "ethnic" Lithuania being given some sort of autonomous position within the Polish state.[64]

The annexationists and the federalists did not differ substantially in their views of the territorial extent of the Polish nation. Their differences arose over the question of how much non-Polish territory was to be incorporated and at what price. Dmowski's program called for boundaries falling substantially short of the frontiers of 1772, the boundaries sought by the

[61] On the activities of the Belorussians, see Vakar, *Belorussia*, pp. 93 ff.

[62] Kamieniecki, *Państwo litewskie*. A discussion of Lithuanian reactions to this plan can be found in Herbačiauskas, *Litwa a Polska*, pp. 22-23.

[63] Mackiewicz, *Istorija Polski*, p. 108: "I do not know whether Pilsudski, in Belvedere, was clear as to how unpopular the federalists were at this time in his 'dear' Vilna."

[64] Dmowski, *Polityka polska i odbudowanie Państwa*, p. 479.

federalists, but some opponents of it called the annexationist program the more imperialistic of the two, since it would bind a large non-Polish population much more tightly to Warsaw. Unsympathetic commentators tended to regard both plans as being imperialistic.

Thus the new government of "Lithuania," organized by the Taryba, found the field anything but open. In the coming struggle for Lithuania, however, the Taryba could count on one supporter, Germany. Heretofore German policy, as directed by Ludendorff, had been aimed at establishing Lithuania as a client state, which would have given the Germans a strong foothold in Russia and also would have opened the way into the Ukraine. This policy, however, was dependent on a strong German army. With the collapse of the German army in the West, the German government now had to reappraise its position in Lithuania. Was it any longer worth while to support the Taryba?

The decision was made to support Lithuanian independence. As a German Foreign Office memorandum later declared, "Germany's interest in the existence of a Lithuanian State stems from two sources, one political and one geographic. Lithuania forms a counterweight against Poland and a land bridge between Germany and Russia."[65] The Germans viewed the newly arising Polish state as a second France, and they had no desire to see it become large and strong:

There is no need to elaborate on how dangerous a union of Lithuania with Poland would be for the future of Germany. It is all the more necessary to support the anti-Polish, nationalistic endeavors of the Lithuanians and to be as helpful as possible, even unobtrusively, to the Lithuanians in the establishment of their state."[66]

Throughout the decisive months after the Armistice, the Germans had many misgivings about Lithuanian policies, the

[65] "Aufzeichnung über die deutsch-litauischen Beziehungen" Berlin, May 2, 1919, Germany, Foreign Office, *Hauptarchiv: Litauen*, Reel 431, frame 201.
[66] Zimmerle (Kaunas) to Foreign Office, February 14, 1919, in Germany, Foreign Office, *Hauptarchiv: Litauen*, Reel 430, frame 274.

Lithuanian designs on Memel in particular, but nevertheless they continued to support Lithuanian independence.[67]

It was not clear, however, just how much aid the Germans, defeated in the war, would be able to give to the embryonic Lithuanian state, which was faced with tremendous problems. In fact, it was even doubtful whether the government could survive its birth pangs.

[67] In the summer of 1919, Zimmerle, the German plenipotentiary in Lithuania, called the original German decision to support an independent Lithuania in 1917 "a politically unfortunate measure." "Denkschrift über die politische Arbeit des Generalbevollmächtigten des Deutschen Reichs für Litauen in der Zeit vom November 1918 bis Juni 1919," Germany, Foreign Office, *Hauptarchiv: Litauen*, Reel 431, frame 474.

III

"We Don't Need a Large Army"

NOVEMBER, 1918–JANUARY, 1919

ON NOVEMBER 3, Augustinas Voldemaras returned from Switzerland, where he had been sent about a week earlier in order to sound out the attitude of the Entente toward the Lithuanian government. He came back without any definite promises of aid from the Entente, but he had been successful in gaining a promise of support from the American Lithuanians.[1]

Voldemaras is another highly controversial personality in Lithuanian history. A brilliant scholar, he had been Docent of History, first at the University of St. Petersburg, later at Perm University, and was fluent in a number of languages. Unfortunately he had a peculiar knack for antagonizing people, which, with his egoism and his quick temper, was a great handicap to his political career.

Nevertheless he had gone abroad with the understanding that he was to be the new Prime Minister, and after his report to the Taryba on November 4, debate ensued on a formal request for the formation of a cabinet under the new constitution. Although Dr. Jurgis Šaulys was proposed as an alternative to Voldemaras for both the Premiership and the Ministry of Foreign Affairs, the decision was finally made in favor of the latter, and he set about organizing his cabinet.[2] That cabinet has come to be known as the "cabinet of talents," or experts (*darbo kabinetas*), and not as a party cabinet,[3] though its final

---

[1] M. Yčas, "Lietuvos vyriausybės sudarymo etapai," in *Pirmasis dešimtmetis*, I, 79-80; Pakštas, "Lietuvių amerikiečių kovos," *Židinys*, XXVII (1938), 643-44; United States, *Foreign Relations: 1918, Russia*, II, 839. Andreev (*Bor'ba litovskogo naroda*, p. 41) claims that he obtained the support of the United States government, but there is no evidence to uphold this claim.

[2] For an account of the formation of the cabinet, see M. Yčas, "Lietuvos vyriausybės sudarymo etapai," in *Pirmasis dešimtmetis*, I, 80-82.

[3] See Šapoka (ed.), *Lietuvos istorija*, p. 546.

make-up must be considered a victory for the Pažanga (Progress) Party, which dominated the Taryba. The cabinet was formally installed by the Taryba on November 11. In addition to holding the posts of Prime Minister and Foreign Minister, Voldemaras served also as Defense Minister.

On the day of the cabinet's installation, the Lithuanian government issued a manifesto appealing for the support of all inhabitants of Lithuania, regardless of language or religion. It was declared that the Taryba would act as the provisional government until the meeting of a constituent assembly. The government pledged itself to seek the return of Lithuanian war prisoners from both Russia and Germany, to seek compensation from the belligerents for war damages in Lithuania, to establish economic order, to prepare the way for land reform by the constituent assembly, and to assure a fair deal for the workers. Declaring that "the principal task, the greatest role of the citizens of Lithuania, will be to maintain order and tranquility in the land," the manifesto called on the people to establish their own local administrations by electing committees of five to seven members and to organize their own militia. In conclusion the manifesto promised the calling of a general conference, the delegates to which would be elected by the people. The conference would review the policies of the government and would also "complete the make-up of the Taryba" by electing additional members to it.[4]

The tasks of the new government came up for debate in meetings of the Taryba on November 14 and 15. In opening the meeting on November 14, Smetona admitted that a gulf had separated the Taryba and the people, but he claimed that the alienation had been caused by the German occupation and that things would now be much better.[5] In his turn, Voldemaras characterized the problem of the new state as that of finding a place in Europe as a small independent nation. He spoke hopefully of the future:

[4] French translation in *Revue Baltique*, I (1919), 202-3.
[5] M. Yčas, "Lietuvos vyriausybės sudarymo etapai," in *Pirmasis dešimtmetis*, I, 87.

The new world brings a new light. From the great American democracy comes joyous news—down with force, replace it with justice. It is clearly written in President Wilson's program: both large and small nations have the same rights.

He saw as the first duty of the government the safeguarding of the state against internal disorder. A declaration of neutrality, he was confident, would suffice to restrain neighbours from invading Lithuanian territory, "and so we don't need a large army to defend our borders."[6] The military issue was to prove the fatal weakness of his short-lived cabinet.

In a speech on November 15, Jonas Vileišis, a member of the Liaudininkai, was not so optimistic about the international situation, maintaining that Voldemaras underestimated the task of gaining recognition. The state had to depend first of all on its own strength, and that strength had to be organized. In conclusion, Vileišis urged the calling of the proposed state conference as soon as possible in order to give the Taryba, as an institution, a mandate from the nation.[7]

The members of the Taryba had already recognized the advisability and the necessity of broadening the base of the Taryba. Two of the dissenters in the Urach affair—Vileišis and Biržiška—had returned to the Taryba after the election of the duke had been annulled, and four other men, including another Socialist were also co-opted. The Taryba leaders hoped in this way to disarm the opposition of the left.[8] Now the Taryba renewed its efforts to secure the representation of the other nationalities in Lithuania. After negotiations extending into December, the Jews and the Belorussians each received a Ministry without Portfolio in the cabinet, while six Belorussians and three Jews were co-opted into the Taryba.[9] The Poles still remained aloof.

[6] *Ibid.*, I, 89-93. See also Dogelis, *Mano gyvenimo prisiminimai*, p. 231; Steponaitis, "Ginkluotų jegų klausimas," *Karo Archyvas*, III (1926), 15.

[7] Yčas, "Lietuvos vyriausybės sudarymo etapai," in *Pirmasis dešimtmetis*, I, 87.

[8] Klimas (Vilna) to Šaulys (Berlin), letter, December 7, 1918, Šaulys Archives, f. 75.

[9] The agreements were mainly on matters of defense, and no definite political commitments were undertaken at this time by the Lithuanian government. See Voronko, *Gudų klausimas*, p. 9; Chambon, *La Lithuanie pendant la Conférence de la Paix*,

With the organization of the cabinet the job of building up th-
administration and the army passed from the Taryba committees, which had made only a few faltering moves, to the new
ministeries. It must be remembered that at this early stage there
could be no firmly established government of law. The constitution had been written by the members of the Taryba, and it
lacked the authority of tradition. Nor had there been any test of
the acceptance of this constitution by the people. Even in such a
fundamental matter as the structure of the government, the
constitutional provisions were not necessarily final. They would
be upheld so long as the men who had produced that constitution were in power. If these men fell, drastic revision of the
structure of government might well follow.

In order to create an apparatus for local government, the
cabinet had called for the establishment of local councils or
committees. Although various members of the Taryba expressed
satisfaction with the way the job was progressing,[10] their confidence does not correspond to eyewitness reports.[11] The country
had been devastated by the war, and with the Germans now
suddenly enfeebled by disintegration within their own ranks, the
people were ready to listen to the various revolutionary agitators.
Many peasants supported soviet rule, believing that this was the
quickest way to effect a land reform.[12] Chaos reigned in the
country, and the problem was compounded by the failure of the
government to organize an effective army.

Since April the Taryba had been operating a registration
bureau in Vilna at which all the returning Lithuanian war
veterans were invited to register. Eventually the Lithuanians
hoped to organize a military force of these registrants. But the

---

pp. 5-6, 67; Garfunkelis, *Žydų tautinė autonomija*, p. 13; M. Zasetski, "Ministerstvo
Belaruskikh Sprau za 10 mesiatsou istanavlan'nia" (The Ministry of Belorussian
Affairs after 10 Months), *Chasopis'* (The Chronologer), No. 1 (1919), pp. 2-5.

[10] Klimas (Vilna) to Šaulys (Berlin), letter, December 7, 1918, in Šaulys Archives, f. 75.

[11] Korzonaj (Telsiai, Lithuania) to Šaulys (Berlin), letter, January 13, 1919, in
Šaulys Archives, f. 76.

[12] See Žadeikis, *Didžiojo karo užrašai*, II, 223.

Taryba did nothing to encourage registration, to organize those who had registered, or even to keep track of the men after registration. By fall the total registration was just 41.[13]

Voldemaras chose as his Deputy Minister of Defense a Russian, General Kondratavičius (Kondratovich). Condemnation of Kondratavičius's policies is one of the few points on which almost all Lithuanian commentators on this period can agree. He was criticized severely in the Taryba, but Voldemaras refused to oust him.[14] Kondratavičius's first concern seems to have been to create an anti-Bolshevik front of all the border governments rather than to concentrate on the defense of Lithuania as an independent state. He favored the creation of a small but trustworthy force which was called a militia but which was organized as an army.[15] Although a call for volunteers was issued on November 23, the organization of volunteer units was hindered by various restrictions, including the requirement that each enlistee have letters of recommendation.[16] The failure of the government to equip itself with a military force deprived the potentially loyal elements in the country of any rallying point. When the revolutionaries opened their offensive, they encountered no opposition on the part of the Taryba and its supporters.[17]

Probably the greatest weakness of the government lay in its lack of funds. Since its founding the Taryba had operated under the patronage of the German authorities, and apart from them had almost no source of material aid.[18] Now the problem arose of financing the work of the independent government. It was impossible to collect any taxes. Aid from the American Lithuanians could not be mobilized in time. A small loan of 30,000 marks was raised among the members of the Taryba, but it could cover

[13] Ruseckas (ed.), *Savanorių žygiai*, pp. 9-10. Some Lithuanian units had organized by themselves in Russia, but they were unable to reach Lithuania or to be of aid to the new state. See Poland, General Staff, *Wojsko litewskie*, p. 32.
[14] Steponaitis, "Ginkluotų jegų klausimas," *Karo Archyvas*, III (1926), 19-21.
[15] *Ibid.*, III (1926), 13. Cf. Waligóra, *Na przełomie*, p. 25.
[16] Uspenskis, "1-as gudų pulkas Gardine," *Karo Archyvas*, I (1926), 161.
[17] See the comments on rural organization in Navakas, *Lietuvai besikeliant*, pp. 28 ff.
[18] See Klimas (ed.), *L'état lituanien*, p. 162.

only a part of the governmental expenditures.[19] When the Germans suggested that the Lithuanians purchase material from the occupation forces, Finance Minister Martynas Yčas seized the opportunity and negotiated a loan of 10,000,000 marks. Yčas later told a story in connection with this loan, which gives some indication of the problems facing the new government:

> I began worrying that someone might rob our State Treasury. So I went to our Vice-Minister of Defense Kondratavičius, asking him to assign a guard to the Treasury. He promised to do this, but several days passed, and still no soldiers came. At a meeting of the Taryba, I said to Kondratavičius, "General, when will you send the soldiers?" And he answered, "You know, Mr. Minister, the situation is such: I gave the order to the commanders of the first and second regiments, but they answered that there are no enlisted men." There was nothing to be done. I spoke with Mr. Prusas, the Director of the Bank of Commerce and Industry, and decided to organize a guard by myself.
>
> Mr. Prusas recommended to me an officer whom he knew, Usanis. I quickly looked up the man and asked him to organize a guard of twelve men. After several hours he brought to me twelve men of different ages and in various uniforms. This army had to be armed. Although we were ministers of an independent state, German military law still prevailed, and it was forbidden to keep arms under penalty of death.
>
> But we got a revolver for each minister and a rifle for each member of the Treasury guard, with a revolver for Usanis. I sent the men over to the arsenal to get their guns. And then the brave Lithuanian army, with twelve rifles, marched over Gediminas Hill, past the Cathedral, and turned in to St. George Prospect, where the Finance Ministry was at No. 3. Suddenly a German patrol met them, disarmed them, and threw them all into jail.
>
> Several hours passed before we could free them. The guns were returned, but on the condition that no bullets be kept in them. The soldiers I had organized stood proudly at the doors of the Finance Ministry, saluting us as we passed, but the Treasury was in danger. Two armed bandits would just have to break in, and the Treasury would be emptied.[20]

Many complications arose from the fact that while the Ger-

---

[19] Yčas, "Lietuvos vyriausybės sudarymo etapai," in *Pirmasis dešimtmetis*, I, 109 ff.

[20] *Ibid.*, I, 110-11.

mans had surrendered in Western Europe, they still stood as conquerors in Eastern Europe.[21] There had been some hope that Allied troops would be sent into Eastern Europe to replace the Germans, but this proved unfounded.[22] The Entente, foreseeing some of the problems which would arise from the lack of authority in Eastern Europe, had inserted a provision into the Armistice which called for the withdrawal of German troops behind Germany's border of 1914, but only when the Entente considered it feasible with reference to the internal conditions in the territories concerned.[23]

The Armistice also annulled the Treaty of Brest-Litovsk, which had been based on German military strength. The Russian Soviet government was quick to denounce the treaty in turn, proclaiming,

The toiling masses of Russia, Lithuania, Estonia, Poland, Latvia, the Ukraine, Finland, the Crimea, and the Caucasus, freed by the German revolution from the yoke of an oppressive treaty dictated by the German militarists, are now called upon to decide their own fate.[24]

Having already declared self-determination an integral part of its program, the Russian government did not claim Lithuania and the other areas for itself. Instead, it gave aid to the various Communist parties which had already been formed in the different regions. On November 15, the Western Red Army, consisting of three divisions, was formed out of former Red Army units.[25] This Western Red Army supposedly was made up of volunteers from the various western border regions.

The revolutionary spirit which swept through Germany on the heels of the military collapse also reached the German armies on the Eastern front. On November 11 the Soldatenrat der 10. Armee (the Soldiers' Council of the Tenth Army, the occupation army in Lithuania) held its first meeting in Minsk. On November 12 the council took over the army newspaper, *Die Zeitung der 10.*

---

[21] See Dmowski, *Polityka polska*, pp. 398-400.
[22] See the comment in Palmer, *Bliss*, p. 375.
[23] See United States, *Foreign Relations: 1918, Russia*, II, 838.
[24] Bunyan (ed.), *Intervention*, pp. 153-54.
[25] Andreev, *Bor'ba litovskogo naroda*, p. 44.

Armee, converting it into an organ of the council, and made arrangements to work with AOK (Armee Oberkommando), the High Command of the Tenth Army.[26] The same procedure was followed in all the German armies on the Eastern front, and in Kaunas the Zentralrat der Ostfront was formed, to which all the smaller councils were invited to send delegates. On November 13 the Zentralrat issued a manifesto, laying out the ideas of the council movement (*Rätebewegung*):

The German Council Government [*Räteregierung*] is anti-Bolshevik. The council movement on the East front greets the Russian people but refuses any connection with destructive and bloodthirsty Bolshevism. We do not want your bread . . . but rather we simply desire that among you the will of the entire people will rule and not just the terrorism of a minority.[27]

The best German troops had been sent to the Western front after the formal conclusion of hostilities in the East, and morale was low among the soldiers who had remained there during the summer and fall of 1918. In November the German High Command decided to consolidate its front, and the War Ministry ordered AOK to withdraw its troops to the line Gontsevichi-Molodechno-Baranovichi-Dvinsk, which would still leave all of Lithuania under German occupation. The new line was to be held only by volunteers.[28]

Under these circumstances it was natural that the Lithuanians should work in close understanding with the Germans. The German government was the only power which had recognized the Taryba, and the German forces in Lithuania still controlled almost all aspects of political and economic life there. Once having decided to continue support of an independent Lithuania, the Germans, on November 15, converted the military administration of Lithuania into a civil administration, headed by Dr. Zimmerle. Zimmerle's task was to direct the transfer of all

[26] Protokollbuch des Soldatenrats der 10. Armee (MS in Šaulys Archives, f. 27), pp. 1-5.
[27] Šaulys Archives, f. 26.
[28] The line marked the extent to which the Germans had introduced their standard-gauge railway tracks. See *Die Post*, No. 602 (November 25, 1918).

national and local functions of government to the Lithuanians. In this role he naturally had to maintain very close relations with the Lithuanian government. It has been claimed that he was in fact directing the policies of the Lithuanian government, but while he certainly did his best to influence the Lithuanians, there is no evidence that he was dictating to them.[29] The Lithuanians, for their own part, acted quickly to broaden their contacts with the German government, and on November 20, Jurgis Šaulys was named Minister Plenipotentiary to Berlin, thereby becoming the first diplomatic representative of the Lithuanian government.

The Lithuanians realized, however, that their future no longer lay with the defeated Germans but with the Entente. The first move of the Voldemaras government on November 11 was to send a radio broadcast to the Allied Conference at Spa, announcing the formation of the cabinet and appealing for aid against the Bolsheviks.[30] A delegation under Father Konstantinas Olšauskis was then sent to the War Council at Spa to seek arms. The Lithuanians realized that their past ties with the Germans might prejudice their cause in the eyes of the Allies, and therefore Petras Klimas, the secretary of the Taryba, began assembling a collection of documents on German-Lithuanian relations from 1915 to 1918,

since in this way the Lithuanian question can be clarified for the Entente, which apparently still considers the Taryba a German creation. Is it possible that the Entente would refuse to recognize us just because of that?[31]

[29] The Poles were particularly antagonistic toward him. See below, chapter VIII. Zimmerle's communiqués to the German Foreign Office give no indication that he thought himself to be the real authority in Lithuania. See his report on a conversation he had with various leaders of the Lithuanian government in Vilna on November 20, 1918; Germany, Foreign Office, *Hauptarchiv: Litauen*, Reel 430, frame 18.

[30] M. Yčas, "Lietuvos vyriausybės sudarymo etapai," in *Pirmasis dešimtmetis*, I, 108.

[31] Klimas (Vilna) to Šaulys (Berlin), letter, December 7, 1918, Šaulys Archives, f. 75. A German edition of this collection was published in December, 1918, at the same time that a Lithuanian introduction was brought out. The French edition cited in this study, *L'état lituanien*, was published later.

In the latter part of December, Šaulys, then in Bern, addressed an appeal to the Entente asking for the recognition of Lithuania.[32]

In early November there had been some speculation that the Entente would shortly recognize the independence of the Baltic States,[33] but that proved incorrect. The Entente was in no position to embark on an active policy among the Baltic peoples at this time. Furthermore, the Lithuanian case had been compromised gravely by the continued dispute between the members of the Taryba and Gabrys. In September, after the controversy at Lausanne, Gabrys had begun a campaign to discredit the Taryba in Western eyes, seeking a mandate to go to Lithuania with Entente or American backing to organize a government there by himself. He offered no definite program, waiting instead to see what his proposed patrons favored, so that he could adopt their ideas as his own.[34] His important role in Switzerland during the war gave his arguments a great weight, despite the fact that he himself was known to have worked with the Germans.[35] All in all, this controversy only resulted in further confusing the Lithuanian question.

The Lithuanian government achieved one very important success in mid-December, when the American Lithuanians announced their formal recognition of the Vilna government and asked the United States government to recognize it. At the same

[32] See Jurgis Šaulys, *La Formation du Gouvernement Provisoire Lituanien* (Geneva, 1919).

[33] *Neue Zürcher Zeitung*, No. 1454 (November 1, 1918); *Der Bund*, No. 553 (December 29, 1918).

[34] See the reports sent between November, 1918, and January, 1919, to the American Mission in Paris by Francis MacNutt, a strong supporter of Gabrys (United States, National Archives, 861L.00/11, 15, and 33). Several close associates of Gabrys were sure that he was for federation with Poland, while the Lithuanians who supported him were sure that he stood unswervingly for complete independence. See Jurgela, Lithuania and the United States, p. 111; *Le Temps*, January 25, 1920; Gabrys, *Vers l'indépendance*, p. 234.

[35] See report dated September 27, 1918, from Kazys Pakštas in Switzerland to the Lithuanian National Council in America, United States, National Archives, 861L.00/3. Although he now denounced the Taryba as a German creation, Gabrys himself continued to maintain very friendly relations with the German Foreign Office. See the report by Müller (Bern) to the Foreign Office, February 27, 1919, Germany, Foreign Office, *Hauptarchiv: Litauen*, Reel 431, frame 358.

time the American Lithuanians announced that they would send delegates to present Lithuania's claims to the various delegations attending the peace conference at Paris.[36] In late December, while at Bern, Šaulys sent a letter to the American Lithuanians, explaining the situation in Lithuania more fully and naming the Lithuanian Executive Committee, made up of representatives of the Catholics and the Tautininkai, as the diplomatic representative in America of the Lithuanian government.[37] The American Lithuanians had earlier participated in the Mid-European Union, a project sponsored by Thomas Masaryk, with the hope that that group might aid them in putting their case across to the American public. These hopes were disappointed when the union proved hardly able to survive the withdrawal of the Poles over the dispute with the Ukrainians in Galicia and Marsaryk's own departure for Paris.

The Lithuanian government looked hopefully to America, both because of Wilson's reputation and because of the influence that the emigration might be able to exert. To the American experts concerned with the drafting of the peace, however, the Lithuanian problem was either a part of the Polish problem or the Russian question, without any merits of its own. They thought Lithuania should either be united with Poland or else become an autonomous part of Russia. There was no plan to support complete independence.[38] The Lithuanians, nevertheless, hoped to persuade the American government of the righteousness of their cause. In the meantime they complained about the conduct of the German troops in Lithuania, asking for a Western occupation army to be sent, or else for permission to organize the 10,000 Lithuanian-Americans in the AEF for

[36] Lithuania, Delegation to Paris, *Composition,* IV, 4-A5; *Der Bund,* No. 548 (December 25, 1918).

[37] *Vienybė Lietuvninkų,* No. 5 (January 29, 1919). When Šaulys arrived in Switzerland, he was greeted by newspaper articles, apparently planted by Gabrys, attacking him as a monarchist who was going to sell out Lithuania to the Germans. See *Neue Zürcher Zeitung,* No. 1672 (December 16, 1918); Šaulys's answer in No. 1730 (December 27, 1918); see also *Der Bund,* No. 553 (December 29, 1918).

[38] Report of the Intelligence Section of the American Mission to the Paris Peace Conference, January 21, 1919, United States, National Archives, 861L.00/145.

service in Lithuania, as well as for equipment and military stores for 20,000 men.[39]

Acting independently of Vilna, the Lithuanian National Council, representing the American Lithuanian Catholics, in a letter dated November 14, asked the Secretary of State for recognition of Lithuanian independence, the unification of Lithuania Major and Lithuania Minor, representation for Lithuania at the peace conference, a United States military mission to help in organizing an army, and dispatch of an occupation army.[40] In addition, the Lithuanians bombarded the White House with various statements on the Lithuanian problem.[41]

The United States government refused to commit itself in the matter of Lithuanian independence, although it realized that aid to Lithuania was necessary in order to contain the threat of Bolshevism in Europe. In a memorandum dated December 30, 1918, Allen W. Dulles called attention to the importance of Lithuania and Poland as the last dam against the Bolshevik threat and stressed the need for helping them. He came out in favor of some sort of cooperation between the two nationalities, pointing out that Piłsudski's federalism and Gabrys's apparent inclination toward federalism opened the way for an agreement.[42] Despite all this debate, the Lithuanians still received no direct aid from the United States in these first few months of paper independence. In a letter of December 5, 1918, to the Lithuanian National Council, the Department of State declared that, while the American government was not unmindful of Lithuanian aspirations,

at the same time, you are informed that the Department is not prepared to recognize any new government in Lithuania at present and

---

[39] United States, *Foreign Relations: Paris Peace Conference*, II, 24-25.

[40] United States, *Foreign Relations: 1918, Russia*, II, 845-849.

[41] The American government was not completely ignorant of Lithuanian claims before this campaign. At least five documents in the House Inquiry were written from a pro-Lithuanian point of view: No. 171, The Lithuanian-Baltic Question; No. 185, Lithuania; No. 268, Geography and Population of Lithuania; No. 461, The Peoples of the Baltic Provinces and Lithuania; No. 476, Poland and Lithuania.

[42] United States, *Foreign Relations: Paris Peace Conference*, II, 481-83.

is furthermore of the opinion that the [question?] of military assistance is one for consideration by the War Council in Versailles.[43]

Nor was any more abundant aid secured from the British or the French. The French would listen to no Lithuanian spokesman but Gabrys, and he opposed any moves which would strengthen the position of the Taryba.[44] The British showed more signs of being helpful, but they too were hesitant about supporting the German-tainted Taryba, although they had already granted *de facto* recognition to the new regimes in Estonia and Latvia.[45] When a British admiral, Sir Edwyn S. Alexander-Sinclair, landed in Liepaja in early December, a Lithuanian delegation was there to greet him, but although he promised aid, nothing concrete was settled.[46] The most the British would do was to recommend an agreement with the retreating Germans.[47]

The failure of the Entente to provide immediate aid, together with the blockade now imposed by the victors in the Baltic Sea, forced the Lithuanians to continue to rely on the Germans. But the Germans proved to be less dependable than had been hoped. The volunteers who were to take over the front from early December failed to arrive, and the German troops continued

[43] United States, *Foreign Relations: 1918, Russia*, II, 856-57.

[44] He was not opposed to the principle of sending aid to Lithuania, having himself already made an unsuccessful effort to persuade the Swiss to send a military mission there. See the letter to Gabrys from the Political Department of Switzerland, December 10, 1918, in the archives of Juozas Gabrys, Vevey, Switzerland. The author is deeply indebted to Mrs. Juozas Gabrys for permission to examine these archives.

[45] The British recognized Latvia on November 11, 1918, a full week before the Latvian State Council declared its independence. (November 18). This recognition was explicitly provisional and was to be effective only until a decision had been reached by the peace conference on the political future of Latvia. Mejerovič to the Committee on Baltic affairs, Paris Peace Conference, in Conférence de la Paix, *Recueil*, IV, C, (7) Commission des Affaires Baltiques, 75.

[46] Morris (Stockholm) to American Mission in Paris, telegram, December 29, 1918, United States, National Archives, 861L.00/13. See also M. Yčas, "Lietuvos vyriausybės sudarymo etapai," in *Pirmasis dešimtmetis*, I, 108; Žadeikis, *Didžiojo karo užrašai*, II, 219; Birontas, *Bermontininkams Lietuvą užpuolus*, pp. 24-26; Dopkewitsch, "Zur englischen Politik im Baltikum," *Deutsches Arkhiv für Landes- und Volksforschung*, VI (1942), 138.

[47] United States, *Foreign Relations: 1918, Russia* II, 840. Cf. Von Hehn, "Die Entstehung der Staaten Lettland und Estland," *Forschungen zur osteuropäischen Geschichte*, IV (1956), 153 and 169.

their retreat homeward over the anguished protests of the Lithuanians and the Entente.[48] Behind the Germans, at a distance of some fifteen to twenty kilometers, came the Bolshevik Red Army. There was little fighting between the Germans and the Russians, and in fact there seems to have been some sort of agreement between the two forces concerning the German retreat.[49] Actually the Germans could not have resisted the Communist advance. The fighting value of their troops had "sunk almost to zero because of known influences,"[50] and when the promised volunteers failed to arrive in December, retreat remained the only course.

The Germans now faced a serious problem. By the terms of the Armistice, they were to hold the Eastern front until the Entente decided otherwise. With the disintegration of the German forces, a substitute had to be found to oppose the Bolsheviks. The Lithuanians were unable to assume this role, and so there remained only the Poles. Piłsudski was already demanding that the Poles be allowed passage to the front, and his protests grew in vehemence when it became clear that the Germans were planning to evacuate Vilna.[51]

The Polish-Lithuanian dispute over Vilna was now being sharpened by the changing military situation. The Lithuanians claimed the guberniyas of Vilna, Grodno, Suwalki, and Kaunas, part of Courland, and Lithuania Minor, all on the grounds that the population was "purely Lithuanian." When pinned down to facts, they would admit that Grodno was overwhelmingly Belorussian,[52] and that they claimed Vilna primarily on histori-

[48] See Jakštas, "Saksų savanorių dalys," *Karo Archyvas*, VI (1935), 184.

[49] See *ibid,,* p. 56; Schröder and Heygendorff, *Die sächsischen Freiwilligen-Truppen*, p. 4; United States, *Foreign Relations: Paris Peace Conference*, IV, 11; Noske, *Von Kiel bis Kapp*, p. 176.

[50] AOK report to Kriegsministerium, Berlin, December 23, 1918, Šaulys Archives, f. 26. In a report to the Foreign Office on December 31, the army command declared, "Only a few volunteers on hand. Great number sent back as useless." Germany, Foreign Office, *Hauptarchiv: Litauen*, Reel 430, frame 143.

[51] United States, *Foreign Relations: Paris Peace Conference*, II, 421.

[52] Voldemaras admitted this in an interview with an American official in October, 1919, but he claimed that the people could be "educated" to accept Lithuanian rule. Report of the United States Military Attaché in Warsaw, October 16, 1919, United States, National Archives, 861L.00/127.

cal grounds.[53] As a support for their claims, however, they could now point to the presence of Belorussian and Jewish spokesmen in the Taryba. Voldemaras considered it a major achievement to have secured their participation,[54] since it greatly strengthened the Lithuanian claims to Grodno and especially to Vilna. The Lithuanians scored a victory early in the struggle for Vilna when Father Jurgis Matulaitis-Matulevičius, a Lithuanian, was named Bishop of Vilna by the Holy See.[55]

The Lithuanians wanted complete independence from Warsaw and sought acceptance of this condition by the Poles living in Lithuania. In November, 1918, Voldemaras claimed that the Polish Committee in Vilna had been refused seats in the Taryba because of its "reactionary politics,"[56] but the view that the Poles refused the seats seems more plausible.[57] In any case the Vilna Poles refused to break with Warsaw.

The Polish government in Warsaw, formed by Piłsudski on November 11, favored federation with Lithuania. Speaking to a delegation of Warsaw Lithuanians, Piłsudski, in the middle of December, called the Taryba imperialistic. Asserting that the Poles had no claims to ethnic Lithuanian territory— meaning essentially Kaunas guberniya—Piłsudski expressed the hope for some sort of union between Poland and Lithuania. He warned that the connection with the Germans would hopelessly com-

---

[53] The claims were confused for a long time. In February, 1919, it was finally decided to use the map in Petras Klimas, *Lietuva, jos gyventojai ir sienos* (Lithuania, Its Inhabitants and Boundaries) (Vilna, 1918), which demanded Grodno guberniya north of the Neman River, thus including the city of Grodno. See Sleževičius (Kaunas) to Šaulys (Berlin), letter, n.d. (March, 1919), in Šaulys Archives, f. 28.

[54] Voldemaras (Vilna) to Šaulys (Berlin), letter, November 28, 1918, Šaulys Archives, f. 75. Vakar (*Belorussia*, p. 104) is mistaken when he states that the Germans forced the Lithuanians to accept the Belorussians into the Taryba.

[55] He was consecrated in Kaunas on December 1 and was formally installed in Vilna on December 8. The original Lithuanian candidate for the post, open since 1907, was Father Olšauskis, but he was rejected because of Polish opposition. Cardinal Ratti and the Papal Nuncio in Munich, Eugenio Pacelli, both of whom later became Popes, then suggested Matulaitis to the Lithuanians. See Matulaitis, *Užrašai*, pp. 139 ff.

[56] Voldemaras (Vilna) to Šaulys (Berlin), letter, November 28, 1918, Šaulys Archives, f. 75.

[57] Lithuania, Delegation to Paris, *Composition*, VII, 1.

promise the Lithuanian government in the eyes of the Entente, and so it would be in the best interests of the Lithuanians to come to some agreement with the Poles.[58] At the same time, however, Piłsudski's government lacked Entente recognition. Dmowski's National Committee, located in Paris, had been accepted by the Western powers as the representative of the Poles. The extent to which Piłsudski and Dmowski would cooperate in organizing Poland—personally the two were hardly on speaking terms— was as yet undecided, and accordingly the whole future course of Polish politics was uncertain.

As the German retreat was making ever more urgent the problem of defending Vilna from the Bolsheviks, the Poles sought ways and means of taking over this task. Warsaw asked the Entente to compel the Germans to allow Polish forces to take over the front,[59] and it attempted to reach a direct agreement with the Germans. In mid-December, Piłsudski sent a representative, Captain Górka, to Vilna to discuss the matter with the German command. The Germans referred Górka to the Lithuanian government, and the Polish officer spoke with Voldemaras on December 19. Although he urged the Lithuanians to make a defense agreement with his government, Górka had no powers to negotiate such an agreement.[60] There seems to have been some indication by Voldemaras at this first talk that an accord might be reached, and the Polish government promptly announced that a definite agreement had been made for the defense of Lithuania by the Poles.[61] On December 23, Górka again approached the Lithuanians, this time as an official plenipotentiary of the Polish Foreign Ministry. But Voldemaras, Yčas, and Smetona had now left Vilna, and the cabinet was in the process of being reorganized. When Górka announced that

[58] Piłsudski, *Pisma zbiorowe*, V, 42; Wielhorski, *Polska a Litwa*, pp. 288-89; Kasakaitis, "Lietuviai Varšuvoj," in *Pasaulio lietuviai*, pp. 189-90.

[59] Poland, Ministry of Foreign Affairs, *Documents diplomatiques*, I, 5-6.

[60] Lithuania, Delegation to Paris, *Composition*, VII, 1. The Polish accounts of these talks do not usually mention the fact that Górka had spoken with the Lithuanian government before December 23.

[61] *Die Post*, No. 6 (January 4, 1919); *New Europe*, March 20, 1919, p. 237; *Revue Baltique*, I (1919), 143.

news of an agreement had already been sent to Foch, Šilingas, a member of the presidium of the Taryba and Acting Chief of State, protested, declaring that only the cabinet of ministers could make such a decision and so this must be a misrepresentation of Voldemaras's statement. The matter was thereupon brought before the cabinet—the make-up of the cabinet at this time is not clear—and an answer was given Górka by telephone that evening. While the Lithuanians expressed their thanks for the proffered help, they asserted that they could accept it only on the condition of complete recognition of the independence of Lithuania with its capital in Vilna. The Poles gave no answer to this proposal, and the matter was dropped.[62]

The Communists were becoming increasingly active during the month of December. Kapsukas and Zigmas Aleksa-Angarietis, together with several other Communists, had arrived in Vilna in the beginning of December with instructions from Moscow. They were immediately co-opted to the Central Committee of the Communist Party of Lithuania and Belorussia, and in a meeting on December 8 the Central Committee organized the Provisional Revolutionary Workers' Government of Lithuania.[63] According to Kapsukas himself, the move was made on instructions from Moscow, for in fact the Lithuanian Communists were loathe to declare their independence of Russia.[64] The draft of the manifesto of the government, drawn up by Kapsukas, stressed the need for close bonds with Russia with the proclamation, "Long live union with the RSFSR."[65] In reviewing the manifesto, the Central Committee of the Russian Communist Party eliminated the reference to union and also

[62] *Vyriausybės Žinios* (Kaunas), No. 2/3 (January 16, 1919); Poland, Ministry of Foreign Affairs *Documents diplomatiques*, I, 1-2, 5-6; Wielhorski, *Polska a Litwa*, pp. 289-90.

[63] See Mickevičius-Kapsukas, "Bor'ba za sovetskuiu vlast'," *Proletarskaia Revoliutsiia*, No. 108 (1931), p. 76n.

[64] *Ibid.*, pp. 77-78. The Estonian and Latvian Communists were similarly hesitant about declaring their independence. See Von Hehn, "Die Entstehung der Staaten Lettland und Estland," *Forschungen zur osteuropäischen Geschichte*, IV (1956), 159.

[65] Mickevičius-Kapsukas, "Bor'ba za sovetskuiu vlast'," *Proletarskaia Revoliutsiia*, No. 108 (1931), p. 81. See also Andreev, *Bor'ba litovskogo naroda*, p. 49.

changed the name of the government to the Provisional Revolutionary Workers' and Peasants' Government of Lithuania.[66]

Although Vilna was still occupied by the Germans, on December 15 a soviet was formed for that city by a gathering of some 220 delegates, presided over by Dr. Andrius Domaševičius, one of the founders of the Lithuanian Social Democratic Party. The Communists held only 96 seats, but they dominated the meeting, gaining five of the nine seats in the presidium of the soviet, as well as electing their own candidate, Pranas Eidukevičius, as chairman.[67] On the initiative of the Communists the soviet declared that it was "the sole agent of government which all citizens must obey."[68] The Communists proved unable to direct the meeting entirely, however, and when a resolution greeting the RSFSR was passed only in a watered-down form, and then only by a close vote, the Communist faction announced that it would send its own greetings.[69]

On December 16, the day on which the soviet announced its decision to take power in Vilna, the Communist Party announced the formation of the Provisional Revolutionary Workers' and Peasants' Government of Lithuania, headed by Kapsukas and Angarietis.[70] The government considered itself free of responsibility to the soviet. It was responsible only "to the Central Committee of the Communist Party of Lithuania and Belorussia."[71] The Central Committee in turn had the "rights" of a regional committee of the Russian Communist Party and was "completely subordinate to the Central Committee of the

[66] Mickevičius-Kapsukas, "Bor'ba za sovetskuiu vlast'," *Proletarskaia Revoliutsiia*, No. 108 (1931), p. 81.

[67] *Komunistas*, No. 1 (December 20, 1918). Eidukevičius had worked personally with Lenin before 1914. See Paleckis, *Sovetskaia Litva*, p. 25. The Russian word *sovet*, the Lithuanian word *taryba*, and the German word *Rat*, all mean "council." In 1918 and 1919 *taryba* was used to designate both the nationalist and the Communist councils in Lithuania. For the sake of clarity, "Taryba" is used in this study only in reference to the nationalist organization, while "soviet" is used for the councils organized by the Communists and their sympathizers.

[68] *Komunistas*, No. 2 (December 22, 1918). See also Mickevičius-Kapsukas, "Bor'ba za sovetskuiu vlast'," *Proletarskaia Revoliutsiia*, No. 108 (1931), p. 84.

[69] *Komunistas*, No. 1 (December 20, 1918).

[70] *Ibid.*, No. 3 (December 24, 1918). [71] *Ibid.*, No. 5 (December 29, 1918).

Russian Communist Party."[72] The Russian Communists made no effort to hide their role in the formation of the Lithuanian government. *Izvestiia* declared, "Soviet Russia . . . has followed the path of least resistance, namely that of creating independent Soviet republics of Estonia, Lithuania and Latvia."[73]

In actual fact, the Communist government was only a shadow government. Immediately after its organization on December 8, its members had split up—some remained in Vilna; others, taking the name of the government with them, went to Vileika. Beyond the attempts to gain recognition by the soviets, this government seems to have done nothing but publicize its program. The purpose of its formation was simply to prepare the way for the Red Army.[74]

Although the Lithuanian Communist government was successful in gaining the recognition of many rural soviets, it met with opposition from the Vilna Soviet. On December 22, the Vilna Soviet, opposing the "dictatorship of the Communist Party over the soviets," refused to recognize the Communist government, claiming the supreme power in Lithuania for itself until the meeting of a congress of soviets.[75] Seeing that they would be defeated, the Communist faction refused to participate in the vote on this question, but did manage to block a move aimed at dislodging its hold on the top posts in the soviet.[76]

The German authorities in Vilna refused to recognize either the Communist government or the soviet. When the soviet attempted to go ahead and organize its own administration, the Germans arrested forty railroad workers, all of whom were

[72] From the program of the Russian Communist Party, adopted in March, 1919. *Kommunisticheskaia Partiia Sovetskogo Soiuza v resheniiakh s"ezdov, konferentsii i plenumov TsK* (The Communist Party of the Soviet Union in the Decisions of its Congresses, Conferences, and Plenums of the Central Committee) (Moscow, 1953), I, 443.

[73] *Izvestiia*, No. 283 (December 25, 1918).

[74] See the comment in *Komunistas*, No. 2 (December 22, 1918).

[75] Mickevičius-Kapsukas, "Bor'ba za sovetskuiu vlast'," *Proletarskaia Revoliutsiia*, No. 108 (1931), p. 87; *Komunistas*, No. 3 (December 24, 1918).

[76] See *Przełom*, No. 2 (December 28, 1918); Kellor and Hatvany, *Security against War*, I, 61.

members of the Communist faction in the soviet.[77] On December 24 the soviet led a strike in retaliation, demanding release of the prisoners, recognition of the authority of the soviet in the city, and permission to organize a militia. On December 25 the occupation authorities released the prisoners, but they refused to yield to the other demands.[78] The Communists were extremely disappointed in the refusal of the German Soldiers' Council to recognize the soviet.[79]

The growing strength of the Communists underlined the weakness of the Lithuanian government, and the decision of the German High Command, on December 14, to evacuate Vilna because of a lack of capable troops[80] added to the troubles of the Taryba. Rumors were rife that the government was preparing to flee to Western Europe, but on December 20, Smetona denied this in a talk with Mykolas Sleževičius, the leader of the Liaudininkai (Populists), who had just arrived in Vilna as a refugee from Soviet Russia. At the same time, however, Smetona confirmed reports that the government would have to evacuate Vilna, and that the new capital was to be Grodno, which Kondratavičius considered easier to defend than Kaunas.[81] Meetings were held by various political parties that very evening to consider this news. Some of the hotter heads demanded the disbanding of the Taryba, but calmer counsel prevailed, since the Taryba had now become known abroad as the chief organ of the Lithuanian government and its destruction might cause confusion harmful to the national cause.[82]

---

[77] *Komunistas*, No. 3 (December 24, 1918). The railway workers were an extremely powerful group because of their control of transportation facilities.

[78] *Ibid.*, No. 4 (December 28, 1918); Mickevičius-Kapsukas, "Bor'ba za sovetskuiu vlast'," *Proletarskaia Revoliutsiia*, No. 108 (1931), pp. 86-88. Andreev credits the Communist Party with having organized the strike (*Bor'ba litovskogo naroda*, p. 60).

[79] See *Komunistas*, No. 3 (December 24, 1918); proclamation of the Soldatenrat, undated, Šaulys Archives, f. 26.

[80] Zimmerle to Foreign Office, December 14, 1918, in Germany, Foreign Office, *Hauptarchiv: Litauen*, Reel 430, frame 43.

[81] Būtėnas and Mackevičius, "Gyvenimas ir darbai," in *Mykolas Sleževičius*, pp. 77-78.

[82] *Ibid.*, pp. 79-80.

On December 21 it was discovered that Yčas, Smetona, and Voldemaras had left the city during the night. Their departure has been the subject of much debate. Their political opponents have maintained that they fled in fear, deserting the government.[83] Their later defense was that they had gone abroad on official business, as they in fact did. Yčas and Voldemaras went to Berlin, where a few days later they completed negotiations for a loan of 100,000,000 marks, an extremely important prop for the tottering Lithuanian government.[84] Smetona went to Sweden and the other Scandinavian countries where he sought to organize the recruitment of volunteer forces for Lithuania.[85] Yčas later claimed that all proper preparations had been made and that Petras Leonas had been charged with running the government.[86] But Stašinskis, the Minister of Internal Affairs, and not Leonas, headed the caretaker government,[87] and the adequacy of the preparations is doubtful. Furthermore, the dangers which the government was facing were well known, and the three men must have realized that their departure would contribute to sharpening the crisis.

On December 22, Kondratavičius announced that the government would now be evacuated to Kaunas, but that the defense staff would go as planned to Grodno. He furthermore allowed the army officers to go home for Christmas; those who so desired were later to reassemble in Grodno, the others apparently being free to do as they wished.[88] The Lithuanian nationalists within the officer corps objected to this strange policy and "mutinied." They demanded a reorganization of both the military staff and the government.

---

[83] The same charge was leveled at Ulmanis in Latvia for a similar action at this time. See Tallents, *Man and Boy*, p. 289.

[84] Text of agreement in Annex 5 of report on the Lithuanian situation by Colonel Dawley (Warsaw), May 20, 1919, United States, National Archives, 184.01502/29.

[85] *Die Post*, No. 7 (January 4, 1919).

[86] M. Yčas, "Lietuvos vyriausybės sudarymo etapai," in *Pirmasis dešimtmetis*, I, 113.

[87] Dogelis, *Mano gyvenimo prisiminimai*, p. 232.

[88] Ruseckas (ed.), *Savanorių Žygiai*, p. 12.

Ideas for a dictatorship were bandied about, but no acceptable leader was to be found.[89] On December 23, Sleževičius agreed to head a new government, but he rejected the idea of a dictatorship as being impracticable, since the Lithuanian government was far too weak. He accepted the premiership of a coalition cabinet and dismissed the much attacked Kondratavičius. The Social Democrats now reversed an earlier stand against participating in the cabinet and thus opened the way for similar participation by the Liaudininkai, who, as a party, had refused to accept the sole responsibility of government.[90]

On December 26, Stašinskis resigned on behalf of the Voldemaras cabinet, and Sleževičius was formally invited to organize a new cabinet. Voldemaras, then abroad, had no say in this change of government and later proved bitterly resentful. But his government was hopelessly discredited; as one Lithuanian put it, "Voldemaras's government was not a complete success. He did not effect a single step in the foundation of Lithuania. He was replaced, not by way of resignation, but of expulsion, by the cabinet of M. Sleževičius."[91] Sleževičius reached an agreement with the leaders of the Taryba whereby that group was not to interfere with the work of the cabinet until the meeting of the proposed state conference, now planned for mid-January. The new cabinet took office on December 27.[92]

The Lithuanians were very careful to make the change appear to outsiders a routine reorganization rather than a revolution. Voldemaras was kept as Foreign Minister, probably because he was in the West on government business, and the position of the Taryba in the government was not formally altered. Neverthe-

[89] Škirpa, "Pakeliui su Mykolu Sleževičium," in *Mykolas Sleževičius*, pp. 206-7.

[90] *Ibid.*, pp. 208-10. The coalition was based on the Christian Democrats and the Liaudininkai, the two leading peasant parties. Andreev claims that Kondratavičius only now entered the government (*Bor'ba litovskogo naroda*, p. 63).

[91] Jurkunas (Stockholm) to Šliupas (London), letter, February 26, 1919, United States, National Archives, 183.9 Lithuania/13.

[92] Būtėnas and Mackevičius, "Gyvenimas ir darbai," in *Mykolas Sleževičius*, p. 84. The account of the cabinet change given in Sapoka (ed.), *Lietuvos istorija*, p. 548, is completely erroneous.

less, news leaked out that Voldemaras and Smetona had been overthrown, and official denials could not completely dispel the resulting confusion.[93]

One participant in the turnover characterized it as a change from the "conservatism" of Smetona and the Pažanga to the "dynamic liberalism" of Sleževičius.[94] The new cabinet formally charged that the Voldemaras government had proved "unable to rouse the country to the productive enthusiasm so necessary at this hour."[95] On December 29 the government issued a new call for volunteers. Asserting that "Lithuania is in danger," the announcement urged, "Boldly, without fear, as our fathers and forefathers, let us stand against our enemies, and raise our efforts for our Mother Fatherland [*sic*—"Motin Tėvynė'], for the Lithuanian State!"[96] These efforts were still too little and too late to affect the Germans' plans to turn Vilna over to the Poles.

Bypassing the Lithuanian government, which was totally incapable of defending Vilna by itself, the Germans decided to revive the local communal government in Vilna, which they had suppressed upon occupying the city in 1915. This move avoided a ticklish political decision, and at the same time answered the demands of the Entente and of Warsaw, since the city administration was dominated by the Poles.

Since the end of October, great numbers of Polish legionnaires had been pouring into Vilna, and now they prepared to take over the defense of the city. Although the Germans continued to prohibit the carrying of arms by civilians for fear of incidents involving the German forces, plans for turning the city over to the Poles went ahead.

With the aid of men sent by the Warsaw government, the Poles already had organized a civil administration for the Vilna

[93] A Havas dispatch announcing the change reported that Voldemaras had been thrown out of the government altogether. *Neue Zürcher Zeitung*, No. 140 (January 29, 1919). An official denial pointed out that he was still Foreign Minister. *Ibid.*, No. 162 (February 3, 1919).

[94] Škirpa, "Pakeliui su Mykolu Sleževičium," in *Mykolas Sleževičius*, p. 202.

[95] *Vyriausybės Žinios*, No. 1 (December 29, 1918).

[96] Būtėnas and Mackevičius, "Gyvenimas ir darbai," in *Mykolas Sleževičius*, p. 92.

area.[97] On December 31, 1918, Warsaw appointed a military administration, which in turn issued a mobilization order proclaiming, "Whoever believes in God is with us, whoever believes in Satan is against us."[98]

In the face of all this, Sleževičius's government made one last attempt to secure the support of the Vilna Poles. On December 30 the Lithuanian representatives, headed by J. Vileišis, opened talks with a delegation of five Poles. The Poles demanded that the Lithuanians, "faithful to tradition centuries old, agree to enter into a political union with Poland."[99] The Lithuanians, on the other hand, demanded the recognition of the independence of the Lithuanian state with its capital in Vilna. In answer to this, the Poles agreed to recognize the independence of Lithuania, but maintained that its territory could be decided only by a formal agreement between the Polish and the Lithuanian governments.[100] In other words, they refused to endorse Lithuanian claims to Vilna.

On January 1 the Lithuanian government completed its preparations for the evacuation of Vilna. The move involved the dispersal of the cabinet, since several of its members refused to leave the city. Mykolas Biržiška, the Minister of Education, was appointed Governor of Vilna, and Augustinas Janulaitis, the Acting Minister of Foreign Affairs, Jakob Vygodski, the Minister of Jewish Affairs, and Dr. Basanavičius all joined him. A token force of some fifty soldiers was left in Vilna as a symbol of the Lithuanian claim to sovereignty over the city. The government left on January 2.

On the same day as the government's departure, the Vilna Poles were given a final note—Polish writers always refer to it

---

[97] *Monitor Polski*, No. 9 (January 15, 1919); Budecki, *Stosunki polsko-litewskie*, p. 17.

[98] *Monitor Polski*, No. 2 (January 3, 1919). See also No. 238 (December 27, 1918)' No. 3 (January 4, 1919); *Dziennik Narodowy*, No. 296 (December 29, 1918); *Kurjer Polski*, No. 2 (January 3, 1919). General Wejtko headed the defense of the Vilna district, and General Mokrzecki was commandant of the city. See Waligóra, *Na przełomie*, p. 39.

[99] Zoltowski, *Border of Europe*, p. 192.

[100] Wielhorski, *Polska a Litwa*, p. 290; Poland, Ministry of Foreign Affairs, *Documents diplomatiques*, I, 2.

as an "ultimatum"—demanding recognition of Lithuanian independence, with Vilna as the capital, stating that this was the *sine qua non* for further talks.[101] On that same day the Poles took over control of the city from the Germans and broke up the Vilna soviet after a pitched street battle which lasted over twelve hours.[102] The token force left by the Lithuanian government refrained from any participation in the struggles for the city, and on the evening of January 5, just before the Red Army's entry into Vilna, quietly left for Kaunas.

Friction arose between the Poles and the German troops, and there was some open fighting between them before the final evacuation of the city by the Germans. The Germans reported that numerous Poles had been disarmed, and that five Poles had been killed and six to eight wounded, while five Germans had been wounded. The German army withdrew its last forces at 2:00 A. M. on January 4 "in orderly fashion and without any further incidents."[103]

On the evening of January 4 the Poles realized that they would be unable to hold the city against the advancing Red Army, and set their own evacuation for the next day. The Poles charged that the refusal of the Germans to free supply lines had caused a shortage of ammunition and that this had made resistance to the Bolsheviks impossible.[104] On the night of January 5 the Red Army occupied the city.

The fall of Vilna made a great impression on all concerned. The German soldiers and the Lithuanians were more upset at yielding the city to the Poles than they were by the Bolshevik occupation. Twelve members of the Soldatenrat der 10. Armee resigned in protest against the High Command's decision to

[101] Wielhorski, *Polska a Litwa*, p. 290; Poland, Ministry of Foreign Affairs, *Documents diplomatiques*, I, 3.

[102] Mickevičius-Kapsukas, "Bor'ba za sovetskuiu vlast'," *Proletarskaia Revoliutsiia*, No. 108 (1931), pp. 89-91.

[103] Report of the Soldatenrat der 10. Armee to Ober-Ost, January 4, 1919, Šaulys Archives, f. 26.

[104] *Kurjer Polski*, No. 9 (January 11, 1919); Wejtko, *Samoobrona Litwy i Bialorusi*, p. 92.

evacuate the city.[105] A report of the Soldatenrat criticized the High Command for having "done everything humanly possible to play Vilna into the hands of the Poles."[106] The Lithuanian government protested against the presence of Polish troops and officials in Vilna in two notes, one delivered to Wejtko by Biržiška on January 2 and the other, dated January 4, sent to Warsaw by courier.[107] The fall of the city to the Bolsheviks was a great disappointment to Piłsudski. Wasilewski later reminisced, "It was the first—and last—time I saw the Commandant crying."[108]

The reorganization of the Lithuanian government in December had not come in time to save Vilna. But it is also a debatable point whether even a more vigorous policy by Voldemaras and Kondratavičius in November could have accomplished more.[109] The financial situation was a tremendous obstacle to any action. Whether the Taryba might have organized a force secretly during the summer of 1918 is an entirely different question, but such speculation or judgment is beyond the province of this study.

The hope for the future lay with the new premier. Sleževičius was a popular figure, well established as a political leader and head of the Liaudininkai, a peasant party. The Christian Democrats, another party drawing the major part of its support from the peasantry, backed the Liaudininkai, largely, it would seem, because they lacked capable leaders of their own at this time. The peasant parties were much more capable of establishing some control over the rebellious countryside than was the Pažanga, which was made up of intellectuals and enjoyed little popular backing.[110] Of course, whether this potential of even the peasant parties could be realized, yet remained to be seen. The

---

[105] *Zeitung des Soldatenrats der 10. Armee,* January 7, 1919.

[106] Cited in Vydunas, *Siebenhundert Jahre deutsch-litauischer Beziehungen,* p. 375.

[107] Wielhorski, *Polska a Litwa,* p. 295; Poland, Ministry of Foreign Affairs, *Documents diplomatiques,* I, 3; Natkevičius, *Lietuvos kariuomenė,* p. 21; Waligóra, *Na przełomie,* p. 43.

[108] Wasilewski, *Józef Piłsudski,* p. 166.

[109] Lithuanian writers have tended to exaggerate the strength of the Lithuanian army in 1919 and 1920, thus heaping greater condemnation on Voldemaras.

[110] See Wasilewski, *Litwa i Białoruś,* pp. 205-8.

government lacked any means of self-defense, and the possibility was great that the government would be able to spend only a few days in Kaunas before being forced by the advancing Red Army to move on to Tilsit.

IV

"Standing Room Back Against the Wall"

JANUARY–APRIL, 1919

AT THE beginning of January, when the Provisional Revolutionary Workers' and Peasants' Government of Lithuania took power in Vilna, the Communists appeared to be almost invincible. Their opposition had simply melted in front of the Red Army, and there seemed nothing to stop their advance on the Prussian border. Suddenly, however, the picture changed; the German lines stiffened.

Sleževičius, in Kaunas, had appealed to the Entente to bring pressure to bear on the Germans to halt their withdrawal on the grounds that the retreat constituted a violation of the terms of the armistice.[1] The German army command in Lithuania, however, asserted that it was powerless; Zimmerle, at the beginning of January, told Sleževičius that nothing could be done so long as the army refused to obey the commands of its officers. On the other hand, a leading member of the Soldatenrat informed Sleževičius, in Zimmerle's presence, that the soldiers had been ordered to retreat, and that they were ready to fight when called upon to do so.[2]

Sleževičius thereupon instructed Šaulys in Berlin to ask the German government to step in. The Germans at this time were faced with the Bolshevik threat from several directions. The difficulties in evacuating the Ukraine, the Red terror in Riga and among the Baltic Germans, and revolutionary disorders in Berlin all served to bring the German government around to a policy of action. On January 8 or 10, Šaulys reported back to Kaunas that the German government had decided against

[1] *Vyriausybės Žinios*, No. 2/3 (January 16, 1919).
[2] Būtėnas and Mackevičius, "Gyvenimas ir darbai," in *Mykolas Sleževičius*, pp. 100-1.

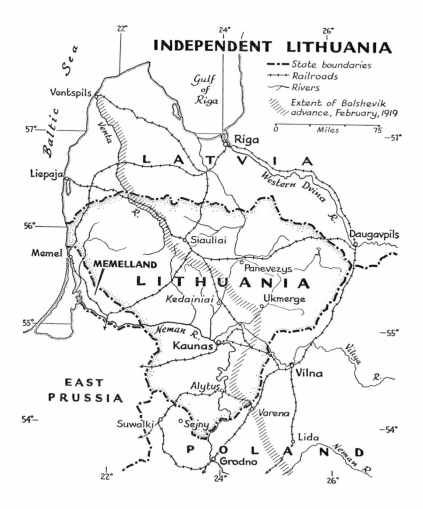

INDEPENDENT LITHUANIA

— · — State boundaries
+—+—+ Railroads
～⌒～ Rivers

▨ Extent of Bolshevik
advance, February, 1919

0 ———— Miles ———— 75

Note: The boundaries shown on this map are those that existed between 1920 and 1939. The Memel Territory, separated from East Prussia by the Treaty of Versailles, was joined to Lithuania in 1923, but was returned to Germany in 1938. The southeastern boundary with Poland, resulting from Zeligowski's seizure of Vilna in 1920, was formalized by the Conference of Ambassadors in 1923, although the Lithuanians recognized it only in 1939.

evacuating Kaunas.[3] The German military authorities then drew up a line of demarcation before Kaunas and notified the Communists, with whom open conflict had thus far been avoided, that "crossing this line will be considered a hostile act."[4]

The successes of the Communists had been based more on the weakness of their opposition than on their own power, and with the stiffening of the German lines, the Red Army was stopped.[5] At the beginning of January the long-awaited German volunteers had finally begun to arrive in Kaunas, coming mainly from Saxony, and by the end of the month there were about 4,000 of them in Lithuania. The Lithuanian government agreed to pay each volunteer four marks per day and to provide equipment for 10,000 men. On January 7, Šaulys signed an agreement in Berlin with a semiofficial German trade organization, Banga, which was established for the express purpose of supplying equipment to the Lithuanians,[6] and on January 28, Sleževičius himself traveled to Berlin where he negotiated an agreement in principle with the Germans on joint military action against the Bolsheviks.[7]

There are indications that the Germans might not have acted if the German government had had any assurances that the Red Army would stop when it reached the East Prussian border.[8] This action by the Germans must therefore be considered as primarily defensive, although throughout the following months the German troops were feared to have political ambitions within

[3] *Ibid.*, p. 101. The date of Šaulys's reply is uncertain.
[4] Report of the German Plenipotentiary in Lithuania, January 23, 1919, Germany, Foreign Office, *Hauptarchiv: Litauen*, Reel 430, frame 207.
[5] There were just 500 men in the force which took Vilna. See *Komunistas*, No. 17 (January 29, 1919).
[6] Text of the agreement with Banga in Annex 6 of the report by Colonel Dawley, May 20, 1919, United States, National Archives, 184.01502/29. On the agreement on volunteers, see Dawley's report of May 5, 1919, United States, National Archives, 184.01502/29. See also Jakštas, "Saksų savanorių dalys," *Karo Archyvas*, VI (1935), 186.
[7] German Foreign Office memorandum, January 31, 1919, Germany, Foreign Office, *Hauptarchiv: Litauen*, Reel 430, frame 218.
[8] See Noske, *Von Kiel bis Kapp*, p. 176.

Lithuania.[9] There is, however, no evidence in the German Foreign Ministry archives of actual participation by German officials in any plots against the Lithuanian government, and despite any threat the Germans might have posed to the political future of the country, the presence of the German troops was absolutely essential to the Lithuanians. Without them, Kaunas probably could not have been held.[10]

Behind the now stabilized front the Communist regime in Vilna worked feverishly to consolidate its position. In late December it had organized the Vilna Military Revolutionary Committee, which, although it was meant only to deal with counterrevolutionary matters, now supplanted the intransigent Vilna Soviet as an administrative organ. In the countryside similar committees, made up only of Communists and their sympathizers, replaced soviets which disagreed with the Communists' land policy. These committees were all subordinate to the Military Revolutionary Committee of Lithuania, headed by Kapsukas.[11]

The Communists did not intend to create a Lithuanian national state, but planned instead to appeal to the population along class lines. As Kapsukas told a group of Vilna Lithuanians:

We do not recognize a state coat of arms or state and national colors. We have struggled too much for the Red flag to tolerate beside it such "stripes." We do not recognize the Lithuanian language as a state language, for in our order there is no state nation or state language— or more precisely, all of them are official languages: Lithuanian, Polish, Belorussian, and Yiddish.[12]

[9] *Pravda*, No. 45 (February 27, 1919), reported that the Germans were openly threatening to break up the Lithuanian government and seize power for themselves. In a letter to Šaulys on February 24 (Šaulys Archives, f. 28), Sleževičius expressed his fear that the Germans were conspiring with the Christian Democrats, and he requested Šaulys to do what he could to "paralyze this policy."

[10] German forces were also decisive in saving Latvia, while Estonia was helped by Finnish volunteers. See Von Hehn, "Die Entstehung der Staaten Lettland und Estland," *Forschungen zur osteuropäischen Geschichte*, IV (1956), 160.

[11] *Komunistas*, Nos. 10 and 12 (January 12 and 17, 1919). See also the reports given to the Congress of Military Revolutionary Committees, *ibid.*, No. 20 (February 5, 1919).

[12] Juozas Tumas-Vaižgantas, *Vaižganto Raštai* (The Writings of Vaižgantas) (Kaunas, 1924), IV, 237.

In organizing the governmental apparatus, the Communists found that because of a shortage of capable party workers they had to invite non-Communists into the government. Although the Communists naturally reserved the top posts for themselves, three Lithuanian Social Democrats thus entered the Council of People's Commissars. These men in turn brought other Lithuanian intellectuals into the government with the result that the Communist regime was actually giving some help to the Lithuanian nationalists. [13]

The Bolsheviks were at first pleased by the decision of the Lithuanian intellectuals to cooperate, and they made an attempt to use them as a go-between in negotiating an agreement with the Kaunas government. [14] But as the month of January wore on, it became clear that the divergence of interests between the two sides was not to be bridged. The "bourgeois" elements in the government worked assiduously for national ends, and the Communists found their own edicts almost impossible to enforce. In early February, an article in the party organ, *Komunistas*, denounced the "arch opportunist" policy of the intellectuals in joining the government, [15] and many non-Communists were soon dropped from the government. Embarking upon a campaign to suppress its opposition, the Communist government closed down the opposition press, prohibited gatherings in the street of more than five persons under threat of the use of armed force to disperse them, reimposed the death penalty, which had been abolished in the first days of the regime, and arrested Lithuanian nationalists as hostages for Communists imprisoned in Kaunas. [16]

The Bolshevik agrarian policy, laid out by Zigmas Aleksa-

[13] The Social Democrats were Vaclovas Biržiška, Vladas Požela, and Vaclovas Bielskis. See the discussion of Biržiška's work in the Commissariat of Education, in *Nepriklausomoji Lietuva*, Nos. 2-4 (April 26, 27, and 29, 1919). The Poles were especially strong in the Commissariat of Defense.

[14] See *Komunistas*, No. 11 (January 14, 1919); *Lietuva*, No. 129 (June 18, 1919).

[15] *Komunistas*, No. 22 (February 9, 1919). The article was unsigned, but the author may well have been A. A. Joffe, assigned by Moscow as advisor to the Lithuanian Communists.

[16] *Ibid.*, Nos. 23, 24, and 29 (February 12, 14, and 26, 1919).

Angarietis along the lines of that in Russia, was arousing great discontent in the countryside which had at first welcomed the Red Army as a relief from the Germans. The Communists called for keeping the large estates intact for collective cultivation, a program which ran directly counter to the desires of the peasantry to divide the land as soon as possible. In early January the government nationalized the land, allowing small holders to keep the land which they were already working by themselves, but prohibiting transfers of land.[17] Angarietis warned that immediate division of the estates would profit only the wealthy, the fatnecks (*storkakliai*).[18]

Angarietis hoped first to organize large-scale cultivation on the estates and then to convince the small holders that they should voluntarily unite to form collectives.[19] Soviets favoring division of the land were suppressed and replaced by the more dependable military revolutionary committees. The Commissariat of Internal Affairs organized special "flying squads" of Communists to protect the estates from the peasants,[20] and the Communist press fulminated vigorously against the "demagogy" of the nationalist parties in advocating land reform.[21]

Nevertheless the Communists were unable to realize their program. Peasants favoring division of the estates began to take over the military revolutionary committees as well as the soviets.[22] By March the government was calling on the farm workers to suppress not only the soviets but also the revolutionary committees wherever the latter opposed the policies of the government.[23] Angarietis even came to categorize the small holders as "undependable."[24]

---

[17] *Ibid.*, No. 12 (January 17, 1919).   [18] *Ibid.*

[19] *Ibid.*, No. 2 (December 22, 1918) and No. 11 (January 14, 1919).

[20] *Ibid.*, No. 12 (January 17, 1919).

[21] See Mickevičius-Kapsukas, "Bor'ba za sovetskuiu vlast'," *Proletarskaia Revoliutsiia*, No. 108 (1931), p. 104.

[22] *Komunistas*, No. 33 (March 8, 1919).

[23] *Ibid.*, No. 41 (March 30, 1919)l

[24] *Ibid.*, No. 37 (March 1, 1919); see also Nos. 33 (March 8, 1919) and 38 (March 21, 1919).

The failure of the agrarian program was especially disastrous because Vilna had always depended on the Kaunas area for its food. Now cut off from its regular sources of supply, the region was suffering from famine.[25] Although food was imported from the Ukraine and Belorussia, and the bread ration was cut by half in mid-February, at the end of February there was still only a two-day supply of food in Vilna.[26]

The Lithuanian Communist state had no real basis for life. As a workers' state, it lacked a proletariat; as an agricultural state, it lacked food and had aroused the enmity of even the poor peasantry; as a Communist state, it lacked a strong party. Furthermore, its national policy satisfied no one. Accordingly, in the course of January, the Communists decided to revise their political policy radically. On February 3, the First Congress of Soviets of Belorussia called for the merger of the Lithuanian and Belorussian states.[27] The Second Conference of the Communist Party of Lithuania and Belorussia, meeting at this same time in Vilna, welcomed this proposal "in the belief that the union will be the first step toward a larger united federation of all the Soviet Republics."[28]

The First Congress of Soviets of Lithuania, meeting in Vilna February 18 to 23, approved the union and adopted a constitution based on the model of that of the Russian Soviet Republic.[29] With this move, the Communist experiment in establishing an independent Lithuanian state ended. The agrarian policy had been the fatal weakness of the government, which lacked the strength to impose its will on the peasantry. The policy of opposing division of the estates not only alienated the population in the area held by the Communist government, but it also

[25] Andreev, *Bor'ba litovskogo naroda*, p. 71.
[26] *Izvestiia*, No. 47 (March 1, 1919).
[27] *Pravda*, No. 25 (February 4, 1919).
[28] *Komunistas*, No. 23 (February 12, 1919). The new state was meant eventually to become part of a single RSFSR. *Pravda*, No. 41 (February 22, 1919).
[29] *Komunistas*, No. 30 (February 28, 1919). For an account of the unification of the Communist parties of the two states, see *ibid.*, Nos. 31, 33, and 40 (March 2, 8, and 25, 1919).

destroyed the Communists' appeal to the peasantry in the area held by the nationalist government.[30]

On the other side of the frontier, the nationalist government in Kaunas was much more successful in winning the support of the people, mainly through advocating land reform. The Liaudininkai had already espoused this program, and in January the Central Committee of the Christian Democratic Party came out for land reform for the landless and small-holding peasants, directly contrasting this to the measures of the Communist government in Vilna which sought to keep the estates together.[31] In this way the two major Lithuanian peasant parties, together with the government in which they participated, established their power over the Lithuanian public.

The Polish parties, based on city labor and on the great landlords, could not have any appeal for the Lithuanians, and in fact were the targets of the Lithuanian parties, whose policy of land redistribution was now a basic tenet of their programs. Most of the Polish landowners had withdrawn from Lithuania with the Russians in 1915 and, rather than return to their estates now, had gone to Poland, where they undoubtedly had great influence in urging the Warsaw government to establish some sort of control over Lithuania. The Germans had no appeal at all for the Lithuanian populace. Their presence in the country was dictated by military needs, and the German army was hated because of the deprivations imposed by the occupation. It was, in fact, necessary for the Lithuanian government to end its dependence on the Germans as soon as possible in order to present a better appearance to the West and to avoid being compromised in the eyes of the peasantry.

The long-awaited State Conference finally met at Kaunas from January 16 to 23, 1919. The make-up of the conference was disappointing to the Socialists, who had been the strongest advocates of convoking the assembly. The Christian Democrats

---

[30] For a more detailed account of the existence of the Communist government in Vilna, see Senn, "Die bolschewistische Politik in Litauen," *Forschungen zur osteuropäischen Geschichte*, V (1957), 93-118.

[31] *Neue Zürcher Zeitung*, No. 235 (February 16, 1919).

held a clear majority of the deputies, 93 of 160, and supported the Taryba, calling on the cabinet to work in closer cooperation with that body. The Liaudininkai opposed this demand, and Jonas Vileišis raised the question of the competence of the conference, since the disorderly conditions had made a uniform procedure for the election of deputies impossible.[32] The conference, however, maintained that it had the right to debate the policies of the government. It elected eight new members to the Taryba and insisted on closer cooperation between the cabinet and the Taryba. The cabinet refused to obey this demand, and the conference ended with the structure of government still undecided.[33]

One of the major criticisms leveled at Sleževičius during the conference was aimed at his liberal policy on civil rights, because, the Christian Democrats charged, he viewed the Bolsheviks as an ordinary party rather than as conspirators and agents of a foreign power. The Christian Democrats wanted a stricter rule. Sleževičius at first refused to act, but the anarchy in Kaunas and the Communist threat finally forced him to crack down. On February 16 the Lithuanian government proclaimed martial law with the penalty for treason being death,[34] and, in order to hinder Bolshevik infiltration into Lithuania, it declared that Russian money was unacceptable as legal tender.[35]

Throughout the first months of 1919, the government worked

[32] *Antroji Lietuvos Valstybės Konferencija* (Kaunas, 1919), p. 6. *Pravda*, No. 16 (January 24, 1919), speculated that the Socialist government would negotiate with the Bolsheviks rather than bow to the demands of the conference.

[33] No stenograms were kept of the conference. One account—*Antroji Lietuvos Valstybės Konferencija*—was published under the supervision of the presidium of the Taryba, but since it is not a verbatim account, it must be used with caution. Cf. the account in Būtėnas and Mackevičius, "Gyvenimas ir darbai," in *Mykolas Sleževičius*, pp. 102 ff. In accordance with the policy of keeping domestic disagreements out of the foreign press, the reports issued by the governments on the proceedings of the conference were noncommittal. Cf. *Neue Zürcher Zeitung*, No. 150 (January 31, 1919).

[34] Būtėnas and Mackevičius, "Gyvenimas ir darbai," in *Mykolas Sleževičius*, p. 109.

[35] *Neue Zürcher Zeitung*, No. 327 (March 6, 1919). Later, tsarist rubles—but not Kerensky rubles—were again declared acceptable as currency. See Šapoka (ed.), *Lietuvos istorija*, pp. 574-575.

feverishly to organize its army. It had issued a new call for
volunteers on December 29, 1918. The volunteers were to receive 100 marks per month, with allotments for their families.
In addition, they were promised land.[36] On January 15, 1919,
the government announced the mobilization of all former
officers of the Tsarist Russian army up to the age of forty-five.[37]
On January 25 a military school was opened, and on February
13 the clases of 1897 and 1898 were mobilized.[38] The mobilized
men did not receive the privileges of the volunteers. Some discontent arose when men arriving from Bolshevik-occupied territory were considered to have been mobilized, and the ruling was
subsequently revised so that all such refugees could become
volunteers.[39]

It has been said that the organization of the army in January
was the final step in the organization of the state, and so from
then on Lithuania enjoyed a *de facto* existence.[40] However, paper
organization must not be confused with real organization. The
army was still too small to be an effective instrument. It was
only at the battle of Kedainiai, on February 10, that Lithuanian
troops first had direct contact with the Bolsheviks. The Germans
continued to bear the brunt of the warfare, and the partisan
movement behind the Bolshevik lines, working independently
of the Kaunas government, was more important than the regular
army. Therefore, it is only in late April and May, when the
partisan forces were incorporated into the regular army, that the
Lithuanian state can be considered a reality.[41]

The Lithuanian government realized that German aid offered
at best a temporary salvation. The cabinet wanted Entente in-

---

[36] See Dogelis, *Mano gyvenimo prisiminimai*, p. 234; *Vienybė Lietuvninkų*, No. 12
(March 19, 1919); Natkevičius, *Lietuvos kariuomenė*, p. 25.

[37] *Vyriausybės Žinios*, No. 2/3 (January 16, 1919).

[38] *Vienybė Lietuvninkų*, No. 18 (April 30, 1919).

[39] Raštikis, *Kovose del Lietuvos*, I, 132. See also *Neue Zürcher Zeitung*, No. 220
(February 14, 1919); Šapoka (ed.), *Lietuvos istorija*, p. 549.

[40] See Rutenberg, *Die baltischen Staaten und das Völkerrecht*, pp. 63-66. See also
Natkevičius, *Lietuvos kariuomenė*, pp. 58-59.

[41] Navakas, *Lietuvai besikeliant*, pp. 91-92; Ruseckas, *Savanorių žygiai*, p. 18. There
are no figures available as to the size of the partisan forces either in February, or
in May, 1919.

tervention to relieve it of this one-sided dependence: "All our policy must be directed toward the Entente . . . . For the future of our country, we must depend especially on England and America, and not on Germany."[42] In February, Sleževičius instructed Šaulys in Berlin to work for the establishment of an Allied commission for Lithuania which would help to control the Germans as well as aid the Lithuanians directly.[43]

The early months of 1919 saw a great expansion of Lithuanian representation abroad. In December, 1918, Šaulys had installed a formal representative in Switzerland. One American Lithuanian later criticized this move, maintaining that Kaunas should have first reached an agreement with the American Lithuanians.[44] The fact was that the conflict with Gabrys was continuing unabated, and the Lithuanian government feared his influence. There were even two Lithuanian Press Bureaus in Switzerland at this time, Gabry's and one established by Šaulys.

Cooperation with the emigration was more quickly achieved in London. Arriving there from America in early February, Šliupas and Tomas Naruševičius organized a Lithuanian Information Bureau.[45] In March the Lithuanian government sent Čepinskis and K. Bizauskas to London to establish formal representation there, and the transfer of functions from Šliupas to them was carried out smoothly.

Šaulys continued in his post in Berlin. His main job, after the German decision to aid Lithuania against the Bolsheviks, was to conclude a state treaty with Germany, but agreement could not be reached because of the Lithuanian refusal to renounce all designs on Lithuanian East Prussia.[46] Šaulys apparently made

---

[42] Sleževičius to Šaulys, January 7, 1919, quoted in R. J. Šarmaitis (R. Ia. Sharmaitis), "Interventsiia anglo-amerikanskikh imperialistov v Litve v 1918-1920 gg.," *Istoricheskie zapiski*, No. 45 (1954), p. 268. There is no copy of this letter in the Saulys Archives.

[43] Sleževičius (Kaunas) to Šaulys (Berlin), letter, undated, Šaulys Archives, f. 28. See also the report of Grant-Smith (Copenhagen) to Polk (Washington, D. C.), March 8, 1919, United States, *Foreign Relations: 1919, Russia*, pp. 672-73.

[44] Bartuška, *Kryžiaus keliais*, pp. 299-300.

[45] *Neue Zürcher Zeitung*, No. 271 (February 23, 1919).

[46] Šaulys Archives, f. 30.

an effort to persuade the Lithuanian government to make Berlin
the center for all the foreign missions, probably on the grounds
that Kaunas had no direct contact with Western Europe. Smetona refused this in the name of the Presidium on the grounds
that thus raising the importance of one post would be improper,
and, even more important, that the location in Berlin would
surely antagonize the Entente.[47] Care was also taken in other
corners to avoid an excessive connection with Berlin in the eyes of
the Entente. The press agency in Switzerland asked Šaulys to
hold up all communiqués for the press in Berlin until after they
had been released in Switzerland. Otherwise, the Western press
services would refuse to carry them, and it was impolitic to be
connected only with Wolff, the German agency.[48]

In January, 1919, Smetona and Voldemaras toured the
Scandinavian countries, and in February, Voldemaras proceeded to London and then to Paris, where he took charge of the
Lithuanian delegation to the peace conference. Although Lithuanian missions and information bureaus were established in Den-
mark and Sweden in January and in Finland in February,
Smetona continued to represent the Lithuanian government in
Scandinavia as something of an envoy-at-large.[49] His role in this
particular period was important, but he was not an active leader
in the government.[50]

In March the Lithuanian government sent a special delegation
to the other governments of the eastern Baltic area to set up
economic and political relations. The mission was well received
in Latvia, Estonia, and Finland, and reportedly concluded
several trade agreements.[51] How significant these agreements
were is unclear in view of the continued Entente blockade of
Lithuania.

[47] Smetona (Copenhagen) to Šaulys (Berlin), letter, March 4, 1919, Šaulys
Archives, f. 76.
[48] Chadakauskaitė (Bern) to Šaulys (Berlin), letter, January 25, 1919, Šaulys
Archives, f. 76.
[49] See Savickis, "Skandinavija," in *Pirmasis dešimtmetis*, I, 76.
[50] His letters to Šaulys in Berlin and to Olšauskis in Paris, contained in the
Šaulys Archives, ff. 75 and 76, indicate that he was out of touch with current events.
[51] See *Kurjer Polski*, No. 152 (June 18, 1919); *Nepriklausomoji Lietuva*, Nos. 27-28
(May 27 and 28, 1919). See also Tallents, *Man and Boy*, p. 290.

While in Stockholm in early February, Smetona opened negotiations with Latvian Prime Minister Ulmanis on the matter of a loan from the Lithuanians to the Latvians.[52] Apparently the Letts were in even more dire straits than the Lithuanians, and an agreement was concluded in late February during a visit by Ulmanis to Kaunas. In return for granting a loan of 5,000,000 marks, the Lithuanians received extensive rights in the use of the Latvian port of Liepaja.[53] The potential advantages of this agreement were also neutralized by the Entente blockade.

The Lithuanian Executive Committee represented the Kaunas government in America. Although the Lithuanian Catholics in America were still sympathetic to Gabrys, whom they had financed during the war, they now threw their support to the Kaunas government, hoping that some sort of a compromise might be reached. The Tautininkai backed the Kaunas government without any reservations. The Executive Committee continued to make representations to the United States government in support of the Lithuanian cause, but it was at Paris that the American Lithuanians made their greatest contribution at this time.[54]

Gabrys was the first Lithuanian political figure to arrive in Paris, coming at the end of December, 1918, at the invitation of the French government.[55] The French hoped for a quick agreement between the Lithuanians and either the Poles or the Russians, and so they suggested to Gabrys that he speak with Polish and Russian representatives in order to see what might

[52] Smetona (Stockholm) to Šaulys (Berlin), letter, February 15, 1919, Šaulys Archives, f. 76.

[53] Dailidė, *Lietuvos sutartys*, I, 3-5. For some reason the loan was not announced abroad, although Ulmanis's visit was widely reported. See *Der Bund*, No. 103 (March 9, 1919); *Neue Zürcher Zeitung*, No. 353 (March 9, 1919). The loan was only announced in mid-summer. See *Vienybė Lietuvninkų*, No. 32 (August 6, 1919). Andreev claims that Latvia loaned money to Lithuania (*Bor'ba litovskogo naroda*, p. 118).

[54] A collection of the notes sent the United States government by the Lithuanian Executive Committee can be found in the documents relating to the Lithuanian national movement, listed under Dr. Julius Bielskis's name, at the Hoover Institution, Stanford, California.

[55] Gabrys, *Vers l'indépendance*, p. 238. See Voldemaras's comment on French policy in his *Lithuanie et Pologne* (Berlin, 1920), pp. 22-23.

be done. In his memoirs, Gabrys is noncommittal on the results
of these conversations, although he does say that he found agreement with Roman Dmowski impossible.[56] He seemed much
more favorably inclined toward the Polish federalists, and he
seems actually to have reached some sort of agreement with
Dłuski, a Polish federalist and the alternate Polish delegate to the
peace conference. On February 5, appearing before a committee
headed by Noulens—this committee later became the Peace
conference's Commission on Polish Affairs—he reported that he
had made an economic and military agreement with Polish
representatives, a copy of which he would submit confidentially
to the members of the committee.[57] The text of this agreement
is not available. In his memoirs, Gabrys makes no mention of the
agreement, maintaining that at this meeting he had argued only
for independence.[58]

The first representatives of the Kaunas government to arrive
in Paris were Father Olšauskis and the rest of the delegation
originally sent in November to Spa. On their arrival in early
January, another Lithuanian denounced them to the French
police as German spies, and they were arrested. Gabrys rescued
them from jail and joined them in forming a Lithuanian delegation; Olšauskis became chairman and Gabrys secretary.[59] The
American-Lithuanian delegation arrived soon after this and
joined forces with Olšauskis and Gabrys.

The Lithuanian government was very upset at the announcement that Olšauskis was working with Gabrys. It claimed that

[56] Gabrys, *Vers l'indépendance*, pp. 238-45.
[57] Report of the American representative in the committee, United States, National Archives, 181.2130/12. Cf. the comments by Charles Rivet in *Le Temps*,
January 25, 1920.
[58] Gabrys, *Vers l'indépendance*, p. 253. He recounted that he was not able to convince Noulens, who was from the Pyrenees, that Lithuania could not be considered
Poland's Brittany or Alsace. See also *Die Post*, No. 105 (February 26, 1919). There
is nothing on this matter in his archives.
[59] M. Yčas, "Lietuvos vyriausybės sudarymo etapai," in *Pirmasis dešimtmetis*, I,
118. Gabrys's memoirs do not mention Father Olšauskis's having been arrested
(*Vers l'indépendance*, p. 251). Actually Gabrys and Olšaukis were old friends, and
their personal friendship continued throughout the following years, even when
Gabrys was *persona non grata* in Lithuania.

the delegation to Spa had proceeded to Paris without authorization and announced the formation of a special delegation for the peace conference.[60] Smetona was to head this delegation, but the French refused him a visa on the grounds that he was a Germanophile.[61] Voldemaras was then named head of the delegation, and he entered Paris from London at the beginning of February, seemingly without too much trouble.[62] Martynas Yčas in Switzerland was unable to get a French visa, probably through Gabrys's maneuvering, and went to Paris illegally.[63] In March, Petras Klimas also experienced great difficulties in getting permission to enter France from Switzerland.[64]

By mid-February the official delegation of the Lithuanian government was established at Paris. Father Olšauskis and the American Lithuanians immediately recognized its authority, and Gabrys was left out in the cold.[65] Balys Mastauskas, the leader of the American Lithuanians, sought to heal the breach; at one stage he reported to his superiors in America that he had succeeded in persuading Voldemaras to accept Gabrys's counsel as "a private person."[66] But it must have been an uneasy

[60] *Vienbyė Lietuvninkų*, No. 7 (February 12, 1919).

[61] M. Yčas, "Lietuvos vyriausybės sudarymo etapai," in *Pirmasis dešimtmetis*, I, 116-17.

[62] This may have been due to the influence of Šliupas, who was a firm supporter of the Kaunas government and who was apparently influential in British circles. In the French press some criticism of Voldemaras did appear because of his participation in the peace talks at Brest-Litovsk. See the letter from Charles Rivas in *La Lithuanie Indépendante*, No. 1 (August 1, 1919).

[63] M. Yčas, "Lietuvos vyriausybės sudarymo etapai," in *Pirmasis dešimtmetis*, I, 117. Yčas asked the American representative in Bern for aid in obtaining a visa (United States, Archives, 861L.00/31). MacNutt, Gabrys's stanch supporter, demanded that the American delegation in Paris urge the French not to permit Voldemaras and Yčas to come to Paris. See his report of January 29, 1919, United States, National Archives, 861L.00/33.

[64] Klimas (Bern) to Šaulys (Berlin), letter, March 6, 1919, Šaulys Archives, f. 76.

[65] The American Lithuanians had gone to Paris with an autonomous mandate, which the Lithuanian Executive Committee in Washington, D. C., now transferred to Voldemaras. Širvydas (New York) to Šliupas (London), letter, March 3, 1919, United States, National Archives, 861L.00/61.

[66] Quoted in Jurgela, Lithuania and the United States, p. 138. For his cooperation with Gabrys, Mastauskas underwent considerable attack from the *Tautininkai*, who even demanded his recall, claiming that he was not properly supporting the Kaunas government. See *Vienybė Lietuvninkų*, Nos. 7 (February 12, 1919) and 31 (July 30, 1919).

truce. Gabrys's departure for Kaunas in March with a French military mission eased the situation considerably.

Voldemaras's own character created further problems for the delegation. He refused to recognize that he had been replaced as Premier by Sleževičius—even though the latter had been the one to empower him to go to Paris—and insisted that he himself was still Prime Minister since he had never resigned. The American Lithuanians preferred not to challenge him on this and Mastauskas at first introduced him to the United States delegation as the "Prime Minister of Lithuania." A report from Smetona finally clarified the situation, and Voldemaras was forced to back down.[67]

The role of the American Lithuanians in the formation and operation of the delegation was a very large one. The delegation was financed almost exclusively by the American Lithuanians, and technical help such as stenographers, together with typewriters, had to be sent from America.[68] The American Lithuanians were very useful also in the matter of making unofficial contacts, which were especially important to the Lithuanian delegation since it was not officially admitted to the conference.

Unofficial contacts came through a number of channels. Balys Mastauskas had worked for George Creel's Committee of Public Information during the war and was even relied on by the United States delegation for information about the Lithuanian situation.[69] Other contacts were made through residents of Paris, such as O. W. Lubicz-Milosz, a French poet of Lithuanian background, and Henri de Chambon, editor of *Revue Parlementaire*,[70] who offered their services to the delegation. Another émigré who joined the delegation was Ernestas Galvanauskas, a participant in the Vilna Congress of 1905, who after

---

[67] Jurkunas (Stockholm) to Šliupas (London), letter, February 26, 1919, United States, National Archives, 183.9Lithuania/13.

[68] *Vienybė Lietuvninkų*, No. 14 (April 2, 1919).

[69] When Colonel Reboul asked Mastauskas to accompany his French military mission to Kaunas, the American delegation unofficially encouraged him to remain in Paris. See the file in the United States National Archives, 184.1Mostowski.

[70] Chambon, *La Lithuanie pendant la Conférence de la Paix*, pp. 15-16.

his emigration had worked as an engineer for a French concern in Serbia. These informal channels were extremely important, but their role cannot be detailed fully because of the lack of adequate memoir material.

Two other important members of the delegation were Simon Rosenbaum and Domonik Semashko, the Jewish and Belorussian representatives respectively. They both had originally been a part of Father Olšauskis's delegation to Spa and had accompanied him to Paris. They remained with the delegation through several reorganizations. Their participation constituted direct evidence for the claims of the Lithuanian government that it was territorial rather than narrowly national in character. In the course of 1919, these two, through their Lithuanian chairman, made numerous protests to the conference against what were described as Polish violations of the national rights of the Jews and the Belorussians.

The Lithuanian demands at Paris fall into three categories: first, recognition of the independence of the Lithuanian state within the territorial limits defined by the Lithuanians themselves; second, admission of the Lithuanian delegation to the conference; and third, aid against the Bolsheviks in the form of men, advisers, and equipment.

The delegation demanded recognition of the independance of Lithuania within the territorial limits defined by the Lithuanians themselves on the ground that Lithuania comprised a distinct national unit and that the Taryba had declared its independence on February 16, 1918.[71] Recognition would also bolster the morale of the Lithuanian forces fighting the Bolsheviks, they said.[72] The territorial claims were somewhat inconsistent, however. In a letter to the conference on March 24, the Lithuanians officially defined their territorial claims as the *guberniyas* of Vilna, Grodno, and Suwalki, as well as parts of Courland and

---

[71] Letter from Voldemaras to the peace conference, March 24, 1919, in Lithuania, Delegation to Paris, *Composition*, III, 1.

[72] Voldemaras to the peace conference, letter, March 17, 1919, United States, National Archives, 861L.00/54.

East Prussia, but in a speech on March 29 to a private audience, Milosz extended the claims into Minsk *guberniya*.[73] The Lithuanians also placed strong emphasis on the support of the Jews and the Beiorussians,[74] and they claimed Memel on the grounds that the population was Lithuanian and that it formed the Lithuanian outlet to the Baltic Sea.[75] Without Memel, they maintained, Lithuania would be "un torse sans tête" or "un homme privé de l'usage de ses bras,"[76] and they requested the admission of a delegation of Prussian Lithuanians to the conference.[77] The Lithuanian government in Kaunas had forsaken active propaganda in Lithuania and Germany in favor of the annexation of Lithuania Minor for fear of complicating its relations with the Germans. It was hoped that the Lithuanian delegation at Paris would be able to achieve this aim by itself.[78] In addition to their demand for recognition of the Lithuanian state, the delegation also sought admission to the conference. When he first organized a delegation, Father Olšauskis did not demand admission as a principal. He stated that his delegation wanted only to offer information on the Lithuanian situation.[79] He humbly declared, "We do not seek a seat at the table, but we do ask in our pride for standing room back against the wall— where we have stood so long—waiting to be heard when the

[73] O. W. Milosz, *Conférence de M. O. W. de Lubicz-Milosz à la salle de la Societé de géographie* (Paris, 1919), p 8. Rosenbaum was being severely criticized in Lithuanian circles for a similar claim. Smetona (Copenhagen) to Šaulys (Berlin), letter, March 5, 1919, Šaulys Archives, f. 76.

[74] Chambon, *La Lithuanie pendant la Conférence de la Paix*, p. 21; Lithuania, Delegation to Paris, *Composition*, III, 1. See also Dmowski, *Polityka polska*, p. 478; Wasilewski, *Litwa i Białoruś*, pp. 199-200.

[75] Lithuanian, Delegation to Paris, *Composition*, VIII, 1. [76] *Ibid.*, III, 8, 3.

[77] *Ibid.*, III, 3. A separatist movement by Lithuanians in East Prussia had started in November and December, 1918, with the organization of a Prussian Lithuanian National Council. See *Der Bund*, No. 536 (December 17, 1918).

[78] Šaulys (Kaunas) to Puryckis (Berlin), letter, March 31, 1919, Šaulys Archives, f. 28. In seeking Memel, the Lithuanians got some unsolicited aid from the Poles, who thus sought to weaken the Germans, and who still hoped to gain sovereignty over Lithuania. See Dmowski, *Polityka polska*, pp. 433, 480; United States, *Foreign Relations: Paris Peace Conference*, VI, 193-94.

[79] Letter to Lansing, January 14, 1919, United States, National Archives, 186.81/6.

question of our fate is to be decided."[80] On February 14, Volde-maras formally requested admission to the conference on the grounds that the Lithuanians had fought in the forefront of the Russian army against the Germans and also that the Lithuanians had fought in the American army. He argued that Lithuania should be admitted on the same basis as the Poles, maintaining that since the American Lithuanians had recognized the Kaunas government, it could not be called unrepresentative of the Lithuanian people. He claimed that admission was a separate question from recognition, pointing to the presence of representatives of the British dominions as showing that unrecognized governments could be admitted to the conference.[81] In an interview in late March, Clemenceau expressed his sympathies for the Lithuanian cause but stated that recognition and admission were matters to be considered only by the Great Powers acting together.[82] Voldemaras later claimed that Clemenceau had promised admission to the Lithuanians,[83] but there is no evidence of this.

Finally, the Lithuanians sought aid against the Bolsheviks in several forms. They requested military units formed of Lithuanian volunteers from the American Expeditionary Forces in Europe, and they also asked that Lithuanians be separated out of the various Polish units which had been formed in the West.[84] In addition, they requested Western military missions to aid in the organization of the Lithuanian army, together with equipment and ammunition for the army and transport facilities to take the material to Liepaja.[85] They claimed that such aid was necessary both for defense against the Bolsheviks and for emancipation from Germany.[86]

---

[80] Letter to Lansing, January 23, 1919, United States, National Archives, 183.9Lithuania/4.

[81] Chambon, *La Lithuanie pendant la Conférence de la Paix*, pp. 18-19.

[82] *Vienybė Lietuvninkų*, No. 13 (March 26, 1919).

[83] Lithuania, Delegation to Paris, *Composition*, VIII, 2.

[84] United States, *Foreign Relations: Paris Peace Conference*, XII, 136-37.

[85] Chambon, *La Lithuanie pendant la Conférence de la Paix*, pp. 17-18.

[86] See Wasilewski's sarcastic comments on the Lithuanians' attitude toward Germany, in his *Litwa i Białoruś*, p. 197.

The Lithuanian delegation at Paris found two formidable opponents in the Polish National Committee and the Russian Political Conference. The Polish National Committee had admitted delegates from Piłsudski's government, and thus it became the Polish delegation to the peace conference. Dmowski and the new Prime Minister, Paderewski, were the two official delegates, with Dłuski, a follower of Piłsudski, as an alternate.[87] The National Committee dominated the delegation, and so, despite the various brochures distributed in favor of federation, and even despite Paderewski's own federalist inclinations, Dmowski's territorial program of annexation was the official one for the delegation.[88] On January 29, Dmowski asserted.

Lithuania should comprise the whole government of Kovno [Kaunas] with adjoining districts of Kurland, of the governments of Wilno [Vilna] and Suvalki. It should form a distinct political entity, possessing a generous measure of self-government, but united politically to Poland, as it would be too small to attain genuine independence.[89]

On February 28, in a note to Cambon, he repeated his opinion that Lithuania should be "linked with Poland."[90] The Poles were interested in having "ethnic Lithuania" attached to the Polish state for several reasons. On the one hand, Lithuania could offer Poland a safe exit to the Baltic sea. On the other hand, they thought that an independent Lithuania would probably fall under German or Russian domination and be dangerous to Poland. In a declaration to the Commission on Polish Affairs on March 3, Dmowski noted that in view of the threat of Germany and Russia to Lithuania, the best course for

[87] See Wasilewski, *Józef Piłsudski*, pp. 171-74.
[88] The delegation adopted the annexationist program at a meeting on March 2, 1919, and Paderewski did not arrive till the end of March to take over the chairmanship of the delegation. See Witold Sworakowski, "Granice Polski w Wersalu," *Tygodnik Polski* (New York), No. 52 (December 26, 1943); Wasilewski, *Litwa i Białoruś*, p. 200; Poland, Delegation to Paris, *Akty i dokumenty*, I, 78; Paderewski's testimony before the Commission on Polish Affairs, April 17, 1919, United States. National Archives, 181.2132101/9. Paderewski's federalist views caused some confusion at the conference as to the Polish aims, and some Poles have claimed that he weakened the position of the Polish delegation. See Kozicki, *Sprawa granic Polski*. pp. 118-19.
[89] Quoted in Zoltowski, *Border of Europe*, pp. 194-95.
[90] Reddaway, "The Peace Conference," in *The Cambridge History of Poland*, p. 497.

the Lithuanians would be to accept some special position within a Polish state.[91]

The other major opponent of Lithuanian claims, the Russian Political Conference, was organized by representatives of the various White Russian groups, who had united in this conference after Russia had been refused a seat at the peace conference. In a declaration issued on March 6, 1919, the Russian conference came out against independence for the Baltic states, preferring instead some sort of self-government, the exact form of which could be decided by an all-Russian constituent assembly. The conference suggested that the new border governments be encouraged by the Entente through their recognition as *de facto* bodies, but with the reservation that no final decision on their status could be made "without the acquiescence of the Russian people."[92] While the Baltic governments hoped to gain the proposed *de facto* recognition, the program as a whole held little appeal for them, since they now wanted their independence, and they would hardly be able by themselves to persuade a Russian constituent assembly to grant that.

The Poles and Russians were also in serious disagreement between themselves over the future borders of Poland.[93] The Russians recognized only an "ethnographic Poland" west of the Bug River. The Poles refused to yield their claims to Lithuania and the Ukraine. The Lithuanians thus ran the risk of being swallowed up in either the Russian or the Polish question. In order to establish their own identity, they sought to be associated with the other two Baltic states, Latvia and Estonia, thus becoming a part of a separate "Baltic question."[94]

[91] *Ibid.*, p. 498; Dmowski, *Polityka polska*, pp. 479, 623; Poland, Delegation to Paris, *Akty i dokumenty*, pp. 127 ff. Dmowski is often mistakenly said to have demanded the borders of 1772 in this declaration.

[92] Maklakov Archives, Series B, IV, 2.

[93] On the problem of the conflict between the Polish and the Russian claims, see Kozicki, *Sprawa granic Polski*, p. 115.

[94] In view of the problem of the integrity of Russia, it is significant to note that Japan recognized Lithuania *de facto* in January, 1919, becoming the first participant in the peace conference to do so. See Vitols, *La Mer baltique et les états baltes*, p. 279. A Japanese representative arrived in Kaunas in June, 1919. *Stockhoms Dagblad*, June 20, 1919.

When the idea was put forth of a general conference of all parties in the Russian revolution, the Lithuanians feared that their demands for independence would be compromised if they agreed to send representatives to it. Although the delegation in Paris indicated that it might attend,[95] the *Neue Zürcher Zeitung* reported that the Kaunas government had refused to be present at any such conference on the ground that Lithuania's independence of Russia had already been established by the Taryba's declaration of February 16, 1918, and by the recognition of that declaration by other states. Even Soviet Russia's recognition of the Vilna Communist government was offered as evidence of Lithuania's right to independence.[96]

The Lithuanians found it impossible to persuade the members of the Entente to recognize the Kaunas government. On February 15 the United States Peace Commissioners refused to take action on a Lithuanian request for recognition because of a lack of information.[97] In the first months of the conference the members of the Entente generally leaned toward the Polish view of the Lithuanian question and favored some sort of union between those two nations.[98] The German taint of the Taryba seemed ineradicable.[99] The French wanted protection against Germany and looked to a large and strong Poland as an ally, although there was some hesitancy on their part over whether to support Polish claims to Russian territory.[100] Despite their refusal to recognize the Lithuanian government, however, the Western

[95] A. A. Berle of the United States delegation was of the opinion that they would. United States, *Foreign Relations: 1919, Russia*, pp. 72-73. Cf. Yčas's reservations in *Der Bund*, No. 48 (February 3, 1919).

[96] *Neue Zürcher Zeitung*, No. 245 (February 18, 1919). It is interesting to note that the Lithuanian Communists, now united with the Belorussians, announced that they were willing to attend the proposed conference. *Komunistas*, No. 33 (March 8, 1919).

[97] United States, *Foreign Relations: 1919, Russia*, p. 668.

[98] See Poland, Delegation to Paris, *Akty i dokumenty*, I, 84-86; Mastauskas's report to the American Lithuanians, January 30, 1919, quoted in *Vienybė Lietuvninkų*, No. 10 (March 5, 1919).

[99] The London *Times*, April 25, 1919, declared that German influence was all that was keeping the Lithuanians from agreeing to a union with Poland.

[100] See Lord "Poland," in House and Seymour (eds.), *What Really Happened at Paris*, p. 70.

powers were gradually coming around to informal cooperation
with the Lithuanians, mainly because of the fear of German and
Bolshevik influences there.[101] Preparations were made to send
missions to the Baltic area to gather information and to bolster
the existing governments.

The continuing blockade of the Baltic through the period of
the armistice had serious repercussions in Lithuania, since the
blockade affected the supplying of German forces in the Baltic
area and also restricted trade with the other Baltic countries.
On March 12, because of the unsure conditions in the Baltic, the
Supreme Blockade Council postponed a decision on the question
of raising the restrictions on trade with the Baltic states.[102] The
United States favored opening limited trade, and the British were
opposed to any lifting of the blockade, and the matter drifted
on.[103] On March 28 the Foreign Ministers of the Great Powers
at Paris approved the opening of trade with Estonia but postponed a decision on Latvia and Lithuania until the political
and military situation cleared up.[104] On March 29 the Supreme
Blockade Council approved the opening of Latvia and Lithuania
on condition of guarantees against reexport, of control from
London, and of quotas for imports.[105]

By March each of the three major Western powers was preparing to send representatives to the Baltic area. The British
sent Stephen Tallents to Latvia, whence he was to gather information on the entire region.[106] At the suggestion of Robert
H. Lord, the American delegation to the peace conference was
preparing a commission, to be headed by Colonel Warwick
Greene, which was only to gather information and in no way to
participate in political or military affairs in the Baltic.[107]
Several American Red Cross officials made a brief trip through

---

[101] See the exchange between Polk and Lansing, March 1919, United States,
Foreign Relations: 1919, Russia, pp. 672-73.

[102] Bane and Lutz (eds.), *Blockade of Germany*, p. 239.

[103] *Ibid.*, pp. 242-43, 271-72.

[104] United States, *Foreign Relations: Paris Peace Conference*, IV, 524-25.

[105] *Ibid.*, X, 115; Bane and Lutz (eds.), *Blockade of Germany*, p. 317.

[106] *Neue Zürcher Zeitung*, No. 367 (March 12, 1919).

[107] United States, *Foreign Relations: Paris Peace Conference*, XII, 136-37.

Lithuania in mid-March and came away with a rather unfavorable impression of its political instability and of German domination.[108] The most important mission at this time was that sent by the French under Colonel Reboul. Gabrys was the inspiration for the mission, which was officially instructed to collect information and also to help organize the Lithuanian army.[109] On his way to Kaunas with the mission, however, Gabrys told the German Foreign Office that the real purpose of the mission was to investigate the possibilities of union between Lithuania and Poland,[110] a fact not publicly known. The mission arrived in Kaunas on March 19 and was greeted with great enthusiasm. The Lithuanians realized that these missions meant a change for the better in their own relations with the Germans, and they hoped that the sending of the missions constituted the first step toward recognition of an independent Lithuania.[111]

At this time, too, the Lithuanian government was again in the throes of a serious ministerial crisis. The rivalry between the Taryba and the cabinet had remained unresolved, and in late February a new conflict arose, this time between the cabinet and the army.[112] Acting in direct contradiction to instructions from Kaunas, an army colonel, Glovackis, had executed several civilians in Suwalki after suppressing an insurrection. The cabinet had ordered the prisoners sent to Kaunas and after the executions sought to discipline Glovackis. Although Šilingas, the acting chairman of the Taryba, had at first assured Sleževičius

---

[108] Report of Major Ross to Herbert Hoover, March 22, 1919, United States, National Archives, 861L.00/60. Lithuania was at this time undergoing a serious political crisis which was not resolved until the end of March. Jurgela (Lithuania and the United States [MS], pp. 234-41) gives a very interesting account of the special preparations the Lithuanians made in order to impress their visitors.

[109] Gabrys, *Vers l'indépendance*, p. 249.

[110] Germany, Foreign Office, *Hauptarchiv: Litauen*, Reel 430, frame, 412.

[111] Šaulys (Kaunas) to Puryckis (Berlin), letter, March 31, 1919, Šaulys Archives, f. 30. One of the first results of the arrival of the Entente missions was the discharge of the German advisers in the Lithuanian army. See Schröder and Heygendorff, *Die Sächsischen Freiwilligen-Truppen*, pp. 47, 72-74.

[112] For an account of the continuing constitutional crisis, see Römer'is, *Paskaitos*, pp. 60-63.

that the presidium of the Taryba would assume no role in the dispute, he later did an about-face and supported the army, thus bringing about the fall of the cabinet in early March.[113] The Christian Democrats now sponsored a new cabinet, headed by Pranas Dovydaitis, a university professor, which took office on March 12. The program of the new cabinet emphasized the role which the army was to play in political affairs.[114] The cabinet suffered severely from a shortage of capable men. The Socialists refused to participate in such a "clerical-dominated" government, and Dovydaitis himself was doubtful of his own talents, saying, "I am not suited for politics, and maybe that's why no one wants to work with me."[115] Gabrys claimed that when he arrived with the French military mission, the Christian Democrats offered him the premiership, but that, when they rejected his demand that he be free to pick his own ministers, he turned down the offer, despite the fact that Reboul urged him to accept.[116]

On March 20, Šaulys was recalled from the ministry at Berlin to aid in resolving the crisis. By the time he arrived in Kaunas, Dovydaitis had already withdrawn from the government, and the Minister of the Interior, Stulginskis, was serving as Prime Minister. Šaulys gathered the leaders of the various parties to-

---

[113] See Gabrys, *Vers l'indépendance*, pp. 262-63; Sleževičius (Kaunas) to Šaulys (Berlin), letter, March 3, 1919, Šaulys Archives, f. 30. A conservative militaristic account can be found in *Tägliche Rundschau*, No. 175 (April 8, 1919).

[114] *Kurjer Polski*, No. 79 (April 3, 1919). The military question, and not "constitutional socialism," was the key issue in the cabinet change. Cf. Graham, *New Governments of Eastern Europe*, p. 375.

[115] Bartuška, *Kryžiaus keliais*, p. 305.

[116] Gabrys, *Vers l'indépendance*, pp. 264-65. Gabrys supported the army, which he thought had "an obligation to participate in politics" (p. 264) and which should not be hindered by civil authorities in its basic task of defending the country. In June, the government newspaper, *Lietuva*, No. 128 (June 17, 1919), denied that Gabrys had been offered a cabinet. In April, Gabrys suffered another setback when he split with Reboul because the Frenchman disapproved of his friendship with Baron von der Ropp, a Balt. *Vers l'indépendance*, pp. 265-68. The Communists also attacked him, publishing a letter which he had allegedly written Kapsukas in September, 1918, inviting the latter to join him in establishing a new government in Lithuania. See *Komunistas*, No. 23 (February 12, 1919). Nevertheless he continued to have strong support among the Chrissian Democrats.

gether and gradually formulated the reforms which would be necessary to reorganize the government on a coalition basis.[117]

By March 28 agreement had been reached on these changes, which meant the drawing up of a new constitution. Under the new system of government, the direct powers of the Taryba were limited to the approval of treaties and loans. All other powers, including legislation on internal affairs, were vested in the cabinet of ministers, which was still constitutionally responsible to the Taryba. The presidium of the Taryba was replaced as the head of the state by an independent "State President." Smetona was understood to be the choice for the presidency.[118]

Sleževičius was chosen to head the new cabinet, Lithuania's fourth. On April 1, Smetona returned from Scandinavia, and on April 4 he was unanimously elected President of Lithuania.[119] Sleževičius's cabinet took office on April 12.

One of the first problems facing the new government was that of establishing relations with Poland. The Lithuanian note of January 4, protesting the Polish occupation of Vilna, had been answered by the Polish government on February 12.[120] The Poles asserted their desire that all peoples be free to decide their own fate, and therefore they refused the Lithuanian government the right to speak for areas claimed to be Polish. But they suggested the opening of talks between the two governments.[121]

[117] Writing from Paris on March 20, Klimas complained to Šaulys that the one-party cabinet was prejudicing the Lithuanian cause in Paris, and he urged the reestablishment of coalition rule as soon as possible. Šaulys Archives, f. 76.

[118] Šaulys (Kaunas) to Puryckis (Berlin), letter, March 28, 1919, Šaulys Archives, f. 30. See also *Neue Zürcher Zeitung*, No. 561 (April 15, 1919). Text of the constitution in A. Merkys (ed.), *Lietuvos istatymai* (Kaunas, 1922), p. 11n.

[119] Smetona's title was "State President," not "President of the Republic." See Römer'is, *Paskaitos*, pp. 65-66. There was a report that the Socialist members of the Taryba walked out of the hall in protest against Smetona's election, but it must be viewed skeptically, since by this time there seem to have been no Socialists left in the Taryba. See *Baltische Blätter*, II, No. 7/8, 62.

[120] The Polish government had been reorganized after an abortive coup by Prince Sapieha on the night of January 5. Paderewski, then in Cracow after a triumphal tour of Poland, was invited to head a new cabinet, replacing Mokrzewski, and he also took the post of Foreign Minister, formerly held by Leon Wasilewski.

[121] Poland, Ministry of Foreign Affairs, *Documents diplomatiques*, I, 3-4; Wielhorski, *Polska a Litwa*, p. 295.

Sleževičius called the note unclear but hopeful. He expected to send a delegation immediately to open relations, but when the Lithuanian governmental crisis arose, the mission had to be postponed.[122] Finally, at the end of March, the cabinet named Šaulys to head a mission to Warsaw. An old friend of Sleževičius, Šaulys was also a key figure in the Lithuanian foreign service, as was testified by his appointment to the critical post at Berlin in November, 1918.[123]

A Polish policy toward Lithuania was in the process of formation throughout the first months of 1919. Piłsudski's freedom of action had been checked by the elections in January to the Polish Constituent Assembly (*Ustawodawczy Sejm*), which returned an overwhelming majority for the National Democratic bloc, and a National Democrat, Stanisław Grabski, headed the Committee on Foreign Affairs.[124] The delegates repeatedly expressed their intention of including all "ethnographic Polish territory" in the Polish state, but, in addition, they hoped for an agreement with Lithuania. All shades of opinions, from federation to annexation, were heard. One deputy spoke of union as the "most perfect creation of our spirit," and stressed the fact that the incorporation of "ethnographic Lithuania" was essential to the economic and strategic rounding out of the Polish eastern lands.[125] Another deputy noted that while all ethnic Polish territory must be united, should Lithuania agree to a union, the borders could be adjusted "according to the real needs of both nations."[126] Forceful incorporation of Lithuania was repudiated by all. As one deputy declared,

To deny the Lithuanians the right to their own statehood would obviously be a mischievous move, but the Lithuanians must come down somewhat from their megalomania and renounce their claim that Vilna is their capital.[127]

[122] Sleževičius (Kaunas) to Šaulys (Berlin), letter, undated, Šaulys Archives, f. 28.
[123] His letters indicate that he was on intimate terms with both Sleževičius and Smetona.
[124] See Graham, *New Governments of Eastern Europe*, pp. 112-13.
[125] Kamieniecki on March 28, *Monitor Polski*, No. 72 (March 29, 1919).
[126] Rataj on March 26, *ibid.*, No. 70 (March 27, 1919).
[127] Dąbski, Peasant Party, *ibid.*, No. 77 (April 4, 1919).

On April 1 Grabski reported that the Committee on Foreign Affairs, while not wanting to prejudice the decisions of the peace conference on the boundaries of Poland, stood by

the principle that the lands in which the Polish population, by strength of numbers or by centuries-long work of civilization, has put the imprint of Polish character, must be brought together into a single political unit.[128]

On April 3 the Deputy Minister of Foreign Affairs, Wróblewski, stated that the government expected to be able to reach an agreement with the Lithuanians soon:

It is neither our fault nor the Lithuanians' that we have had to wait so long for this; it is the fault of our enemies, who for centuries have wanted to set us against each other. Soon those intrigues will cease, the way will be cleared, and a common program will be found. In that common program we must have one guide and one rule, that Polish Wilno [Vilna] cannot be separated from us. [Voices: "Bravo!"][129]

On April 4 the Sejm passed two important resolutions. One called on the government to free the Vilna territory from the Bolsheviks so that it might be united closely with Poland.[130] The other, introduced by the Socialist Niedzialkowski, proclaimed the readiness of the Sejm to recognize the right of the Lithuanians and the Belorussians to decide their own fate, but maintained that neither the Communist government nor the government "organized" by the Germans was representative.[131]

During the first part of 1919 the question of Polish-Lithuanian relations passed rapidly from the stage of mutually isolated discussions in each country to that of direct contact as the Polish army moved eastward, replacing the German forces and pushing back the Bolsheviks. The "Lithuanian front" was mentioned for the first time in the communiqué of the Polish General Staff of January 28, 1919, and from February 10 on it was included

[128] *Ibid.*
[129] *Ibid.*
[130] Poland, Ministry of Foreign Affairs, *Documents diplomatiques*, I, 9-10.
[131] *Ibid.*, I, 9. The reservation of the right to determine what government was "representative" disproves Budecki's claim that this resolution made Poland one of the first states to recognize Lithuania (*Stosunki polsko-litewskie*, p. 24). See also Zoltowski, *Border of Europe*, p. 197; Wielhorski, *Polska a Litwa*, p. 296.

regularly.[132] By the middle of April, Polish forces were advancing on Lida. With the Germans still occupying Grodno and the Bolsheviks Vilna, the way was clear for the Poles to realize their territorial ambitions without any open conflict with the Lithuanians.

The Lithuanians meanwhile were pushing their own plans for taking Vilna. On March 25, Alexandras Stulginskis, the Acting Prime Minister, asked the German government for food supplies with which to feed the populace of Vilna once the Lithuanian army had taken the city.[133] On March 30 the German government threw a wrench into the Lithuanian plans by ordering German troops to cease offensive action against the Bolsheviks and to avoid any conflict with the Poles.[134] Stulginskis then asserted that the Lithuanians would take Vilna by themselves but that they needed two battalions of infantry and two batteries of artillery to support them. He promised to prevent any clash between the Germans and the Poles.[135] The German High Command, however, preferred to let the Poles go ahead. Since the Poles had the blessings of the Entente in their campaign against the Bolsheviks, the Germans saw no reason to interfere at this time in the Vilna question.[136] Furthermore, they had grave misgivings that the French military mission in Kaunas might turn the Lithuanians against the Germans.[137]

Although its relations with Poland were now about to enter a critical stage, by the middle of April the Lithuanian government had risen from its nadir in the beginning of January to the most stable position as yet attained. The Entente still refused recognition, but the first indications of a change were to be seen in this

---

[132] Pomaranski (ed.), *Pierwsza wojna polska*, pp. 26, 33 ff.

[133] Šaulys Archives, f. 30.

[134] Report by Colonel Dawley (Warsaw), May 20, 1919, United States, National Archives, 184.01502/29. See also Schröder and Heygendorff, *Die sächsischen Freiwilligen-Truppen*, p. 48.

[135] Undated, Šaulys Archives, f. 30.

[136] Military report, signature illegible, to the Chief of Staff for the Defense of Lithuania, April, 1919, Šaulys Archives, f. 25.

[137] Zimmerle to the Foreign Office, March 26, 1919, Germany, Foreign Office, *Hauptarchiv: Litauen*, Reed 430, frame 563.

quarter. The arrival of the Western missions and the promises of lifting the blockade brought hopes of relief from the dependence on the Germans. Domestically the power struggle within the government had been settled for the time being, and the Bolshevik threat was abating. A national army was being formed, and the government's stand on the land question had won the support of the peasantry. All in all, the future seemed reasonably bright.

V

"With Its Capital in Vilna"

APRIL–JUNE, 1919

BARELY A WEEK after the installation of the new cabinet under Sleževičius, the national ambitions of the Lithuanians suffered a tremendous blow. Piłsudski had been steadily advancing eastward, and by April 18 his forces were in Lida.[1] On the morning of Holy Saturday, April 19, a regiment of cavalry under Lieutenant Colonel Beliny-Prazmowski suddenly appeared in Vilna and seized the railway station. By Easter Monday, April 21, when Polish infantry arrived, the Poles were in complete control of the city.[2] The victory was hailed with great jubilation in Poland, where it was recalled that Vilna had been retaken from the Russians on Easter Sunday in 1661 and had been captured by Kościuszko on April 22, 1794.[3] The Lithuanians were enraged and chagrined by the Polish maneuver and at first they even tried to deny its success.[4]

The victory of the Poles was real. Piłsudski had found the Bolsheviks unprepared to meet a push north from Lida. Although some of his officers had advised waiting for the arrival of Polish troops then en route from Western Europe, he had decided in favor of the bolder move and had sent the cavalry north along the railroad. With the aid of the Polish railroad workers in Vilna, the cavalry had arrived secretly in the city's railroad station at 5 A.M. and had quickly seized control of that sector of the city. The Communist government, caught by surprise, fled hastily to Daugavpils, but several of its members were arrested before they could escape.[5] A part of the Polish population of Vilna

[1] Pomaranski, *Pierwsza wojna polska*, p. 89.   [2] *Ibid.*, p. 93.
[3] *Kurjer Polski*, Nos. 99 (April 25, 1919) and 104 (April 30, 1919).
[4] See *Die Post*, No. 207 (April 29, 1919).
[5] See *Izvestiia*, No. 93 (May 3, 1919).

rose in support of the attackers, while the opposition came mainly from the Jewish population. The Communists claimed that
this resistance showed the support of the Jews for the Bolshevik
regime,[6] and Polish writers have tended to agree with this.[7] In
fact, the national and religious antagonisms between the Jews
and the Poles must have been a contributing factor in this acute
situation.[8]

Although the Communists still held the northeastern part of
Lithuania, the fall of Vilna signified the virtual end of Communist rule in Lithuania, and a polemic immediately arose in
the Communist press as to the reasons for this collapse. A.
Miasnikov, who had been the head of the Belorussian Communist
Party at the time of the Lithuanian-Belorussian merger, claimed
that the Lithuanian Communists had been lax in their organizational work and had allowed opposition forces to flourish in
Vilna.[9] Kapsukas, on the other hand, hotly defended his government, saying that the job of organization had just been too great
for the limited time and resources of the party.[10] Another writer
maintained that the Lithuanians had simply not had enough aid
from Moscow and were unable to stand against the Poles by
themselves.[11] Whatever the lessons the Communists could draw
from their experiences in Lithuania, it was now too late to save
the situation.

In Vilna there arose the problem of what the role of the Polish
army should be, since none of the conflicting national claims to
the region had as yet been generally recognized. The Lithuanians
maintained that the Poles were invaders, stationed in Lithuanian
territory without any agreement on the part of the Lithuanian
government. Voldemaras reported to the peace conference on
April 29 that the Lithuanians had suggested an alliance between

[6] See *Pravda*, No. 95 (May 6, 1919).
[7] See *Neue Zürcher Zeitung*, No. 813 (June 2, 1919).
[8] See Schröder and Heygendorff, *Die sächsischen Freiwilligen-Truppen*, p. 74.
[9] *Izvestiia*, No. 93 (May 3, 1919).   [10] *Ibid.*, No. 97 (May 8, 1919).
[11] *Pravda*, No. 95 (May 6, 1919). The lack of aid may have been partly due to
the overly optimistic reports of Joffe, who seems to have completely misjudged the
strength of the Poles. See *Izvestiia*, No. 82 (April 16, 1919).

the Poles and the Lithuanians against the Bolsheviks. The condition for this agreement was to be the recognition by the Poles of an independent Lithuanian state with its capital in Vilna. The Polish troops in Lithuania would then be considered expeditionary forces, sent there to fight the Bolsheviks. In the absence of such an agreement, Voldemaras concluded, the Polish troops could only be considered invaders.[12]

Piłsudski had already made preparations for the administration of the area, apparently discounting in advance any such protests against the Polish action. In March he organized the Civil Government of the Eastern Territories (*Zarząd Cywilny Ziem Wschodnich*), under Jerzy Osmołowski, a known federalist.[13] The government was to be made up of representatives of the local populations and was to administer all the territories of historic Lithuania taken by the Poles from the Bolsheviks. Osmołowski was directly responsible to Piłsudski, not to the Polish Council of Ministers.[14] Thus the Polish army could be described as only an expeditionary force.[15]

In mid-April, several days before the move on Vilna, Piłsudski had sent an unofficial delegation to Kaunas to sound out the Lithuanian government on a joint campaign against the Bolsheviks. The Lithuanians rejected the plan, which included a program for federation.[16] In a famous speech at Vilna on April 22, Piłsudski announced his intention of allowing the population of the grand duchy to choose its own government; the military occupation was in no way to prejudice the future political disposition of the region. He made no mention of the possibility of federation or annexation.[17]

---

[12] Voldemaras claimed the guberniyas of Kaunas, Vilna, Grodno, Suwalki, and parts of Courland and East Prussia. Text in Lithuania, Ministry of Foreign Affairs, *Documents diplomatiques: Conflict polono-lithuanien: Question de Vilna*, pp. 17-18. The Lituanians gave this letter the widest possible publicity, sending it to all parties at the peace conference, as well as to all the major press agencies.

[13] See Wielhorski, *Polska a Litwa*, p. 301.   [14] *Le Temps*, May 17, 1919.

[15] See the account of an interview with Paderewski, *Monitor Polski*, No. 120 (May 31, 1919).

[16] See Pobóg-Malinowski, *Najnowsza Historia Polityczna Polski*, II, Part 1, 184n

[17] Text in *Monitor Polski*, No. 95 (April 28, 1919).

Piłsudski's actions seem to have been a definite though cautious step toward realizing his hope of federation. The National Democrats criticized him vehemently for his failure to annex the territory immediately.[18] On the other hand, he drew warm support from the federalists.[19] His move was actually something of a stopgap compromise between the federalist and the annexationist programs. It also relieved the Poles of some of the pressure from Paris, where there was still strong sentiment against the Poles' having crossed the Bug River, since this move might mean a violation of the territorial integrity of Russia.[20]

The Polish victory at Vilna was a shock to the Lithuanians. Opponents of Sleževičius bitterly denounced him for his failure to reach Vilna first.[21] The attacks in one newspaper, *Žaibas*, were so sharp that Sleževičius suppressed the paper and arrested the editor, Father V. Bartuška.[22] Vilna now became the focal point in Lithuanian foreign policy. Writing on April 24, Sleževičius urged Juozas Puryckis, the acting Lithuanian Minister at Berlin, to seek increased German aid in clearing Lithuania of Bolshevik forces. He emphasized that the Germans would not be asked to fight the Poles, but he clearly anticipated conflict between the Lithanians and the Poles: "Get everyone on their feet. Vilna must be ours. We cannot leave it to the Poles."[23]

At the end of April the Lithuanians suffered another diplomatic defeat when the Germans began their withdrawal from Grodno *guberniya*. After the fall of Vilna in January, Foch had

---

[18] A review of the National Democratic press can be found in *Kurjer Polski*, No. 106 (May 2, 1919). See also Devereux, *Poland Reborn*, pp. 96-97; Zoltowski, *Border of Europe*, p. 197.

[19] *Kurjer Polski* supported the plan as being democratic and at the same time as not abandoning Poles to the Lithuanians. See Nos. 100 (April 26, 1919), 103 (April 29, 1919), and 106 (May 2, 1919).

[20] See Przybylski, *La Pologne en lutte pour ses frontières*, p. 191.

[21] Communist writers now claim that Sleževičius cooperated with the Poles in their campaign on Vilna. See Žiugžda, "Draugas J. V. Stalinas ir lietuvių tautos kova del nacionalinės nepriklausomybės," in *Lietuvos Istorijos Instituto Darbai*, I, 18.

[22] See Bartuška, *Kryžiaus keliais*, pp. 308 ff. Father Bartuška was an American Lithuanian and a supporter of Gabrys.

[23] Sleževičius (Kaunas) to Puryckis (Berlin), letter, April 24, 1919, Šaulys Archives, f. 30.

ordered the Germans out of Grodno, though plans for the withdrawal were not completed until early April. Since the Polish supply lines to Vilna passed through Grodno, occupation of that area was essential to the Poles in order to hold Vilna. The Lithuanians protested loudly, but the Poles found little opposition to their advance and in fact were welcomed by many. Over the objections of the Lithuanian government, some officers of the Lithuanian-Belorussian regiment in Grodno joined the Poles.[24]

The Allied leaders in Paris now feared the outbreak of hostilities between the Lithuanians and the Poles.[25] Their fears were also aroused by the news of a German coup in Liepaja in mid-April, whereby Ulmanis was replaced by Niedra at the head of the government of Latvia. The Allies were still uncertain as to whether the Kaunas government was a German tool or not, and accordingly they followed an ambiguous policy. They did not want to force anything upon the Lithuanians, continuing to hope that the Poles and the Lithuanians might reach a direct agreement by themselves.[26]

This policy was self-defeating since the Lithuanians took advantage of the Allies' unwillingness to use pressure and refused to reach an agreement with the Poles. As the weaker party, the Lithuanians wanted to avoid negotiating directly with the Poles, especially since the latter already held Vilna. From the Lithuanian point of view, Bolshevik rule in Vilna seemed preferable to Polish rule there, since the Bolsheviks would at least be unable to marshal as much support in the West. The Lithuanians wanted outside aid and so, while making an ostensible effort to negotiate, they avoided any agreement which might compromise the demands which they were pressing in Paris for the recognition of their independence with Vilna as their capital.

[24] The Poles later disarmed the Lithuanian-Belorussian regiment. See Uspenskis, "1-as gudų pulkas," *Karo Archyvas*, I (1925), 169 ff.
[25] The first conflict came on May 8, 1919. See Ruseckas, *Savanorių žygiai*, p. 19.
[26] See the letter from Dutasta to Dmowski and Voldemaras, April 26, 1919, in United States, *Foreign Relations: Paris Peace Conference*, IV, 628-29.

On the other hand, the Polish government wanted to keep its relations with the Lithuanians free of any interference from Paris, and therefore it sought to keep the negotiations going at any price. If a direct agreement could not be reached, at least a show of progress had to be made in order to postpone any intervention by the Entente. The Russian Political Council at Paris, the continuing body set up by the Russian Political Conference, was working assiduously to prevent an expansion of Poland into what was considered Russian territory, and some Polish writers have maintained that the Lithuanians and the Russians were cooperating against the Poles.[27] That the objections of the two against Polish expansion coincided cannot be denied, but there was no definite agreement.

The policies on both the Lithuanian and the Polish sides can be seen clearly in the negotiations conducted by Šaulys's mission to Warsaw. It is perhaps symbolic that Šaulys arrived in Warsaw on April 19, the day the Poles entered Vilna. The mission was empowered to negotiate with the Poles for recognition, to establish diplomatic and economic relations with Poland, and to adopt a plan of common action against the Bolsheviks. The mission was authorized to conclude preliminary treaties on any of these points.[28] Apart from the abortive talks conducted by Captain Górka in December, 1918, this was the first official contact between plenipotentiaries of both governments.

On Tuesday, April 22, Deputy Minister of Foreign Affairs Wróblewski received Šaulys. Paderewski was in Paris at this time. Also present at the meeting was Grabski, still the Chairman of the Foreign Affairs Committee of the Constituent Assembly. The talks at that first meeting laid down the line for all the talks to come.[29]

Šaulys presented the proposal which was to be outlined by Voldemaras in his letter to the peace conference on April 29,

[27] See Wasilewski, *Litwa i Białoruś*, pp. 197, 200; Dmowski, *Polityka polska*, pp. 478, 482.

[28] Poland, Ministry of Foreign Affairs, *Documents diplomatiques*, I, 7-8.

[29] This account is based mainly on Šaulys's report to his government, May 31, 1919, Šaulys Archives, f. 32.

demanding the recognition of the Lithuanian state with Vilna as its capital.[30] The Poles were still split between the federalist sympathies of the government and the annexationist demands of the Constituent Assembly. Since it could not act in direct contradiction to the wishes of the assembly, the government had to tread carefully. Wróblewski answered Šaulys's demands cautiously, saying that the conditions would be "difficult" to meet. On the other hand, Grabski flatly rejected the idea, maintaining that the eastern lands were an integral part of the Polish state and therefore could not be alienated in this manner. When these stands were made clear, Šaulys declared that there seemed to be nothing which could be done and so all that remained for him to do was to document what had been stated. After arrangements had been made for a formal exchange of notes, the meeting ended. Šaulys did not expect his mission to remain much longer in Warsaw.

On April 25, Šaulys sent a letter to the Polish government, presenting the Lithuanian stand. After noting the desire on both sides to open relations, he stated that the Lithuanians held their minimum condition to be the recognition of their independence with their capital in Vilna: "Only after the acceptance of this condition of the recognition of the Lithuanian state, the basic condition for good relations between the two states, can the mission pursue further negotiations."[31] On April 24 Sleževičius wrote to Šaulys, telling him of the situation in Grodno. Noting that the Poles were seeking a direct agreement with the Lithuanian forces in Grodno, Sleževičius stated that he had forbidden any negotiations until the results of the talks in Warsaw were clear.[32]

A week later, still having received no answer to his note of April 25, Šaulys sent a second note, dated May 2, the text of

---

[30] An American representative in Warsaw, Frederic Dolbeare, wrote to Robert Lord on May 15, 1919, "I have never seen a communication from any Lithuanian delegation which did not speak about the independence of Lithuania and its capital Vilna." United States, National Archives, 186.3116/63.

[31] Poland, Ministry, of Foreign Affairs, *Documents diplomatiques*, I, 8.

[32] Šaulys Archives, f. 32.

which is not available. He then made preparations to leave Warsaw on May 8, and he notified Kaunas of this intention. On the morning of the eighth he finally received a message by mail from Wróblewski, dated May 2. It had been delayed because of a strike of Polish government couriers. The note simply stated that Šaulys's note of April 25 had been forwarded to Paderewski in Paris; without the latter's approval, nothing could be done. That afternoon, Šaulys paid a visit to the Ministry of Foreign Affairs in order to get some explanation of the course of events. When he was informed that Paderewski was expected back within the next few days, he decided to remain in Warsaw in order to speak with the Minister.

Just at this time Šaulys received another letter from Sleževičius, announcing that the Lithuanian-Belorussia regiment in Grodno had made a separate agreement with the Poles despite the express orders of Kaunas to the contrary. Even more important, long-awaited news had been received from Paris,[33] warning against Polish machinations and strongly advising against making any agreement with the Poles which would suggest to the Entente that the Lithuanians had any inclination toward union with Poland:

The Poles now want to make an agreement with us in order to show the Entente that they are not aggressors, but rather that we Lithuanians very much want to make an agreement and to live together with them in a single state.

Sleževičius instructed Šaulys to hold unswervingly to the basic condition of the recognition of Lithuania's independence with its capital in Vilna: "If this is not fulfilled, there can be no agreement with the Poles."[34]

Paderewski returned to Warsaw on May 10. On May 12 he reportedly had an important conference with Piłsudski on the Lithuanian question.[35] On May 13, Šaulys obtained an inter-

[33] A telegraph line had just been opened from Kaunas to the West. See *Vienybė Lietuvninkų*, No. 20 (May 14, 1919).

[34] Sleževičius (Kaunas) to Šaulys (Warsaw), letter, May 7, 1919, Šaulys Archives, f. 32.

[35] *Kurjer Polski*, No. 117 (May 13, 1919).

view with Paderewski, and the two spoke at length. After declaring that the frontier question was one for the peace conference, Paderewski stated that it could be resolved "to the advantage of the Lithuanians" if they would agree to federation, which would involve union of railroads, post, telegraph, finance, army, and foreign policy.[36] That this offer had been planned in advance is indicated by the fact that Paderewski repeated it on May 23 and that Piłsudski made an identical proposal in a talk with Šaulys on May 21.[37] It was, of course, in contradiction to the policy, which was publicly advocated by the Polish government. In his speech of April 22, Piłsudski had promised some form of self-determination to the residents of Vilna, and early in May h∍ was quoted as saying that the Poles would never cede Vilna outright without first holding a plebiscite.[38] On May 23, Paderewski told Šaulys that all the talk about a plebiscite was simply "a necessary concession to our bawlers" (*dawka niezbędna dla naszych krzykaczy*) and that there would never be such a plebiscite.[39]

The Polish government may have been working in this manner in order either to present the Constituent Assembly and the Entente with a *fait accompli* in the form of an agreement with the Lithuanians in favor of federation, thereby overriding any objection by the Russians or the National Democrats, or else to deceive the Entente and the Lithuanians by dragging out the talks while preparing the way for other maneuvers. The Lithuanians believed that the latter was the intention, claiming that the federalists and the annexationists were working hand in hand.[40]

In a personal letter to Šaulys on May 16, Sleževičius expressed

---

[36] Terms stated in a letter to Colonel Dawley from Šaulys, May 20, 1919, Šaulys Archives, f. 32. In his report on May 20 from Warsaw, Dawley stated that he was expecting a letter from Šaulys telling the terms offered by the Poles, but the letter is not to be found in the United States, National Archives. Cf. United States, *Foreign Relations: Paris Peace Conference*, XII, 195n.

[37] Šaulys's report to his government, May 31, 1919.

[38] *Journal des Débats*, May 13, 1919.

[39] Šaulys's report to his government, May 31, 1919. The Polish quotation was in the original text. Paderewski was apparently referring to the annexationists.

[40] See editorial in *Nepriklausomoji Lietuva*, No. 21 (May 20, 1919).

the belief that the Poles were trying to drag out the talks in order "to blow smoke into the eyes of the Entente." He stated that the Germans opposed an agreement between the Lithuanians and the Poles. The American stand was "very unclear," but seemed to lean toward the Poles, while the French were completely on the side of the Poles. Sleževičius believed that only the English favored the Lithuanians.[41]

In an official letter of the same day, Sleževičius directed Šaulys to demand a straightforward answer to the Lithuanian demands. If the Polish response was unsatisfactory, then Šaulys was to leave immediately; delay under such circumstances could only hurt the Lithuanian cause.[42] In a letter addressed to Colonel E. J. Dawley of the American Commission in the Baltic Provinces, Šaulys declared that the Poles were acting in bad faith and were only seeking to prolong the talks in order to show the Entente that some progress was being made.[43]

On May 15, at Paderewski's urging, the Polish Constituent Assembly passed another resolution on the Lithuanian question disavowing any intention of annexing any part of the former grand duchy against the will of the people concerned.[44] This resolution, however, did not renounce the Polish claim to Vilna, which was considered to be Polish territory and an integral part of the Polish community.[45]

On May 16, Paderewski sent a formal note to Šaulys in which he called the latter's attention to the Sejm resolution of April 4 on the right of the Lithuanians to organize their own state and suggested that the Lithuanians accept it, leaving the border question open.[46] This was of course unsatisfactory to the Lithu-

---

[41] Šaulys Archives, f. 32.   [42] Šaulys Archives, f. 32.
[43] Šaulys Archives, f. 32. There indeed seems to have been some optimism in Entente circles because of the fact that the talks had not been broken off. See Dolbeare (Warsaw) to Lord (Paris), letter, May 15, 1919, United States, National Archives, 186.3116/63.
[44] *Le Temps*, May 18, 1919; Gibson (Warsaw) to American Mission in Paris, May 15, 1919, United States, National Archives, 186.3116/56, and May 16, 1919, United States, National Archives, 186.3116/81.
[45] See Voldemaras, *Lithuanie et Pologne*, pp. 7-8.
[46] Poland, Ministry of Foreign Affairs, *Documents diplomatiques*, I, 10.

anians, for whom Vilna was more than a simple border question. In a letter to the Polish government on May 22, Šaulys expressed his satisfaction that the Polish government was ready to allow the Lithuanians to organize their own state, but he asserted that the Lithuanians wanted a declaration of mutual recognition which would expressly name the capital of each state. He protested against the Polish occupation of Vilna and again demanded the withdrawal of the Polish troops.[47] After personally delivering the note to Paderewski on May 23, Šaulys finally left Warsaw.[48]

During and after his stay in Warsaw, Šaulys was the target of several attacks in the Polish press. His curt statement, in an interview with a reporter of the *Kurjer Polski*, that he considered Piłsudski's address of April 22 "not a manifesto but an address by a conqueror" drew severe criticism.[49] Both *Kurjer Polski* and later the French *Le Temps* attacked Šaulys for his "undiplomatic method of expressing himself about Polish politics."[50] *Kurjer Polski* declared that Šaulys was "far from the humanitarian principles of the Polish tradition."[51] *Le Temps* criticized him sharply for his failure to offer something in return for his demands, a clear indication that the correspondent, probably Charles Rivet, was thinking of federation.[52]

In all, Šaulys's mission accomplished little. The Lithuanians found it preferable to appeal to the peace conference, especially since the Poles were acting from a position of strength.[53] The

[47] *Ibid.*, I, 10-12.

[48] Wielhorski (*Polska a Litwa*, p. 313) claims that Šaulys went in protest, leaving only a consulate to represent the Lithuanians. Actually Šaulys had left because there was nothing more to be done; he had already remained longer than planned. He had not been sent to Warsaw as a permanent representative, and he was still officially Minister to Berlin. The consulate and the information bureau were not left in protest, but rather as a result of the work of the mission. Poland, Ministry of Foreign Affairs, *Documents diplomatiques*, I, 13; *Monitor Polski*, No. 119 (May 30, 1919). According to the consul, Kasakaitis, the consulate was suppressed after the troubles over Sejny in August and September. See Kasakaitis, "Lietuviai Varšuvoj," in *Pasaulio lietuviai*, p. 191.

[49] *Kurjer Polski*, No. 128 (May 24, 1919).

[50] *Ibid.*, No. 129 (May 25, 1919). See *Le Temps*, May 31, 1919.

[51] *Kurjer Polski*, No. 102 (April 29, 1919).

[52] *Le Temps*, May 31, 1919.

[53] Wielhorski (*Polska a Litwa*, p. 307) blames the failure of the talks on the Lithuanian "refusal," under German influence, to allow self-determination to the

Poles wanted to avoid any outside intervention which might weaken their position.[54] The good faith in the proposals advanced by both sides is subject to doubt. Both seem to have concentrated more on impressing the peace conference than on reaching an early agreement.[55]

The offer of federation made to Šaulys was paralleled by a Polish appeal in Vilna for the support of the local Lithuanian organization, the Provisional Lithuanian Committee, constituted immediately after the Polish occupation of the city.[56] In an interview on April 23 with Mykolas Biržiška, the chairman of the Lithuanian Committee, Osmołowski promised the Lithuanians "all the advantages" if they would cooperate with the Polish administration.[57] He hoped eventually to gain their endorsement of federation between Poland and Lithuania. In answer, the Lithuanian Committee drew up a list of civil rights demands, purposely omitting political problems, since, the Lithuanians maintained, only the Kaunas government could handle such matters.[58] When the Lithuanians presented the list to him on April 24, Osmołowski declared that he would take up the demands with the Warsaw government, expressing confidence that an agreement could be reached. The next day Osmołowski left for Warsaw. However, it would seem that the failure of the negotiations with Šaulys had put a damper on further talks along

---

other nationalities in historic Lithuania. But the Lithuanians at this time were intensifying their efforts to reach a final settlement with the Belorussians. See *Le Temps*, June 20, 1919; *Neue Zürcher Zeitung*, No. 875 (June 13, 1919). If Polish writers do not condemn the Lithuanians for acting without considering the other nationalities, as Wielhorski did, they accuse them of sinister motives in cooperating with the other nationalities against the Poles. See Wasilewski, *Litwa i Białoruś* p. 217.

[54] Voldemaras blames the failure on Polish "intransigence" (*Lithuanie et Pologne*, p. 27). Cf. Studnicki, *Państwo kowieńskie*, p. 7: "The Lithuanian government must come to an agreement since it is much weaker than Poland."

[55] On May 23 the Lithuanians appealed for an inter-Allied commission of inquiry to intervene in the dispute. Lithuania, Delegation to Paris, *Composition*, VII, 6.

[56] *Nepriklausomoji Lietuva*, No. 1 (April 25, 1919).

[57] This account is based on information given the author by Professor Biržiška in an interview on August 14, 1956, and also on the published account of the talks in *Nepriklausomoji Lietuva*, No. 5 (April 30, 1919).

[58] The situation is comparable to the negotiations between the Lithuanian government and the Vilna Poles at the end of December, 1918.

this line, for when Osmołowski returned to Vilna in May, he made no effort to communicate with the Lithuanians about this matter.[59]

The Poles followed up the talks with Šaulys by sending their own representative, Deputy Minister of Foreign Affairs Staniszewski, to Kaunas, almost on Šaulys's heels.[60] But this second round of negotiations proved as fruitless as the first. Staniszewski and his mission arrived in Kaunas on May 28 and talks were begun the next day.[61] At the opening meeting, Sleževičius refused to speak Polish, using instead an interpreter to translate from Lithuanian into French.[62] In answer to the charge that the Poles were responsible for the failure of Šaulys's mission, Staniszewski asserted that his presence in Kaunas was ample proof of the desire of the Poles to establish relations between the two countries. He went on to claim that there had never been any question of Poland's refusing to recognize the right of the Lithuanians to an independent existence. The purpose of the current negotiations was to work out the details of the formal recognition. Sleževičius demanded the withdrawal of Polish forces from all the disputed territory and the admission of a Lithuanian civil administration. To this, Staniszewski answered that no territory could be turned over against the express will of its population. Therefore he asked for details of the Lithuanian plans to administer the area and for guarantees that German troops would not be employed in the action.[63] In his report to the Polish

---

[59] When confronted with a direct question from Biržiška on the matter, Osmołowski was evasive. When Biržiška was in Warsaw later, Socialist members of the Constituent Assembly told him they had questioned Osmołowski about the demands of the Vilna Lithuanians but that he had replied only that he had lost the list of demands and so he could not supply the information.

[60] Poland, Ministry of Foreign Affairs, *Documents diplomatiques*, I, 15. The Polish documents offer the most complete account available of these talks.

[61] Wielhorski, *Polska a Litwa*, p. 313.

[62] Poland, Ministry of Foreign Affairs, *Documents diplomatiques*, I, 15. This practice, widely used by the Lithuanians in direct talks, seems to have been extremely irritating to the Poles, who often pointed to the fact that almost all the Lithuanian leaders could speak Polish fluently as being evidence of the Polish culture of Lithuania. See Ruhl, *New Masters of the Baltic*, p. 237.

[63] Poland, Ministry of Foreign Affairs, *Documents diplomatiques*, I, 15-17.

Ministry of Foreign Affairs on his impressions of Lithuania, Staniszewski stated that the first meeting had made a very unfavorable impression on him; it was clear that grounds for an agreement would be difficult to find; and he called the Lithuanian government pro-German and unpopular.[64]

Staniszewski had not at first been empowered to discuss the Lithuanian demand that a Lithuanian civil administration be admitted to Vilna and Grodno.[65] Upon his application to Warsaw, new instructions were sent allowing him to talk about the matter, provided the Lithuanians made their demands more precise. On June 7, Staniszewski held a second meeting with Sleževičius, at which time he found the latter "moins officiel et moins froid." In answer to Staniszewski's request for an exact statement of Lithuanian demands, Sleževičius promised a written note.[66]

Sleževičius's statement was forthcoming on June 11. The demands expressed in the note were essentially those which Voldemaras had outlined in his letter of April 29 to the peace conference. The Lithuanians demanded recognition of their independence with all the territory they claimed. They asked that Lithuanian civil authorities be admitted into Grodno *guberniya* as far as the Neman River; the frontier to the south of that was to be fixed by the peace conference. They would permit the Poles to use the railroads to pass to the Bolshevik front, but would not allow them to take any part in the political affairs of the area.[67] An answer was requested by June 18. Upon receipt of this note, Staniszewski left Kaunas, considering that his mission had done all it could.

On June 24 the Polish Foreign Ministry sent a formal reply to Šaulys's note of May 22 as well as to Sleževičius's note of June 11. Asserting that the Poles had proved that they desired friendly

---

[64] *Ibid.*, I, 17-18.

[65] The Lithuanian Christian Democratic daily, *Laisvė,* No. 55 (June 1, 1919), seized upon this to claim that the Polish mission was simply a band of "jokers" (*juokdariai*), since it had come without authorization to negotiate any agreements.

[66] Poland, Ministry of Foreign Affairs, *Documents diplomatiques*, I, 18-19.

[67] *Ibid.*, I, 21-23.

relations with the Lithuanians, the Polish message stated that the Polish government could recognize the Lithuanian government only after the withdrawal of the German forces and that no more negotiations would be undertaken until that withdrawal. Only those territories could be turned over to the Lithuanians which expressed the desire to be part of the Lithuanian state. In conclusion, the note maintained that the Polish military actions in Lithuania were directed only against the Bolsheviks and were in no way contrary to the interests of the Lithuanian people.[68]

The Lithuanians had kept a close eye throughout these negotiations on the attitude of the Western powers, and the failure of those powers to adopt a single policy either individually or as a group on the Lithuanian question must be considered one of the causes of the failure of the direct talks between Poland and Lithuania to arrive at any solution. In practice, by sending missions and technical aid, the Entente powers were beginning to recognize the existence of the Lithuanian government. Formally, they still refused recognition and would not admit the Lithuanians to the peace conference. This duality, as it became apparent, led the Lithuanians to expect more, and so as not to compromise future possibilities, they became more intransigent.

The Lithuanian delegation in Paris continued its work with varying success during the spring of 1919. On April 19, Voldemaras joined with representatives of Estonia, Georgia, Latvia, and the Ukraine in a declaration demanding a hearing aimed at recognition and admission to the conference.[69] On May 2, Voldemaras wrote to Clemenceau complaining that although the Lithuanians had in March been promised admission, nothing had as yet been done. With the negotiations with the Germans now imminent, he declared, the Lithuanians were repeating their request for action.[70]

On April 23, Voldemaras and Yčas received an invitation to speak before a subcommittee of the Commission on Polish

[68] *Ibid.*, I, 23-25.

[69] Conférence de la Paix, *Recueil*, IV, C, (2) Commission des Affaires Polonaises, 143-44.

[70] Lithuania, Delegation to Paris, *Composition*, VIII, 2.

Affairs. Since they were only invited as individuals "au courant" on Lithuanian affairs, and not as representatives of the Lithuanian government, they delivered a note to the committee expressing gratitude at having been called but asking leave not to speak, since they wanted to be heard for themselves and not just as a part of the Polish question.[71] On May 10 the two appeared before the full commission and spoke of the situation in Lithuania. Their objections to the first call had not been met, but they nevertheless agreed to appear now. At this meeting Voldemaras requested the recognition of Lithuania including the *guberniyas* of Vilna, Grodno, Kaunas, Suwalki, and parts of Courland and East Prussia. Stressing the participation of Belorussian and Jewish representatives in the government, he claimed that Lithuania wanted complete independence, and not federation with either Russia or Poland. He expressed confidence that Lithuania could avoid economic or political absorption by any of its neighbors, and he attributed the Lithuanian antagonism toward the Poles to "the policy of the Poles through the centuries."[72]

After the Lithuanians had left the room, Kammerer, the French member of the commission, expressed the belief that the Lithuanians would be willing to federate with a democratic Russia if the opportunity arose. This opinion was to be found in several commentaries on the Lithuanian question,[73] but it must be based on personal impressions which cannot be documented. It may be that the Lithuanians used federation with Russia as a big "if" with which to ease the pressure for union with Poland, feeling that Russia was beyond rehabilitation. It is highly doubtful that by this time the Lithuanian leaders would have settled voluntarily for anything short of complete independence.

In the terms of peace presented to the Germans on May 7 the Lithuanians found much of interest to them. By Article 433 the

---

[71] United States, *Foreign Relations: Paris Peace Conference*, IV, 626-27, 639-40.
[72] Conférence de la Paix, *Recueil*, IV, C, (2) Commission des Affaires Polonaises, 164-67.
[73] See Wielhorski, *Polska a Litwa*, p. 321; Pobóg-Malinowski, *Najnowsza Historia*, II, Part 1, 141.

German troops were ordered to remain in the Baltic area until the Allies decided to order their withdrawal, a strange situation whereby, as Lansing noted, the Entente and the Germans were in effect acting as allies.[74] Another point of great importance to the Lithuanians was the separation from East Prussia of the Memelland, that is, the territory north and east of the Memel or Neman River. Although Lithuania was not mentioned by name in the treaty, it is clear from Clemenceau's response to the German commentary on the terms that the area was meant to be joined to Lithuania once the political status of that country was settled.[75] The Lithuanians objected to the refusal to name them as the new sovereign of the territory, and they complained because the left bank of the Neman had been kept with East Prussia, arguing that a plebiscite should have been ordered there. Furthermore, they called the internationalization of the Neman unjust.[76] The Allies made no provision for the immediate administrative separation of the Memelland from East Prussia, with the result that the conflict there between "separatists" and "anti-separatists" intensified rapidly.[77]

Although the hope lingered on in Entente circles of a Polish-Lithuanian rapprochement, by May the Lithuanians had succeeded in associating themselves, in the eyes of the west, with Latvia and Estonia, thus constituting the "Baltic question." On May 27 the Entente leaders sent a note to Admiral Kolchak in Siberia, setting forth conditions for the recognition of the Admiral's government as the *de facto* government of Russia. The fifth condition was

[74] Meeting of Foreign Ministers, May 9, 1919, United States, *Foreign Relations: Paris Peace Conference*, IV, 691.

[75] Kammerer to the Commission on Baltic Affairs, May 19, 1919, Conférence de la Paix, *Recueil*, IV, C, (7) Commission des Affaires Baltiques, 18.

[76] Voldemaras to the peace conference, May 20, 1919, Lithuania, Delegation to Paris, *Composition*, III, 4.

[77] Gaigalat was arrested in June for his work on behalf of Lithuania. See *Tilsiter Allgemeine Zeitung*, No. 143 (June 21, 1919); Woodward and Butler (eds.), *British Foreign Policy*, First Series, III, 22-23; Lithuania, Delegation to Paris, *Composition*, III, 5. There were rumors in Lithuania at this time that the English were planning to take over the Memelland as a Baltic "Gibraltar." See *Lietuva*, No. 137 (June 28, 1919).

that, if a solution of the relations between Esthonia, Latvia, and Lithuania, and the Caucasian and Trans-Caspian territories and Russia is not speedily reached by agreement, the settlement will be made in consultation and cooperation with the League of Nations, and that until such a settlement is made, the Government of Russia agrees to recognize those territories as autonomous and to confirm the relations which may exist between the Allied and Associated Governments and the *de facto* Governments of those territories.[78]

The Lithuanians felt that this note would be followed by a *de facto* recognition of their government,[79] but they were again disappointed. Kolchak's answer on June 4 was noncommittal, assuring recognition of the "autonomy" of the existing governments for the present, but reserving for an all-Russian constituent assembly the final decision on the form of government for the territories in question. He agreed to the principle of recourse to the League should a direct agreement not be reached.[80] Despite the exchange, however, the question of the recognition of the Baltic governments just drifted on.

Another move of the peace conference which served to join Lithuania to the "Baltic question" was the formation in May of a Commission on Baltic Affairs. The competence of the commission was not at first clear, and it met with vigorous opposition on the part of the Russians at Paris, who maintained that it could do nothing to violate the integrity of the Russian lands or to prejudice the decisions of a Russian constituent assembly.[81] At the first meeting of the commission on May 15, the French delegate, Kammerer, stated that the task of the commission was to aid the existing governments against the Bolsheviks and against the Germans, but without prejudicing the possibilities of a democratic Russian federation.[82] When the Italian delegate,

[78] United States, *Foreign Relations: 1919, Russia*, pp. 300, 361, 369.

[79] See Lithuania, Delegation to Paris, *Composition*, VIII, 5.

[80] United States, *Foreign Relations: 1919, Russia*, p. 376. See Bakhmetev's explanation of the note, *ibid.*, pp. 684-87.

[81] See the statement made by Maklakov to the commission, May 26, 1919, Conférence de la Paix, *Recueil*, IV, C, (7) Commission des Affaires Baltiques, 41; letter to the peace conference from the Russian Political Council, May 24, 1919, *ibid.*, pp. 48-49.

[82] *Ibid.*, pp. 5-6.

Della Torretta, joined the commission at its third meeting on May 22,[83] he immediately questioned the competence of the commission, claiming that its mandate seemed limitless, and he expressed the fear that the commission was violating Russia's territorial integrity, thereby working against the policies of the Entente governments.[84] Kammerer admitted that there was Russian opposition to the existence of the commission, but he maintained that the commission was essential to curb German influences in the Baltic area.[85] The commission decided to ask for a new mandate, and on May 24 the Council of Four declared "that the commission is authorized to examine the future relations of all the Baltic States with Russia and to submit recommendations on this subject."[86]

On June 10, after the commission had begun to debate a constitutional project for Estonia, Della Torretta again questioned the group's competence, this time pointing out that the exchange of notes between the Entente and Admiral Kolchak may have eliminated the commission's right to deal with political affairs.[87] In answer, Lord Esme Howard, the chairman, and Kammerer both maintained that the commission was not trying to work out a definitive program but was only preparing recommendations which would be needed if the League—which was to evolve from the peace conference—should be called on to intervene.[88] Thenceforth the commission met no more challenges to its *raison d'être* in the somewhat vagrant course of its discussions.

The members of the commission quickly developed a strong sympathy for the Baltic governments and defended the interests of the small nations with great zeal. On May 26, Kammerer declared that there could be no question of allowing the White Russians to take over the Baltic states by force, despite the fact that the existing governments there could not be granted recognition at this time.[89] When an Estonian delegation appeared before the commission on May 28, the members of the commission

[83] *Ibid.*, p. 30.   [84] *Ibid.*, p. 30.   [85] *Ibid.*, pp. 30-31.   [86] *Ibid.*, p. 37n.
[87] *Ibid.*, p. 68.   [88] *Ibid.*, pp. 68-70.   [89] *Ibid.*, p. 46.

were most apologetic for their inability to give the Estonians any substantial aid.[90]

In the early meetings of the commission, the Polish-Lithuanian dispute came up in connection with the problem of curbing German power in the Baltic. In a discussion of a proposed demarcation line between the Polish and the German forces, drawn up by the Commission on Polish Affairs, Samuel E. Morison, the American delegate, questioned whether Lithuanian territory was not being put under Polish occupation and suggested that it might be better to allow the Germans to remain until the Lithuanians were able to handle their own affairs, rather than to foster further conflict between the Poles and Lithuanians.[91] On May 26, Morison again raised this issue, claiming that the Lithuanians had been holding the front by themselves since March 30 and so were able to take over all Lithuanian territory by themselves. Stressing the serious consequences of a Polish-Lithuanian conflict, he suggested the intervention of the commission in order to bring about a settlement.[92]

On June 13 the commission heard a French military report from Kaunas which asserted that the Lithuanians would hold their share of the front alone and to maintain internal order. The report went on to demand the immediate evacuation of the German forces.[93] On June 17, Colonel Warwick Greene, the head of the American Commission in the Baltic Provinces, appeared before the Commission on Baltic Affairs and assured it that the Lithuanian government "is well representative of the popular wishes and corresponds to the views of the various classes of the population."[94] He urged that loans be extended to the Baltic governments in order to relieve their dependence

---

[90] *Ibid.*, p. 53.

[91] *Ibid.*, p. 17. Cf. Lansing's similar comments in a meeting of the Foreign Ministers, May 24, 1919, United States, *Foreign Relations: Paris Peace Conference*, IV, 767-73

[92] Conférence de la Paix, *Recueil*, IV, C (7) Commission des Affaires Baltiques, 44-45. The statement that the Lithuanians had been holding the front by themselves since March 30 was erroneous. The Germans had been forbidden to advance against the Bolsheviks after March 30, but they had remained at the front until the beginning of June.

[93] *Ibid.*, p. 83.   [94] *Ibid.*, p. 93.

on the Germans.[95] Kammerer noted, however, that such loans to unrecognized governments could not be made by the Western powers individually and so would have to be handled by the peace conference.[96]

The financial situation was again becoming serious in Lithuania. The money obtained through the German loan in December, 1918, was rapidly being exhausted, and the internal tax system had not yet begun to produce the needed revenues.[97] The Lithuanians were now looking for another foreign loan, but none was to be had. The British representative in Kaunas, Grant-Watson, apparently raised hopes of aid from Great Britain, but no loan was forthcoming.[98] Vileišis was sent to Berlin to seek a new loan, but he was unsuccessful, since the German price was the renunciation of Lithuanian designs on East Prussia.[99]

Welcome aid did come at this time from the West in the form of food and supplies. Distribution of the first shipment of food for children, sent by the Hoover Commission, began on May 17.[100] Through the efforts of the American Lithuanians, medical supplies also began to arrive in May.[101] The food situation in Lithuania was not so bad as elsewhere in Eastern Europe, and a good harvest in the summer of 1919 relieved the Lithuanians of dependence on outside aid in this regard.[102]

[95] *Ibid.*, pp. 91-92.   [96] *Ibid.*, p. 93.

[97] Greene told the Commission on Baltic Affairs that the Lithuanian government had collected five million marks in taxes, *ibid.*, p. 146, but this was not enough for the needs of the government.

[98] Sleževičius (Kaunas) to Puryckis (Berlin), letter, n.d., Šaulys Archives, f. 30. Sleževičius wrote to Šaulys on May 19 that promises of financial aid had been received from three countries—he did not name them—but that none had as yet made good on its promises. Šaulys Archives, f. 32. Grant-Watson, Chargé of the British legation at Copenhagen, first arrived in Kaunas on April 6, 1919.

[99] Sleževičius (Kaunas) to Šaulys (Warsaw), April 24 and May 16, 1919, Šaulys Archives, f. 32; statement by Greene to Commission on Baltic Affairs, July 7, 1919, Conférence de la Paix, *Recueil*, IV, C, (7) Commission des Affaires Baltiques, 146; Woodward and Butler (eds.), *British Foreign Policy*, First Series, III, 21, 23-24.

[100] On May 20, what seems to have been a well-organized demonstration of thanks by Lithuanian school children took place before the Metropole Hotel in Kaunas. The children cheered the American directors of the food program. *Lietuva*, No. 109 (May 23, 1919). On the organization of relief, see *Neue Zürcher Zeitung*, Nos. 518 (April 8, 1919), 527 (April 9, 1919), and 856 (June 10, 1919).

[101] *Neue Zürcher Zeitung*, No. 759 (May 22, 1919).

[102] *Ibid.*, No. 1455 (September 25, 1919).

The advance against the Bolsheviks continued throughout
April. The German troops were under orders from Berlin not
to attack the Russians, but by calling their forward outposts
"patrols" and then yielding the territory gained to Lithuanian
troops, they evaded this prohibition and thus aided the Lithuanians in taking Ukmerge at the beginning of May.[103] But no
order was forthcoming from Berlin to change the official position,
and the dissatisfaction of the Germans with the terms of the
peace at Paris precluded even any more such informal cooperation as had made possible the capture of Ukmerge.[104]

With Entente encouragement the Lithuanians were seeking to
organize their own forces so as to escape their dependence on the
German volunteers. The French mission was very important in
this regard, but three Swedish officers who came to Lithuania as
volunteers were even more helpful than the French.[105] The
American observer, Colonel Dawley, considered the Lithuanians
to be good soldier material, but he stressed the shortage of junior
officers and equipment and recommended American aid.[106]

In May, General Silvestras Žukauskas was named Chief of
Staff by Smetona, and a mobilization was ordered of all students
so as to provide "intellectual forces for the Lithuanian state."[107]
The Lithuanians now appealed to the peace conference to permit

[103] Jakštas, "Saksų savanorių dalys," *Karo Archyvas*, VI (1935), 214-16.
[104] See report by Colonel Dawley, May 20, 1919, United States, National Archives, 184.01502/29.
[105] Report by Colonel Dawley, May 5, 1919, United States, Archives, 184.-
01502/25; United States, *Foreign Relations: Paris Peace Conference*, XII, 191; *Times*
(London), May 13, 1919; *Neue Zürcher Zeitung*, No. 694 (May 11, 1919). See the
report of the Swedish Colonel Arnsberger, *Svenska Dagbladet*, May 10, 1920. The
British sought Russian approval before sending in their military advisers. Omsk to
Maklakov (Paris), telegram, June 3, 1919, Maklakov Archives, B, II, 2. Šarmaitis's
claim that the Entente missions were running Lithuania from March, 1919, on
cannot be substantiated ("Interventsiia anglo-amerikanskikh imperialistov,"
Istoricheskie Zapiski, No. 45, [1954], p. 269).
[106] United States, *Foreign Relations: Paris Peace Conference*, XII, 190, 191. For an
account of the preparations which the Lithuanians made to receive Dawley, see
Jurgela, *Lithuania and the United States*, pp. 241 ff. See also the report by Colonel
Greene, May 19, 1919, United States, *Foreign Relations: Paris Peace Conference*, XII,
196.
[107] Natkevičius, *Lietuvos kariuomenė*, pp. 27, 36. See also *Le Temps*, June 7, 1919;
Lietuva, No. 113 (May 28, 1919).

the separation of all Lithuanians serving in the various White Russian armies and the return of these men to their "father-land."[108] After all these delays and disappointments, the chief hope of the Lithuanians in their military and financial problems was to secure aid from the American Lithuanians.

The American Lithuanians had already begun organizing military forces in 1918, and in May, 1919, they reportedly informed Smetona that 75,000 men were ready to go to Lithuania.[109] Actually the total came nowhere near that number, and the Lithuanian press spoke only of the possibility of 10,000 men coming.[110] The American Lithuanians now demanded that the Kaunas government send a mission which would handle the military affairs and set up formal contacts with the Lithuanian community in America.[111] Kaunas had been preparing such a mission and had named Šaulys to head it. The mission was to seek financial aid and to help in sending the American Lithuanian military force to Lithuania.[112] It had to be postponed, however, when Šaulys suddenly contracted typhus.[113]

The German coup at Liepaja, the refusal of the Berlin government to order the volunteers to attack the Russians, the presentation of the conditions of peace at Paris, and the organization of local forces in Eastern Europe all brought about a change in the relations between the German occupation forces, the national governments of the Baltic region, and the Entente. In April, Leon Wasilewski, the former Foreign Minister of Poland, claimed that the Polish occupation of Vilna had destroyed the *raison*

[108] Lithuania, Delegation to Paris, *Composition*, VII, 10.

[109] *Kurjer Polski*, No. 129 (May 25, 1919).

[110] *Lietuva*, No. 137 (June 28, 1919). See also Pakštas, "Lietuvių amerikiečių kovos," *Židinys*, XXVII (1938), 642.

[111] *Vienybė Lietuvninkų*, No. 24 (June 11, 1919). On the Lithuanian propaganda campaign in America at this time, see Jurgela, Lithuania and the United States, pp. 251 ff.

[112] Šaulys (Kaunas) to Sleževičius (Kaunas), letter, May 23, 1919, Šaulys Archives, f. 32. See also *Neue Zürcher Zeitung*, No. 964 (June 28, 1919); United States, *Foreign Relations: Paris Peace Conference*, XII, 192.

[113] The health problem was very serious in Kaunas at this time. The government urged the people to cook or boil all food and water before use. *Lietuva*, No. 118 (June 4, 1919). See also *Laisvė*, No. 73 (June 25, 1919).

d'être of the German forces in Lithuania,[114] and the circles which had been the strongest in the condemnation of the Lithuanian government as a German tool were now the loudest in the demands for German withdrawal, expecting that it would be followed by a change in the Lithuanian government.[115]

As the fears grew of German interference in the Baltic, the Entente became more and more convinced that the time had come to exercise the right to demand the withdrawal of the German troops.[116] On June 1 the Supreme Council ordered the immediate evacuation of Latvia, with the evacuation of Lithuania to follow as soon as possible.[117]

The peace conference set up an Interallied Commission, headed by the British General H. P. Gough, to supervise the evacuation, but the group was weakened by several shortcomings in its organization. Only the British assigned members to it, the other powers failing to do so for no clear reason other than sheer lack of interest. The commission had no authority over Allied military missions already at work in the Baltic region, and it had no power to communicate directly with the German government.[118] The evacuation of the eastern areas of Lithuania went ahead with little difficulty, nevertheless, and on June 3 the Lithuanians took over control of the entire Bolshevik front. [119]

---

[114] Quoted in *Le Temps*, April 29, 1919. See also Wielhorski, *Polska a Litwa*, p. 301.

[115] The London *Times*, April 15, 1919, spoke of a "German and Lithuanian condominion supported on the bayonets of the Reserve Corps." *Le Temps*, May 14, 1919, claimed that the Germans needed no Liepaja-type coup in Lithuania since the Taryba was already their agent. See also *Monitor Polski*, No. 123 (June 4, 1919). *Monitor Polski*, No. 139 (June 25, 1919), claimed that Hindenburg was in Lithuania planning a campaign against the Poles.

[116] Greene complained that the Allies were arousing suspicion among the Baltic peoples because of their failure to control the Germans. Conférence de la Paix, *Recueil*, IV, C, (7) Commission des Affaires Baltiques, 72. Cf. Tallents's statement (*Man and Boy*, p. 311) that Greene was considered too friendly to the Germans at this time.

[117] Niessel, *L'évacuation*, p. 19.

[118] See Woodward and Butler (eds.), *British Foreign Policy*, First Series, III, 223-24.

[119] Schröder and Heygendorff, *Die sächsischen Freiwilligen-Truppen*, p. 28.

The problem of reorganizing the Bolshevik front after the withdrawal of the Germans and of preventing Polish-Lithuanian armed clashes was a pressing one for the Entente. On May 20 and 21 military talks were held between Polish and Lithuanian representatives at Vilna. Any agreement reached was to be subject to the Entente reservation that it could not prejudice the future political settlement. Political considerations were to be expressly ignored in the talks.[120] Nevertheless, neither side was willing to compromise on the minimum line it deemed necessary for its own military requirements, and Vilna was again the apple of discord, this time because of its importance as a railroad center. The talks were adjourned without result, and although another meeting was planned for Kaunas, the talks were never resumed.[121]

Claiming that the Germans still stationed in Lithuania constituted a threat to their security, the Poles now undertook to broaden their occupation zone to the north of the Varena-Vilna railroad. The Lithuanians protested this move, and armed clashes resulted between the two armies.[122] On June 6, Sleževičius complained to Colonel Greene that the Poles were moving into purely Lithuanian territory, where there were no Bolshevik troops and that they were mobilizing the local population.[123] On June 13, Voldemaras protested to the Supreme Council against the Polish advance and requested Entente intervention to force the Poles to stop.[124]

On June 18, Colonel Reboul notified the Lithuanian government that a line of demarcation between the Lithuanian and the Polish forces had been drawn which was in no way to prejudice a future political settlement. The Lithuanians protested that the line had been drawn without the participation of any Lithuanian

[120] Sleževičius wrote to Šaulys on May 19, saying that if Šaulys thought the talks would hinder his work in Warsaw, the Lithuanians would break them off. Šaulys Archives, f. 32.
[121] Poland, Ministry of Foreign Affairs, *Documents diplomatiques*, I, 13-15.
[122] See Lithuania, Delegation to Paris, *Composition*, VII, 11.
[123] Chambon, *La Lithuanie pendant la Conférence de la Paix*, p. 91.
[124] Lithuania, Delegation to Paris, *Composition*, VII, 7.

representatives, but they could do nothing but accept it.[125]
On June 23, Sleževičius notified Reboul, that, despite the fact
that the line divided Lithuania, his government was willing to
cooperate in its observance, since it would serve to stop the Polish
advance. Sleževičius went on to request that Polish civil administration be kept out of the disputed territory.[126]

The Lithuanians were now reasonably confident of recognition
by the peace conference. Although the Germans continually
warned the Lithuanians that the Entente would desert them, the
Lithuanians now had the evidence of the Entente missions and
of a greater solicitude toward their complaints against the Poles
to bolster their faith. The drawing of the line of June 18 was itself
a triumph for the Lithuanians, since it denied the Poles the
right to advance without any limit into Lithuania.

Although the moves of the Entente were aimed chiefly at pre-
serving a united front against the Bolsheviks rather than at
satisfying Lithuanian demands *per se*, the victory of the Lithuanians in establishing their right to an existence separate from
the Poles must not be overlooked. Another fact which should not
be ignored is the gradual acceptance of the Lithuanian government as a genuine national institution, rather than a German
creation. Although there were still voices in the West upholding
the Polish interpretations of "Lithuania," the Lithuanian national identity had been fairly well established through the work
of the delegation in Paris, the work of the Lithuanians abroad,
and the reports of the Entente missions in Kaunas.

[125] Chambon, *La Lithuanie pendant la Conférence de la Paix*, p. 105.

[126] Būtėnas and Mackevičius, "Gyvenimas ir darbai," in *Mykolas Sleževičius*, p. 118.

VI

"The Larger Policy of the Conference"
JUNE–AUGUST, 1919

THE LINE of demarcation set up in June proved short-lived. Neither Poles nor Lithuanians were satisfied with it, and the Poles were strong enough not to have to limit themselves to verbal protests alone. Because of the unfriendly and even hostile relations between the two, the Poles wanted at least a broader protective zone to the north and west of the Varena-Vilna railroad.[1] This involved crossing the line of demarcation, and the Lithuanians were quick to protest, expressing the fear that the aim of the advance was to take Kaunas.[2] The situation was made even worse, from the Lithuanian point of view, by the manner in which the German evacuation was being carried out. On July 1 the German command informed the Lithuanian government that Suwalki was soon to be evacuated to the Poles. In a note to Tallents on July 2, the Lithuanians protested strongly against this, seeking British assistance to protect the existing line of demarcation from violations "under any pretext."[3] On July 5, Sleževičius sent an urgent telegram to Puryckis at Berlin:

The Germans are withdrawing from Lithuania. We can keep complete order in our land by ourselves. But news has been received from reliable sources that the Poles, disregarding the line of demarcation set up by the Entente, plan to cross that line into Lithuanian territory. Please make energetic representations to the Entente Governments as quickly as possible, asking that they sternly forbid the Poles to cross the established line of demarcation between the Polish and Lithuanian armies.[4]

[1] Gibson (Warsaw) to Lord (Paris), telegram, June 20, 1919, United States, National Archives, 186.3116/106.

[2] Voldemaras, *Lithuanie et Pologne*, p. 33; United States, *Foreign Relations: Paris Peace Conference*, XII, 217. See Gibson's denial, United States, National Archives, 186.3116/106.

[3] Šaulys Archives, f. 30.

[4] Šaulys Archives, f. 30. Cf. the note delivered to the Swiss government, *Neue Zürcher Zeitung*, No. 1048 (July 13, 1919).

On July 11 the Germans withdrew from Kaunas,[5] but they did not evacuate all of Lithuania. The northwestern part of the country was still held by German forces in order to keep the connection open between East Prussia and Latvia.

On July 10, Clemenceau brought before the Supreme Council the reports of the Polish advance into Lithuania, and his recommendation that Marshal Foch act to halt the advance was accepted.[6] On July 11, Foch ordered the Poles to withdraw behind the line of June 18 as soon as possible.[7] On July 12 the Lithuanians again complained to the Supreme Council that the Poles were continuing to violate the line.[8] On July 18, Sleževičius sent another protest to Tallents, this time against the incomplete German withdrawal as well as against the Polish violations of the demarcation line, and he asked for arms and other aid.[9]

By July 18 the French military officers on the Polish-Lithuanian front had already yielded to the Polish demands, and on that day a provisional new line was drawn, giving the Poles a deeper protective zone along the railroad.[10] Lithuanian-Polish relations were reaching a dangerous stage as the clashes continued between the Lithuanian and Polish armies. On July 24 Kaunas sent another note to the Polish government pointing out that it favored the establishment of formal relations between the two, but that such an event could not be realized unless the Poles ceased their advance and retired behind the line of demarcation, meaning the line of June 18.[11] The same day, the Lithuanians again complained to the Supreme Council against

[5] Before they left, the German troops gathered before the quarters of the French military mission and sang "Die Wacht am Rhein." *Baltische Blätter*, No. 22 (July 19, 1919), p. 155. The Lithuanians claimed that the Germans burned part of the city in their withdrawal. *Neue Zürcher Zeitung*, No. 1116 (July 27, 1919).

[6] Woodward and Butler (eds.), *British Foreign Policy*, First Series, I, 59.

[7] *Neue Zürcher Zeitung*, No. 1097 (July 23, 1919).

[8] Lithuania, Delegation to Paris, *Composition*, VII, 12.

[9] Woodward and Butler (eds.), *British Foreign Policy*, First Series, III, 29-30. Lithuanian press releases at this time claimed that the Poles had launched an offensive against the Lithuanians on July 12, the day after the German withdrawal from Kaunas. See Chambon, *La Lithuanie pendant la Conférence de la Paix*, pp. 105-6.

[10] Budecki, *Stosunki polsko-litewskie*, p. 26.

[11] Lithuania, Delegation to Paris, *Composition*, VII, 14.

the Polish advance, noting that the Poles had given no indication of retiring.[12]

The English and French missions in Warsaw and Kaunas were doing their best to bring about an armistice. It would seem that the French were inclined to yield to the Poles, whereas the British were demanding their withdrawal. For their part, the Poles refused outright to withdraw. On July 24, Piłsudski told the British representative in Warsaw that he would not take the responsibility for withdrawing to the line of June 18.[13]

On July 26, Foch appeared before the Supreme Council, and, after pointing out the Polish violations of the line of June 18, recommended a new line, based on the provisional line of July 18 and on the recommendation of the Commission on Polish Affairs of April 22.[14] The major change in this new line was the assignment to the Poles of the districts of Suwalki and Sejny.[15] In this proposal Foch was backed by members of the Commission on Polish Affairs, and when Clemenceau and Balfour questioned the Polish character of Sejny, the experts of the Commission on Polish Affairs hastened to assure the council that the territory was indeed Polish and not Lithuanian. Lansing and Balfour consistently expressed their fear of placing Lithuanians under Polish occupation, but they lacked "evidence" with which to oppose the statements of the Polish experts, as the new line, like that of June 18, was drawn up without the participation of Lithuanian representatives.[16]

When Balfour objected to the idea of yielding territory to the Poles simply because they had chosen to violate the former line of demarcation, the answer was that the Poles had advanced with

[12] *Ibid.*, VII, 13.

[13] Woodward and Butler (eds.), *British Foreign Policy*, First Series, I, 239-40.

[14] *Ibid.*, I, 195. A map showing the various lines is reproduced in the same volume, facing p. 216.

[15] See Budecki, *Stosunki polsko-litewskie*, p. 26. See the debate in the Polish Constituent Assembly, July 22, 1919, *Monitor Polski*, No. 163 (July 23, 1919).

[16] The German census of 1916 reported 51 percent of the population of Sejny as Lithuanian. See Wielhorski, *Polska a Litwa*, p. 59. Suwalki was unquestionably Polish.

the permission of the French military mission in Warsaw.[17] Balfour commented that he thought the Poles were acting in defiance of the council, but was willing to accept the explanation offered since everyone else did. The line was then agreed upon as Foch had recommended it.[18]

On July 29, Balfour, still incensed over the actions of the Poles, brought up Piłsudski's statement of July 24 and urged pressure to force the Poles to yield. Clemenceau dismissed the matter without debate, pointing out that the new line of July 26 had changed the entire situation.[19]

On August 3, Colonel Reboul notified the Lithuanian government of the new line which had been drawn in Paris, but again he pointed out that the line was not to prejudge the territorial boundaries of Poland and Lithuania, since that decision would be made separately by the peace conference.[20] In his letter to the Supreme Council of August 5, Voldemaras acknowledged receipt of the news of the line of July 18, but he protested that the line had been drawn without Lithuanian participation. He emphasized the willingness of the Lithuanians to accept the new line as a starting point for a settlement but noted that the Poles were refusing to abide even by the new decision.[21] In his letter of August 6, Voldemaras protested against the assignment of Sejny to the Poles by the line of July 26.[22] Answering Reboul on August 8 the Lithuanian government similarly protested the loss of Sejny,[23] but the protests accomplished nothing. Military affairs received first call, and because of their superior strength the Poles held a favored position in Paris. The Lithuanians were

[17] Colonel Reboul had recommended to the Commission on Baltic Affairs that Sejny be assigned to Lithuania. Conférence de la Paix, *Recueil*, IV, C (7), Commission des Affaires Baltiques, 83.

[18] Woodward and Butler (eds.), *British Foreign Policy*, First Series, I, 204; United States, *Foreign Relations: Paris Peace Conference*, VII, 315. Because of delays in the transmission of the news of this decision, Lithuanian writers have often declared that the line was drawn up in August or even September.

[19] United States, *Foreign Relations: Paris Peace Conference*, VII, 378.

[20] Chambon, *La Lithuanie pendant la Conférence de la Paix*, p. 107.

[21] Lithuania, Delegation to Paris, *Composition*, VII, 15.   [22] *Ibid.*, VII, 16.

[23] Chambon, *La Lithuanie pendant la Conférence de la Paix*, p. 108.

too weak either to merit greater consideration from Paris or to offer effective resistance to the Poles.[24]

The Lithuanian government meanwhile was finding the problems of independent existence varied and demanding. As Klimas declared, "Everything now depends on how we organize our own house. The English especially have opened our eyes to this."[25] In early July the first internal loan—30,000,000 marks at 5 percent—was floated.[26] Plans for calling a constituent assembly were announced, but the assembly was not to be called until Vilna was in Lithuanian hands.[27] Though now a reality, the Lithuanian army lacked training and equipment. Appearing before the Commission on Baltic Affairs on July 7, Greene noted that the Lithuanians were still very dependent on some 10,000 to 12,000 German volunteers in their forces. The Lithuanians had mobilized about 15,000 men, but they still needed another two months' training.[28] The other great shortcoming of the army was equipment. The Lithuanians, having no military industry of their own, had to rely on foreign supplies. In a note of June 28, 1919, Greene had recommended to the American delegation that, in order to save Lithuania from German influence now that the Bolshevik threat had lessened, either the Entente should intervene physically or else some sort of cooperation should be set up between the British and the Americans in order to supply the Baltic states with food and equipment.[29]

In Paris, Yčas and Voldemaras had already approached the American delegation, seeking to buy equipment from the American Liquidation Commission of the War Department, an agency

[24] The "provisional" assignment of Sejny to the Poles proved to be permanent. The "Foch line" in that region still stands today as the border between Poland and the Lithuanian Soviet Socialist Republic.

[25] Klimas (Paris) to Šaulys (Kaunas), letter, June 29, 1919, Šaulys Archives, f. 76.

[26] See *Lietuva*, No. 137 (June 28, 1919).

[27] *Neue Zürcher Zeitung*, No. 1048 (July 13, 1919). See Staugaitis's statement on the constituent assembly, July 7, 1919, Conférence de la Paix, *Recueil*, IV, C, (7) Commission des Affaires Baltiques, 145; also *Lietuva*, No. 110 (May 24, 1919).

[28] Conférence de la Paix, *Recueil*, IV, C, (7) Commission des Affaires Baltiques, 146.

[29] United States, *Foreign Relations: 1919, Russia*, II, 682-83.

set up in February, 1919, to dispose of the AEF equipment left in Europe at the end of the war.[30] Demands for the material ran high, and Lithuania found herself competing with other buyers in a seller's market.[31] The Lithuanians managed to conclude an agreement for a purchase of about $5 million worth of equipment, but, according to Yčas, the deal was not completed without a great deal of trouble. The original agreement had been made on July 2, 1919. On July 4 an American, a Mr. Rubinov, visited the office of the Lithuanian delegation and suggested that for a commission of 5 percent he would be glad to aid the Lithuanians in this matter. Through inquiries the Lithuanians learned that Rubinov was not an agent of the commission, but was well known there (he was already representing Latvia and Estonia). At Yčas's suggestion the Lithuanians thanked Rubinov for his solicitude but declined his aid despite his warning that they might regret this move. On July 5 the Liquidation Commission notified the Lithuanians that the deal was off—the French were purchasing the entire remaining stock.

Yčas, now under fire from the delegation for having ruined the transaction by refusing to grease Rubinov's palm, tried to appeal to President Wilson directly but got no farther than the desk of Wilson's secretary. Through Mrs. Šliupas, who was then in Paris, the Lithuanians presented their case at a tea party to the wife of an unidentified American delegate, who advised them to hold off on their direct appeal to Wilson and promised to speak to her husband on the matter. A few days later, the Liquidation Commission notified the Lithuanians that their request would be honored, and that the equipment would be sold as promised.[32] This case is perhaps indicative of the indirect channels which the

[30] See *ibid.: Paris Peace Conference*, X, 374, 381.

[31] See report of commission in U. S. Congress, 66th Congress, 3d Session, *House Committee on Expenditures in the War Department*, Vol. IV, ser. 4, Parts 75-78 (Washington, D. C., 1921), p. 4164.

[32] M. Yčas, "Lietuvos vyriausybės sudarymo etapai," in *Pirmasis dešimtmetis*, I, 119-23. The manner in which the Lithuanians paid for this purchase is not clear. They got some $40,000 from the American Lithuanians, but the source of the rest of the money is not indicated anywhere. See Širvydas, *Bronius Kazys Balutis*, p. 50.

Lithuanian delegation, and probably other delegations too, had to use since they were not formally admitted to the conference.

The railroads were another vital question for the Lithuanians at this time. During the war the Germans had altered the gauge of the Russian-built roads to their own standard gauge and had built new roads with the narrower gauge. The German wartime railroad program had given Lithuania a degree of economic unity which had never been achieved under Russian rule, but at the same time it had tied the country more closely to Germany. The standard gauge tracks restricted movement from Russia while making the Lithuanians dependent on the Germans for rolling stock.[33] The Lithuanians sought to buy the necessary equipment for themselves from the Americans at Paris, but the latter refused to sell and referred the question to the peace conference.[34] The matter came up in the Council of Four at the end of June, and on June 25 the decision was taken to demand that the Germans leave behind their railroad materials then in the Baltic. The stock was to be the property of the Allied and Associated Powers, not of the Baltic states.[35] Furthermore, in line with the desire to keep the Baltic area economically tied to Russia rather than to Germany, the intention was expressed of seeking the restoration of the Russian gauge.[36]

Acting through direct negotiations with the Germans, the Lithuanian government on July 4 signed an agreement with the German authorities in Lithuania (Zimmerle and the chief of the German railroads) on the transfer of control of the railroads. The lines, together with all equipment on the day of evacuation, were to be handed over to the Lithuanian government; the

---

[33] Russian-made wagons could be converted, but locomotives could not. On the German railroad program, see Georg Neumann, "Die Eisenbahnen Litauens und des Baltikums zu russischer Zeit und ihre Entwicklung durch den Krieg," *Zeitung des Vereins Deutscher Eisenbahnverwaltungen*, No. 83 (November 1, 1919).

[34] Chambon, *La Lithuanie pendant la Conférence de la Paix*, p. 94.

[35] The equipment was to comprise part of the reparations due the Allies under Article 375 of the peace treaty. See Kammerer's statement to the Commission on Baltic Affairs, June 24, 1919, Conférence de la Paix, *Recueil*, IV, C, (7) Commission des Affaires Baltiques, 110.

[36] United States, *Foreign Relations: Paris Peace Conference*, VI, 672-73.

amount of compensation was to be negotiated later. All Russian equipment was to be turned over free of charge. Provision was also made for Lithuania to rent additional German equipment.[37] As it turned out, the transfer was not a simple matter because of the presence of independent German forces in northwest Lithuania, but the basic settlement had now been made.

As these agreements were being made and the strength of the new state grew, projects for regulating Lithuania's future relations with its neighbors attracted more and more attention. There were four main lines which these projects would follow: some sort of union with the Baltic states to the north, union with Russia to the east, union with Poland to the south and southwest, or, of course, complete independence. There was no talk in Lithuania of union with Germany, despite various allegations of German domination over the Lithuanian government. Such a course would have been unthinkable both from the point of view of the anti-German sentiments of the mass of the population and also from the point of view of gaining Entente recognition.

In the constitution, the question of future relations with other nations was expressly left to the constituent assembly, but the constitution had already been revised extensively in April and future changes were not inconceivable. Actually, by the nature and manner of its organization and functioning, the Lithuanian government was following a policy of independence, but many rumors of projected unions were being bruited about. The strongest would seem to have been the idea of some sort of union with the other two Baltic states.[38] This idea gained greatly by the appointment on August 15 of Šliupas as the Lithuanian representative at Riga.[39] However, there were serious stumbling blocks in the way of realizing this idea—differences in culture, differences in immediate problems, fundamental disagreements over the proposed extent of the union, and the inertia of existing conditions. The Latvians and the Estonians were historically

---

[37] Dailidė, *Lietuvos sutartys*, I, 6-11.
[38] See Steinmetz, *De Nationaliteiten in Europa*, p. 367.
[39] For Šliupas's ideas see his *Lietuvių-Latvių Respublika ir Šiaures Tautų Sajunga*.

connected with the Germans rather than with the Poles and did not share the Lithuanians' antipathy toward the Poles, while at the same time the Lithuanians looked upon the Germans in a different way than their two neighbors did. The Estonians were advocating a broader union than the Lithuanians would accept. They wanted inclusion of the Poles, so that the new political union would have power of some significance. The Lithuanians naturally opposed this in view of their own differences with the Poles, advocating instead a union of the three Baltic states alone.[40] This narrow concept was in a way self-defeating, since such a union would produce little of the desired increment in power. Therefore, the trend toward independent organization of each state was practically unbreakable. An agreement in principle on a military alliance, made in July,[41] was the only result achieved at this time.

For Lithuania a union with Poland in any form was of course out of the question, as has been shown in the review of the direct negotiations between the two governments. Even without the Polish occupation of Vilna the consummation of such a union is doubtful. Although some Poles continued to hope for some sort of agreement, the power of the National Democrats made the Lithuanians wary of all offers and also fortified Lithuanian intransigence. In August the story was circulated in Polish newspapers that in mid-July the British, after declaring that a recognition of Lithuanian independence was impossible, had urged the Lithuanian government to give serious consideration to the idea of a federation with Poland. In response the Lithuanian cabinet of ministers on July 19 was said to have indicated its preference for federation with Russia, with only four Socialists—Kairys, Sleževičius, Paknys, and Šaulys—opposing. As evidence of this Russophile tendency within the Lithuanian government, the Warsaw newspaper *Kurjer Polski* went on to point to the presence

---

[40] Piłsudski saw this division and hoped to bring the Lithuanians around to an agreement by exerting pressure through the other Baltic states. See Wasilewski, *Józef Piłsudski*, p. 198.

[41] *Times* (London), July 15, 1919; *Svenska Dagbladet*, July 11, 1919.

of ex-Russian officials, such as Veriovkin (former Governor General of Vilna), in the Lithuanian government.[42] The Lithuanian government issued an official denial of this report, calling it "absolutely contradictory to fact" and "a provocation to Polish-Lithuanian relations."[43]

In fact, union with Russia was little discussed in Lithuania, but it was the goal of the Western powers in their plans for Lithuania.[44] The constitutions for each of the Baltic states under consideration by the Commission on Baltic Affairs would have given each state some sort of autonomous position within a new democratic Russia.[45] The commission carried on its work energetically, fully aware that neither the Russians nor the Lithuanians approved, but hoping that the plan would be accepted as a compromise. Finally, however, on July 7, the commission decided to abandon the debate on the ground that the proper moment had not yet come for the conference to occupy itself with the question.[46]

There remained a disinclination at Paris to recognize the Baltic states. Although it was repeatedly pointed out that the mention of the governments in the note to Kolchak had implied *de facto* recognition,[47] the Supreme Council, chiefly because of the stand of the American representatives, refused to take the formal

---

[42] *Kurjer Polski*, No. 202 (August 7, 1919). While Governor-General of Vilna, Veriovkin had been extremely helpful to the Lithuanians in their cultural struggles with the Poles.

[43] *Ibid.*, No. 212 (August 17, 1919). In publishing the denial, *Kurjer Polski* questioned how the report could be construed as "provocative." See also Poland, Ministry of Foreign Affairs, *Documents diplomatiques*, I, 28. It should be pointed out that Šaulys was not a member of the cabinet.

[44] See the discussion in the Commission on Baltic Affairs, June 24, 1919, Conférence de la Paix, *Recueil*, IV, C, (7) Commission des Affaires Baltiques, 104 ff.

[45] The debate mentioned only Estonia, but Lord Esme Howard expressly stated that the draft was to apply to each of the three Baltic states. Conférence de la Paix, *Recueil*, IV, C, (7) Commission des Affaires Baltiques, 135.

[46] *Ibid.*, p. 149. In the course of the talks, the commission found itself contradicting the terms of the notes exchanged with Kolchak and raising issues which could only be settled satisfactorily by the participants directly, if at all, such as the fact that if the Baltic states were given autonomy in advance, they would not be represented in the Russian constituent assembly.

[47] See the debate between Della Torretta and Tyler, Conférence de la Paix, *Recueil*, IV, C, (7) Commission des Affaires Baltiques, 135.

step of recognition, with the result that Lithuania and the other two Baltic governments suffered serious reversals in the official actions of the conference. The recommendation of the Commission on Baltic Affairs that credits be extended to the three Baltic states[48] died in committees, since credits could not be extended to unrecognized governments with such uncertain futures.[49] Another consequence for the Lithuanians was that the conference had to prepare a plan for Allied occupation and administration of Memel, because the territory could not be turned over to an unrecognized government.[50] Repeated efforts by the Baltic commission to force a new Baltic policy, or at least a restatement of current policy, were of no avail as the members of the Supreme Council wished to keep the Baltic policy in line with what Balfour called "the larger policy of the conference," [51] avoiding any definite commitments on the Russian question. Declarations such as those sought by the commission on Baltic Affairs were considered liable only to complicate matters and cause misunderstandings.[52]

Despite these blocks, Lithuania was gradually gaining informal recognition. The Entente was already taking many actions without a formal declaration.[53] The blockade of the Baltic area was gradually lifted, since the Entente realized that the continued resistance of the Baltic governments to the Bolsheviks, as well as to the Germans, was dependent on their receiving supplies from the West.[54] In a report from Tallinn on July 19,

[48] *Ibid.*, p. 110. United States, *Foreign Relations: Paris Peace Conference*, VII, 48.

[49] United States, *Foreign Relations: Paris Peace Conference*, VII, 239.

[50] See the discussions in the Commission on Baltic Affairs, August 8 and 19, 1919, Conférence de la Paix, *Recueil*, IV, C, (7) Commission des Affaires Baltiques, 186-88, 196-98.

[51] United States, *Foreign Relations: Paris Peace Conference*, VII, 734.

[52] *Ibid.*, VII, 324-27.

[53] See statement by E. H. Carr, September 9, 1919, Conférence de la Paix, *Recueil*, IV, C, (7) Commission des Affaires Baltiques, 211.

[54] See United States, *Foreign Relations: Paris Peace Conference*, VII, 102, 131-32; Bane and Lutz (eds.), *Blockade of Germany*, p. 559; Churchill, *The Aftermath*, p. 245. The unfavorable reaction on the part of the Poles to this increasing attention being paid the Lithuanians found expression in an interview with Paderewski published in *Dziennik Berlinski*, August 2, 1919.

Colonel Dawley told the American delegation in Paris that steps must be taken to relieve the dependence of the Lithuanians on the Germans. As the situation stood, the range of action for the Lithuanians was extremely limited: "Any break with Germany takes away the only source of supply aside from American food-stuffs that Lithuania has, and this fact alone renders an alliance with Germany more probable."[55]

The Lithuanian record in Paris during this period was not without some bright spots. On July 7 a Lithuanian delegation testified before the Commission on Baltic Affairs. Voldemaras and Staugaitis claimed that the Lithuanians were in a position to keep order in their own affairs if only the disruptive influences of the Germans and the Poles could be alleviated by action on the part of the Entente. The favorable picture which these two gave of Lithuania was substantiated by reports from Warwick Greene personally and from the French mission in Kaunas through the French delegate in the commission.[56] In August the Lithuanian delegation made an important gain in its own prestige through an agreement with an international Jewish delegation in Paris on the position—one of autonomy—which the Jews were to have in Lithuania.[57]

The British were the first major power to take steps in harmony with the new trend toward recognition. In early July, Curzon still hoped for federation, perhaps through an agreement by a conference of representatives of the border governments and the Russian Political Council, but Crowe and Balfour both felt that

[55] United States, *Foreign Relations: Paris Peace Conference*, XII, 217. Cf. the reports of British representatives in the Baltic area, Woodward and Butler (eds.), *British Foreign Policy*, First Series, III, 21, 23-24; Reboul's statement to the Commission on Baltic Affairs, September 16, 1919, Conférence de la Paix, Commission des Affaires Baltiques, 213.

[56] Conférence de la Paix, *Recueil*, IV, C, (7) Commission des Affaires Baltiques, 144-48.

[57] Lithuania, Delegation to Paris, *Composition*, VII, 7. In Lithuania itself, how-ever, there was a growing threat of anti-Semitism. In June the newspapers carried an appeal from the cabinet for religious understanding. See *Lietuva*, No. 133 (June 24, 1919). Since there were no reports of trouble in the foreign press, it would appear that the situation remained quiet.

the gulf was too broad to be bridged.[58] By August, Curzon favored the *de facto* recognition of Lithuania in order to "regularize the position of Lithuania in the Baltic States."[59] In the middle of August a report coming from Lithuanian sources in London claimed that the Lithuanian representative in London, Čepinskis, had been assured of British recognition.[60]

Elsewhere in Europe, the Lithuanians were having considerable success. On June 26, in answer to a letter of May 23, 1919, from Voldemaras, the Pope, while not formally recognizing the new government, took cognizance of the Lithuanian national movement in a note sent through Cardinal Gasparri to Count Alfred Tyszkiewicz in Rome, asserting that "the Holy See will not fail to favor all that tends toward the realization of the just and legitimate aspirations of Lithuania and the safeguarding of its religious institutions." He expressed confidence in a "bright future" for Lithuania and imparted an apostolic benediction on "all the Catholic sons of Lithuania."[61] In July and August, Lithuania concluded postal conventions with Finland, Latvia, and Estonia.[62] On August 22, Norway granted the Lithuanian government *de facto* recognition.[63]

Also during the month of August, however, a serious new threat to the Lithuanian government was developing in the northwestern part of the country, where German troops still held control. The center of the German forces was the railroad center of Šiauliai. Conflicts between Lithuanian and German troops had been reported there as early as June, but the situation

---

[58] Woodward and Butler (eds.), *British Foreign Policy*, First Series, III, 409-10, 411n.

[59] *Ibid.*, III, 509-10.

[60] *Neue Zürcher Zeitung*, No. 1229 (August 15, 1919).

[61] *Neue Zürcher Zeitung*, No. 959 (June 27, 1919). Text of Voldemaras's letter in Grand Rapids (Mich.) *Herald*, July 13, 1919.

[62] *Neue Zürcher Zeitung*, Nos. 1132 (July 29, 1919) and 1206 (August 12, 1919). On postal relations with the United States, see *ibid.*, No. 1368 (September 10, 1919). The postal system was far from well organized. In a letter in February, 1920, Warwick Greene wrote, "You will probably never hear again of a letter you are incautious enough to trust to the mail. Nobody dreams of entrusting a letter to 'government' post." Hale (ed.), *The Letters of Warwick Greene*, p. 147.

[63] *Neue Zürcher Zeitung*, No. 1488 (September 30, 1919).

became acute only with the formal general withdrawal of the Germans in July, when the unruly and undisciplined elements in the German forces began to act on their own, in disobedience of orders from Berlin. On July 26, Sleževičius sent a protest to Tallents against a reported troop build-up in Šiauliai,[64] and the German forces were accused of hindering the recruitment of men for the Lithuanian army.[65] The Entente commission under Gough, then demanded the complete withdrawal of all German forces from the Baltic area with safeguards against reenforcements or stockpiling of war materials in the Baltic states.[66] On August 16 the Germans notified the Lithuanians that they would be unable to complete the evacuation until October 8, and the Lithuanians vainly protested this delay in a message to the peace conference.[67]

In the latter part of July another threat to the existence of the Baltic government had arisen in the person of Colonel Bermondt-Avalov, a man of uncertain background,[68] who assumed the leadership of a Russian volunteer army in Latvia and Lithuania, with headquarters in Jelgava, Latvia. Declaring himself a patriotic Russian—he always wore a Cossack uniform—this "colonel d'operette et prince de comédie"[69] made no bones about his German sympathies: "I was of the firm conviction that Communism was to be conquered only with the help of Germany, since Germany alone was interested in the reestablishment of a great Russia."[70] Despite this conviction, he found it necessary to criticize the Germans for supporting such separatist movements as the Lithuanian and the Latvian, calling this policy "one of the main reasons for the failure of all our common undertakings."[71]

On July 26 a part of Bermondt's army, headed by Colonel

---

[64] Woodward and Butler (eds.), *British Foreign Policy*, First Series, III, 119.
[65] Niessel, *L'évacuation*, p. 20.
[66] Woodward and Butler (eds.), *British Foreign Policy*, First Series, I, 253-54.
[67] *Ibid.*, III, 76-77.
[68] See the speculations in Von Braatz, *Fürst Anatol Pawlowitsch Lieven*, pp. 128-31.
[69] Vanlande, *Avec le Général Niessel*, p. 27.
[70] Bermondt-Avalov, *Im Kampf*, p. 153.   [71] *Ibid.*, p. 71.

Virgolich, moved into Lithuania from Latvia and seized Kur-senai, about 25 kilometers to the west of Siauliai.[72] Throughout August the antagonism between Bermondt and the Lithuanian government increased. On August 12, Grant-Watson informed Curzon that there seemed to be an agreement between the Letts and the Lithuanians to attack Bermondt if the latter should carry out a planned move toward Daugavpils.[73] At a meeting held in Riga on August 26, which had been called for the purpose of creating a united front against the Bolsheviks, [74] Colonel Benjaševičius, the Lithuanian representative, protested against the disruption caused in Lithuania by Bermondt's forces. Claiming that Benjaševičius was not showing "military correctness" to a "senior officer," Bermondt threatened to at-tack the Lithuanians if they did not stop complaining.[75] The conference assigned then Daugavpils as Bermondt's target in a proposed general offensive in September, [76] which meant that his troops would have to cross through both Lithuania and Latvia to get to the front, and yet neither of those countries trusted him. The Germans backed Bermondt's demand for the use of the Lithuanian railroads, threatening to cut off Lithua-nia's coal supply if the demand should be refused.[77]

Although Bermondt was formally heading an independent Russian army, few doubted that the hand of Von der Goltz and the German army stood behind his actions.[78] German soldiers were being allowed to resign and reenlist in Bermondt's army, thus assuming Russian citizenship.[79] In the eyes of the Latvians and the Lithuanians, Bermondt seemed even more of a threat than the Germans. He openly took a stand against independence for the Baltic governments[80] and showed no inclination to

---

[72] Birontas, *Bermontininkams Lietuvą užpuolus*, p. 74.
[73] Woodward and Butler (eds.), *British Foreign Policy*, First Series, III, 58.
[74] The British sponsored the conference. *Ibid.*, III, 86.
[75] Bermondt-Avalov, *Im Kampf*, pp. 174-76.   [76] *Ibid.*, p. 177.
[77] Woodward and Butler (eds.), *British Foreign Policy*, First Series, III, 81.
[78] *Ibid.*, III, 131-32.
[79] Birontas, *Bermonitninkams Lietuvą užpuolus*, p. 66.
[80] See Bermondt-Avalov, *Im Kampf*, pp. 177-78.

negotiate disputes, claiming the right to dictate.[81] It would seem that conflict was inevitable.

At this time, relations with Poland were also passing through a most serious stage, perhaps a decisive one. There were two distinct trends in Polish thought, both of which found their expression in political events during the month of August. One idea was that German influences were weakening in Lithuania and that the time was now propitious for agreement. With the evacuation of the main German forces, the causes of conflict were thought to have been removed, and the chances for an agreement, possibly even a union, thereby improved. The moment was right to "conform to the requirements of the strategic situation and relieve the Poles from the necessity of being in the wrong."[82]

Others viewed the German threat as being as great as ever, if not even greater. *Kurjer Polski* noted the German evacuation, but claimed that the German secret police had remained behind with Zimmerle. The German troops in the northwest were taken as the proof that the situation had not changed; the Taryba was still considered the tool of the Germans,[83] and it was the duty of the Polish government to protect the Poles yet in Lithuania.[84]

Against this background of continuing hostility, the Polish government now made a new attempt to reach an agreement with the Lithuanians. Piłsudski sent Wasilewski to Vilna in early August to prepare a mission to Kaunas. Wasilewski was instructed first of all to discuss the Lithuanian situation with Mykolas Biržiška, the leader of the Vilna Lithuanians. This he did. On August 3, Wasilewski had a final talk with Piłsudski, who had been in Vilna since August 1, and then he left for Kaunas.[85]

[81] See Poland, Ministry of Foreign Affairs, *Documents diplomatiques*, I, 26.

[82] *Times* (London), August 1, 1919.

[83] *Kurjer Polski*, No. 202 (August 7, 1919). Non-Lithuanian writers persisted in identifying the Taryba with the Lithuanian cabinet despite the facts to the contrary. It would seem that this practice was carried on intentionally in order to have a better propaganda weapon. The true situation in Lithuanian politics was known abroad. See the report in *ibid.*, No. 259 (October 4, 1919).

[84] *Ibid.*, No. 178 (July 14, 1919).

[85] Wasilewski, *Józef Piłsudski*, pp. 203-4.

On August 5, in Kaunas, Wasilewski proposed to the Lithuanian government that separate plebiscites be held in Polish-occupied and in "Kaunas" Lithuania according to identical electoral systems. The delegates so elected were to meet in Vilna in a common assembly which would then establish the juridical and political status of Lithuania and define its relations with Poland.[86] A three-hour debate on that day led to nothing, as Sleževičius categorically rejected the idea of holding a plebiscite in Vilna, claiming that it was ethnic Lithuanian territory: "If Vilna is not recognized as a Lithuanian city, that is death for Lithuania."[87] The Lithuanians promised an answer after a meeting of the cabinet of ministers. That answer was delivered on August 6. In it the Lithuanians rejected the idea of a plebiscite in "ethnographic Lithuania" so long as Polish troops were present there. The Lithuanians further wanted military agreements, with guarantees of demarcation lines, completely independent of political considerations.[88] Wasilewski left the next day, his mission unsuccessful.

One immediate result of the failure of Wasilewski's mission was an intensification of the campaign against the Lithuanian government as a "German tool." *Kurjer Polski* asserted that the disagreement was not with the Lithuanian people but with the German-oriented government, which was not representative of the Lithuanian people. It counseled that the Poles should seek a direct agreement with the Lithuanian people, both through internal and external pressures.[89] Polish press releases abroad

[86] Poland, Ministry of Foreign Affairs, *Documents diplomatiques*, I, 29-30. Wasilewski later claimed that Biržiška had been sympathetic to this plan. See Wasilewski, *Józef Piłsudski*, pp. 203-4. In his report on the work of the mission, he only stated that Biržiška was sympathetic to the idea of an alliance, and no terms were mentioned. See Poland, Ministry of Foreign Affairs, *Documents diplomatiques*, I, 28. In his letter of January 13, 1957, to the author, Professor Biržiška stated that he had refused to give an opinion about the plan to call an assembly. He wanted to avoid any entanglement in Polish-Lithuanian negotiations over political affairs.

[87] Poland, Ministry of Foreign Affairs, *Documents diplomatiques*, I, 29.

[88] Text in *ibid.*, I, 30-32. By "ethnographic Lithuania," the Lithuanians meant the guberniyas of Kovno, Suwalki (north of Augustow), Vilna (with minor exclusions), and Grodno (north of the Neman).

[89] *Kurjer Polski*, No. 217 (August 22, 1919).

were filled with accounts of the powerful positions held in Lithuania by Germans. Zimmerle was said to be working systematically against any agreement with Poland, and a strong hostile sentiment against the government was reported to be growing among the Lithuanian people.[90] The Paris *Temps* declared, "The Taryba in Kaunas is completely under the influence of Berlin, while the Lithuanian people, on the contrary, desire a union with the Polish republic."[91]

On August 17 there was a mass demonstration in Kaunas, which was variously represented abroad. *Pays de France* called it an affirmation by the Lithuanian people of "the bonds of the heart with the Polish nation."[92] Lithuanian sources abroad, on the contrary, claimed that the demonstrators had demanded the evacuation of all Lithuanian territory by both the Germans and the Poles. The instigation for the demonstration was said to be indignation over the loss of Sejny. *Neue Zürcher Zeitung* reported demonstrations before the English and American missions in thanks for aid.[93] A report dated August 17 from the Lithuanian Telegraph Bureau in Kaunas, an affiliate of the German Wolff agency, reported a demonstration of protest before the French mission and asserted that the Germans were hailed as the only supporters of Lithuanian independence.[94] The Russian agency, ROSTA, reported only the demonstration against the French[95] and the Lithuanian representative in London, Čepinskis, declared only that the crowd had demanded German and Polish withdrawal.[96]

Tension was obviously mounting again between the Poles and the Lithuanians. On the night of August 28 came the breaking point, and Polish-Lithuanian relations were strained almost irreparably. On that night Lithuanian authorities carried out

[90] *Le Temps*, September 1, 1919.   [91] *Ibid.*, September 6, 1919.
[92] Quoted in Chambon, *La Lithuanie pendant la Conférence de la Paix*, p. 125.
[93] *Neue Zürcher Zeitung*, No. 1273 (August 24, 1919).
[94] Šaulys Archives, f. 23. Šaulys wrote *démenti* in the margin of his copy of the report. The Wolff agency in Kaunas was disbanded in September. See *Neue Zürcher Zeitung*, No. 1491 (September 30, 1919).
[95] *Izvestiia*, No. 188 (August 26, 1919).
[96] Woodward and Butler (eds.), *British Foreign Policy*, First Series, III, 119.

mass arrests of Poles throughout Kaunas, on the charge of complicity in a plot against the Lithuanian government by the POW (*Polska Organizacja Wojskowa*—Polish Military Organization— organized by Piłsudski during the war as a Polish national army). The arrests continued sporadically for the next several months, but even in early September Polish writers maintained that the actions were an arbitrary policy on the part of the Lithuanian government, which was arresting citizens "to whom no charge can be ascribed other than being Poles."[97] They charged that the arrests were German-inspired[98] and constituted a part of a systematic anti-Polish campaign.[99]

The Lithuanians, on the contrary, had made the arrests under the charge that the Poles were participants in a plot against the government.[100] This charge was dismissed peremptorily by the few Polish writers who deigned even to mention it.[101] The Polish government unofficially admitted that there had actually been a plot, aimed at "freeing" Lithuania from the "German-dominated" government, but maintained that the conspiracy had neither been inspired nor backed by the Polish government.[102] That same view has been taken by Polish writers who, after a lapse of several years, finally admitted the existence of a plot. The plot is represented as a product of purely local initiative, completely independent of the Warsaw government.[103]

The Lithuanians claimed just the opposite. Their position was that the Warsaw government was in close touch with all the events and in full charge.[104] Professor Mykolas Biržiška told

[97] Habdank, *Prześladowanie polaków*, p. 8. Habdank was one of the Poles eventually arrested. This particular quotation refers to a group of Poles who were released without trial, but Habdank obviously meant to imply the innocence of all.

[98] *Kurjer Polski*, No. 230 (September 4, 1919).

[99] *Monitor Polski*, No. 204 (September 11, 1919).

[100] See *Neue Zürcher Zeitung*, No. 1461 (September 25, 1919).

[101] E.g., *Kurjer Polski*, No. 230 (September 4, 1919).

[102] Woodward and Butler (eds.), *British Foreign Policy*, First Series, III, 154.

[103] Wasilewski, *Józef Piłsudski*, pp. 205-6; Wielhorski, *Polska a Litwa*, pp. 318-19. The same stand was taken by the leader of the plot, Kovalecas, at his trial. See Rainys, *POW Lietuvoje*, p. 27. Compare Bermondt's opinion of Polish designs on Lithuania, Woodward and Butler (eds.), *British Foreign Policy*, First Series, III, 278.

[104] Šalčius, *Lenkų Sąmokslas Lietuvoje*, pp. 19-20.

this writer that the plot had originally been uncovered by Vilna
Lithuanians, who obtained secret documents from a Lithuanian
member of the POW. These documents, according to Professor
Biržiška, were written on official Polish government stationery
and signed by government officials, leaving no room for doubt
that the Polish government was involved.[105]

According to the Lithuanian account, the POW on August 28
planned to cut off Kaunas from outside communication and to
seize the members of the government:

> They planned to create their own cabinet of ministers immediately
> and to announce to the world that the country, having risen in re-
> volt, had overthrown the Taryba government set up by the Germans
> and, wanting to remain free, had united with Poland.[106]

The arrests reached into high posts, including an aide of General
Žukauskas. This, combined with Žukauskas's reputed friend-
liness toward the Poles,[107] served to undermine his position and
undoubtedly contributed to his being removed shortly there-
after as head of the Lithuanian army.[108]

Although it had thus survived a major crisis, Sleževičius's
government was far from firmly entrenched. The cabinet was
faced with growing opposition because of its nationalization of
various industries and its other economic policies, and in mid-
August, Zimmerle reported that the Christian Democrats would
probably try to take power.[109] The uncovering of the Polish
plot gave the cabinet a new lease on life as all the Lithuanian
political parties rallied together against their common enemy,
but a showdown was clearly to be expected in the near future.

---

[105] Interview, August 14, 1956. As proof of the connection between the Kaunas
Poles and the Warsaw government, Lithuanian writers point to Wasilewski's talks
with Poles from Kaunas while he was in Vilna in early August. See Wasilewski,
Józef Piłsudski, p. 203; Rainys, *POW Lietuvoje*, pp. 183-84. But cf. Wielhorski, *Polska
a Litwa*, p. 319.

[106] Šapoka (ed.), *Lietuvos istorija*, p. 558. See also Ruseckas, *Savanorių žygiai*,
pp. 27-28; Šalčius, *Lenkų Sąmokslas Lietuvoje*, p. 30.

[107] See Wasilewski's comments on him in Poland, Ministry of Foreign Affairs,
Documents diplomatiques, I, 29.

[108] See the report by General Niessel to French War Ministry, November 21,
1919, United States, National Archives, FW.861L.20/1.

[109] Zimmerle to Foreign Office, August 19, 1919, Germany, Foreign Office,
Hauptarchiv: Litauen, Reel 431, frame 41.

The internal troubles of the government, the fear of the Poles, distrust of Bermondt, and the refusal of the Allies to grant effective recognition all were bringing the Lithuanian government to reconsider its relations with Soviet Russia. The Estonians and the Latvians were also having second thoughts as to where their greatest dangers lay and were considering the possibility of making some sort of settlement with the Communists. The Red Army had been driven out of most of the territory inhabited by the three Baltic nationalities, and without formal recognition from the West, the Baltic governments were unwilling to carry the fight beyond their own national boundaries.

Meanwhile the Bolsheviks were not slow to see the advantages for themselves in the disinclination on the part of the Baltic governments to continue the struggle. The Soviet government still faced serious threats from the Whites in the Ukraine and at Petrograd. Furthermore, the Poles were still dangerous, having the requisites for fighting which the Baltic governments lacked: claims to territory still held by the Bolsheviks and recognition and assistance from the West.

In May the Lithuanians had suggested to the Bolsheviks that an exchange of prisoners be arranged, and this was done in mid-July.[110] The Polish successes had reduced the Bolshevik threat to Lithuania considerably, and in late August and September, as the Lithuanians were slowly approaching the Dvina River, the fighting there was characterized by the American Chargé in Stockholm as "little more than bushwhacking with troops of the lowest class."[111]

The discovery of the Polish plot in Kaunas in August served to convince the Lithuanians that the Poles were now a greater threat than the Bolsheviks. Since Lithuania's two neighbors to the north were also beginning to regard the Bolsheviks as a secondary threat, the way was being opened for a great change in the external relations of the three Baltic governments.[112]

[110] See Dogelis, *Mano gyvenimo prisiminimai*, p. 253.
[111] United States, *Foreign Relations: 1919, Russia*, p. 708.
[112] See Richard Henry Little's report "Baltic Races Waver on Edge of Bolshevism: Lack Confidence in Entente's Queer Policy," Chicago *Daily Tribune*, September 3, 1919.

VII

"The Soviet Serpent"

AUGUST–OCTOBER, 1919

SOVIET RUSSIA made the first move toward the settlement of its differences with the new Baltic republics. On August 31, Chicherin, the Soviet Foreign Minister, directed a radio message to the government of Estonia. After claiming that the government was only a tool of the Entente and that by fighting the Soviet state it was conducting a policy contrary to the interests of its own people, he invited it to open peace negotiations, for the purpose of determining the future boundary between the two states on the basis of the recognition of the Estonian government by that of the RSFSR. After expressing his hope for a quick answer from the Estonians, Chicherin declared that Tallinn would henceforth be responsible for a continuation of the war, since the RSFSR had indicated its desire to conclude peace.[1]

In his answer of September 4 the Foreign Minister of Estonia, Poska, stated that the Estonians were fighting only in self-defense, the conflict having been set off by a Russian invasion, and that therefore, if the Soviet government was ready to make peace, the Estonians were certainly willing to do so. He went on to suggest the opening of talks at Pskov on September 10.[2] On September 6, Chicherin accepted the suggested time and place but he protested against the statement that the RSFSR had attacked Estonia, maintaining that the struggle had only been between "the workers and the bourgeoisie" within Estonia.[3]

As the new Soviet policy unfolded, the Lithuanian government acted quickly. At its suggestion an informal meeting was

[1] *Izvestiia*, No. 193 (September 2, 1919); Shtein, *Russkii vopros*, p. 266.
[2] *Izvestiia*, No. 199 (September 9, 1919).
[3] *Ibid.*, No. 199 (September 9, 1919).

held between representatives of the three Baltic states at Riga on September 10 to discuss the matter of establishing a common Baltic front to deal with the Bolshevik state.[4] Meanwhile the opening of the talks between the Estonians and the Russians had been postponed at the request of the Estonians.[5] The Soviet government was disturbed by this turn of events, and Iurii Steklov, editor of *Izvestiia*, saw the hand of the British behind the postponement, calling it an effort to forestall the conclusion of peace. Attempting to show the conflict between British policies and the national aspirations of the Baltic peoples, Steklov maintained that the Germans were in the Baltic area at the request of the Entente and that England would not force their evacuation since the Germans were "the chief strength of the local counterrevolution." He went on to state the Soviet position:

> But we repeat again and again: the Russian Soviet Republic has absolutely recognized the rights of all nationalities to self-determination and at any moment is ready to enter into talks with any of them on the basis of this principle.
> Let them choose.[6]

The Riga conference discussed the possibility of a union between the three states, but it decided to recommend the holding of periodic meetings of delegations rather than the organization of a common political organ. The forms of union suggested are not revealed in the communiqués.[7] Although the Russians insisted that the British were the force behind the Baltic alliance—*Izvestiia* quoted the German *Vossische Zeitung* as calling the Baltic union "the firm grounding of the English in the Baltic"[8]—it was really the Lithuanians who were the strongest advocates of

---

[4] Šliupas in Riga was the one responsible for the meeting. See Natkevičius, *Aspect politique et juridique du différend polono-lithuanien*, p. 254.

[5] *Izvestiia*, No. 201 (September 11, 1919).

[6] *Ibid.* Just one month before, Steklov had argued that the friendship of the border Communist states toward the Moscow government had shown that those border nationalities did not want to separate from the Russians. *Ibid.*, No. 183 (August 19, 1919). Hence the Soviet proposal represented an essentially new attitude toward the non-Communist border governments.

[7] See *Baltische Blätter*, No. 31 (September 20, 1919), p. 225.

[8] *Izvestiia*, No. 204 (September 14, 1919).

a common front against both the Russians and the Germans,[9] and it was at their urging that another conference was called, to meet at Tallinn on September 14. At the suggestion of the Estonians, however, British observers were invited this time.[10]

When the conference opened at Trompea Castle in Tallinn, Prime Ministers and Foreign Ministers of four states were present —Latvia, Estonia, Lithuania, and Finland. (The Finns had sent a representative despite their not yet having decided on the future orientation of their foreign policy between the Scandinavian and the Baltic states.[11]) Lithuania was represented by Sleževičius, who in addition to being Prime Minister was also Acting Minister of Foreign Affairs, and by Jonas Šimkus, the Minister of Industry and Commerce. The delegates were not plenipotentiaries; they had to report the decisions back to their governments for consideration. Although the proceedings were confidential, the conference issued official reports and representatives of the Entente were consulted at almost every step.[12]

The avowed purpose of the conference was the discussion of the peace proposals by the Bolsheviks.[13] The Lithuanians and the Latvians had received offers from the Bolsheviks similar to that already sent to the Estonians.[14]

The decisions of the conference were communicated to the peace conference at Paris by the chairman of the Estonian delegation in a letter dated September 29. They were: (1) to negotiate in a common front with the Bolsheviks; (2) to insist that the Bolsheviks accept this front; (3) to agree that the specific conditions demanded by each member of the front would be worked out in advance of talks with the Russians; (4) to call a new conference in Tartu within fifteen days, after the delegates had had

[9] *Monitor Polski*, No. 210 (September 18, 1919).

[10] *Times*, (London), September 19, 1919.

[11] *Monitor Polski*, No. 210 (September 18, 1919).

[12] See Tallents's report on the conference to Curzon, September 15, 1919, Woodward and Butler (eds.), *British Foreign Policy*, First Series, III, 554; *Baltische Blätter*, No. 32 (September 27, 1919), p. 234.

[13] *Times* (London), September 18, 1919.

[14] Text of the Russian note to Lithuania, September 11, 1919, in *Izvestiia*, No. 203 (September 13, 1919).

a chance to report back to their governments; (5) to inform the Entente of all steps taken; and (6) to make it clearly understood that the proposed negotiations with the Russians were only for the conclusion of an armistice, since the negotiation of peace was possible only through a general settlement of the Russian question.[15]

On September 16, the Estonian representatives arrived in Pskov to begin the postponed talks with the Russians.[16] The Bolsheviks were jubilant about the opening of the talks. Steklov declared that the meeting marked a tremendous failure for the Entente: "The Soviet serpent apparently has seduced the unstable Eve (Estonia)."[17]

The talks rapidly turned into a disappointment for the Russians as the Estonians stood by the decisions of the Tallinn conference and sought Russian agreement to a general conference between Moscow and the Baltic governments. At the first session, held on the morning of September 17, Krassin, the chairman of the Russian delegation, admitted that the Russians had economic reasons for wanting peace, such as gaining access to the Baltic Sea, but he hastened to declare that the "memory" of the united struggle of the proletariat of Estonia and Russia against tsarism was reason enough for making peace.[18] After a recess during which he prepared his answer, the chairman of the Estonian delegation, Birk, stressed the fact that the Estonians were fighting a defensive war. Furthermore, he declared that the basic condition for peace was a common settlement by the Russians with all the Baltic states.[19] The Estonians refused to be pinned down

[15] United States, *Foreign Relations: 1919, Russia*, pp. 715-16. See also *Neue Zürcher Zeitung*, No. 1437 (September 22, 1919); *Pravda*, No. 209 (September 20, 1919). An account of the conference by the Latvian Foreign Minister, Mejerovič, is reported in *Pravda*, No. 217 (September 30, 1919). Finland and Latvia reportedly abstained from the vote on Point 3. Haynes (Helsinki) to American Mission in Paris, telegram, September 16, 1919, United States, National Archives, 861E.00/-165.

[16] The Russian delegation included Krassin, Litvinov, and Bogolepov. *Izvestiia*, No. 206 (September 17, 1919).

[17] *Ibid.*, No. 208 (September 19, 1919).   [18] *Ibid.*

[19] *Pravda*, No. 209 (September 20, 1919).

to any agreements by the Russians and constantly expressed their desire to communicate with Tallinn on all matters. Piqued by an Estonian request to be permitted to check with Tallinn so as to verify the Bolshevik claims that peace offers had been made to the other Baltic states, Litvinov handed them copies of the offers. Nevertheless the Estonians demanded and obtained a recess.[20]

On the next day Krassin claimed that talks must be conducted with each country separately because of the special problems of each. Birk declared that he understood the existence of distinct problems for each country, but he maintained that a general conference was nevertheless the essential condition for further negotiations. The talks then ended abruptly that evening as the Estonians gained a "temporary adjournment" and returned to their own country.[21]

The Russians did not conceal their disappointment over the results of the talks. They maintained that peace was essential for the "White Guard" and "White-Guard Menshevik" governments because it would be suicide for them to continue the fight against Soviet Russia, whereas the Bolsheviks' love of peace was said to be beyond question in the light of the "events of the last two years."[22] Therefore, the Russians argued, the responsibility for the failure to conclude peace and for the continuation of the war obviously rested with the Estonians and their allies. In an article entitled "The Blood Will Be on Them," Steklov pointed out that the talks had been adjourned by the Estonians and not the Russians. He proclaimed the willingness of the Russians to hold a general conference with all the Baltic states, but pointed out the problems for future action if any one of the states concerned should refuse to attend. "The matter is clear," he stated. "These small states do not trust us. But we have greater cause for not trusting them." He asserted that the Bolshevik government

[20] An account of the talks of the first day can be found in *Izvestiia*, No. 207 (September 18, 1919) and No. 208 (September 19, 1919). A verbatim record is given in *ibid.*, No. 215 (September 27, 1919).

[21] *Pravda*, No. 209 (September 20, 1919).

[22] *Ibid.*, No. 208 (September 19, 1919).

was free to run its own policy as it wished and questioned the freedom of the Baltic governments to act in contradiction to the will of the Entente.[23]

Another Soviet writer maintained that the Estonian demand for a general conference was a violation of the original agreement on opening the talks, since it had not been mentioned before. Because the fulfillment of this new demand was dependent on third parties, the Soviet government refused all responsibility for the continuation of hostilities; at the same time it declared itself willing to participate in the general conference.[24] In an interview published by *Izvestiia*, Litvinov claimed that peace was essential to the Estonian government because of the pressure of the working classes and the threat presented by Von der Goltz and the followers of Kolchak, but he doubted that the Baltic states would act independently of the Entente, charging that England was behind the demand for a general conference. He felt sure that the Baltic states could not refuse peace, but he speculated that the English would sponsor terms which could not be met.[25]

Undaunted by these and other challenges to accept the terms of the Bolsheviks, Sleževičius on September 24 radioed to Chicherin the Lithuanian answer to the Bolshevik proposal. In it he informed the Russians that the Lithuanians would not make a formal response to the peace proposals directed to them until after talking with their neighbors who had received similar proposals—an indirect reference to the proposed Tartu conference.[26] On September 27 the Latvians sent a similar statement.[27]

These events were not without their impact in the West. By exploiting the Western fears of the Bolsheviks, the Baltic governments now hoped to gain the recognition which they had so far been unable to secure on their own merits. On September 12 the representatives of Estonia, Latvia, and Lithuania sent to

[23] *Izvestiia*, No. 209 (September 20, 1919).
[24] *Pravda*, No. 209 (September 20, 1919).
[25] *Izvestiia*, No. 212 (September 24, 1919).
[26] *Ibid.*, No. 214 (September 26, 1919).
[27] *Ibid.*, No. 217 (September 30, 1919).

the chairman of the peace conference a joint appeal for recognition, maintaining that acknowledgement of their independence was a necessary condition for the continuation of the struggle against the Bolsheviks.[28] A week later, however, the Lithuanian delegation in Paris stated further that the Lithuanian government would make no agreement with the Bolsheviks without first reaching an understanding with the Allies.[29]

The problem of dealing with this question in Paris was complicated by new conflicts between the Lithuanians and the Poles, as well as between all three Baltic nations and the Germans. At the end of August, the Poles had moved into Sejny and Suwalki, in accordance with the line of July 26. The Lithuanian troops stationed there resisted the advance, and several pitched battles followed.[30] It has been claimed that the fighting wrought greater havoc in Sejny than had been seen during the war just ended the year before.[31] Protests were sent to Kaunas by a Lithuanian priest in Sejny, Narjauskas, against the closing by the Poles of the Lithuanian seminary in Sejny.[32] On October 27 the Lithuanians carried Father Narjauskas's protest to the peace conference, claiming that they had proposed a mixed commission, made up of representatives of France, Great Britain, Poland, and Lithuania, to examine the problem, but that the Poles had given no answer.[33]

In addition, Bermondt was becoming an ever greater threat. On September 5, Iudenich recognized Bermondt and his troops as part of the White Russian forces.[34] On September 6, Benjaševičius had been in Siauliai to speak with Bermondt's repre-

[28] *Le Temps*, September 13, 1919; *Izvestiia*, No. 208 (September 19, 1919).

[29] Letter to peace conference, September 19, 1919, Lithuania, Delegation to Paris, *Composition*, VIII, 10.

[30] Chambon, *La Lithuanie pendant la Conférence de la Paix*, pp. 127-28. See also *Kurjer Polski*, No. 246 (September 21, 1919), *Monitor Polski*, No. 262 (December 1, 1919).

[31] Chambon, *La Lithuanie pendant la Conférence de la Paix*, p. 127.

[32] *Ibid.*, pp. 129-30. Narjauskas was arrested by the Poles shortly after this. He later became the first official Lithuanian representative to the Holy See. See M. Yčas (ed.), *Lietuvos Albumas* (Berlin, 1921), p. 362.

[33] Chambon, *La Lithuanie pendant la Conférence de la Paix*, p. 130.

[34] Bermondt-Avalov, *Im Kampf*, p. 182.

sentatives, but he left before the delegates arrived.[35] Bermondt blamed Entente intrigues for the failure of all such efforts at agreement,[36] but the Lithuanians had their own ideas on Bermondt's objectives. Benjaševičius reportedly called him an "adventurer" who had no intention of sending his troops to the front,[37] though Bermondt later maintained that at this time he was only trying to clear the way for his planned advance against the Bolsheviks at Daugavpils but that the Lithuanians refused to yield to him either the Panevezys railroad or the Tilsit-Daugavpils line.[38]

Yet another complication for the Lithuanian government was the practice by which German troops who did not want to leave the Baltic area "renounced" their nationality and joined Bermondt's "Kolchakist" forces.[39] The Lithuanians, protesting to the West, reported conflicts between the "Bermondtists" and the Lithuanian forces.[40] At this same time, representatives of Kolchak were reported to be in Lithuania, attempting unsuccessfully to negotiate for coordination of the forces of both.[41]

The Lithuanians now claimed to have uncovered a German plot aimed at installing a new government in Kaunas more favorable to the Germans, which would be consolidated by a loan of 300,000,000 marks.[42] Later the Lithuanian government charged that Gabrys and Baron von der Ropp were involved in a grandiose plot to form a new state of "Ost-Deutschland." East Prussia would secede temporarily from Germany in order to escape pressure from the Entente and would unite with Latvia, Lithuania, and Estonia.[43] Gabrys's personal archives, however,

---

[35] *Ibid.*, pp. 180-81. [36] *Ibid.*, p. 180.

[37] *Baltische Blätter*, No. 32 (September 27, 1919), p. 234. Cf. the editorial comment on Bermondt in *Neue Zürcher Zeitung*, No. 1587 (October 16, 1919).

[38] *Ibid.*, pp. 178-79.

[39] See Woodward and Butler, (eds.), *British Foreign Policy*, First Series, III, 130-31; Niessel, *L'évacuation*, pp. 22-23.

[40] Woodward and Butler (eds.), *British Foreign Policy*, First Series, III, 132.

[41] *Kurjer Polski*, No. 241 (September 16, 1919); *Pravda*, No. 201 (September 11, 1919).

[42] Woodward and Butler (eds.), *British Foreign Policy*, First Series, III, 133.

[43] See *ibid.*, III, 206.

give no evidence to support this charge of his complicity in any German plot, and his correspondence with Von der Ropp during this period is free of any allusions to such conspiracies. More than likely his name was brought into the matter simply in an effort to discredit him, although the plot itself may have been real. In his memoirs, Von der Goltz claimed that he would indeed have executed a coup against the Lithuanian government in October but for fear of retaliation on the part of the Entente. [44]

Lithuania's relations with the Bolsheviks had a direct connection with the conflicts with the Germans and the Poles. On September 15, Čepinskis in London, stated,

There is a great inclination among our people to make peace as we suffer from Kolchak on the one side and from the Poles on the other. This, combined with the attitude of the Entente, had made it impossible for us to continue military operations against the Bolsheviks, for we had absolutely nothing in the way of assistance from the allies. [45]

The dangers of this situation were at last forcing the Entente powers to work out a more active policy toward the Baltic states. [46]

The Western powers increased their pressure for a German withdrawal and also sought to cut off supplies from Germany to Bermondt. At a meeting of the Supreme Council, held on September 15, Lloyd George asked Foch about the "right" of the Entente to demand a German withdrawal. Foch answered that such a demand was fully justified and that the sooner the withdrawal was ordered the better; he pointed out that the

---

[44] Von der Goltz, *Meine Sendung*, p. 254. Cf. Woodward and Butler (eds.), *British Foreign Policy*, First Series, III, 188. On September 29, Zimmerle reported that Gabrys had made some sort of agreement with the Russo-German forces, but he did not specify the nature of that agreement. Zimmerle himself felt that Gabrys had lost his chance at political power in April and that he now was no longer an important figure in Lithuanian affairs. See Germany, Foreign Office, *Hauptarchiv: Litauen*, Reel 432, frames 89 and 182.

[45] *Times* (London), September 17, 1919. Sablin, the White Russian representative in London, claimed that it was the fear of Denikin's advance in the Ukraine that was pushing the Baltic states into peace talks with Soviet Russia. Sablin (London) to Sazonov (Paris), telegram, September 15, 1919, Maklakov Archives, B, II, 2.

[46] See Churchill, *The Aftermath*, p. 269.

German government was now claiming that the troops refused to obey its orders.[47] Although the American representative in the council, Frank Polk, continued to express his doubts that the German government was responsible for recruiting the new volunteers in the Baltic Russo-German forces, the council decided to exert pressure on the German government to cut off all aid to the Baltic forces.[48] On September 26 the council renewed the blockade of the German Baltic coast.[49] In a note of October 3 to the Supreme Council, the German government reported that on September 25 it had stopped pay for the Baltic troops and had closed the Courland border to volunteers. Von der Goltz had also been recalled. The government stated that it was unable to do more, disclaiming any connection with the enlistment of German forces in Russian units. The note went on to protest against the renewal of the blockade and suggested the creation of an inter-Allied commission to organize and supervise the evacuation.[50] On October 10 the council approved in principle the actions of the German government but reserved the right to judge the responsibility of the German government for the existing situation.[51]

The case of Poland hardly lent itself to the use of blockade or other pressures. On the contrary, the Allies were anxious to hasten the regularization of Poland's new position and to strengthen it. On September 1 the Commission on Polish Affairs suggested that the line proposed by it in April be used to designate the line "to the west of which the Polish government for the time being can legally exercise all sovereign rights."[52] On September 25, Polk suggested that either the line should be left undecided pending a direct agreement between the Poles and the Russians, or else a "minimum line" should be drawn for the Poles,

[47] Woodward and Butler (eds.), *British Foreign Policy*, First Series, I, 696-98.
[48] *Ibid.*, I, 723.   [49] Niessel, *L'évacuation*, p. 22.
[50] Woodward and Butler (eds.), *British Foreign Policy*, First Series, I, 872-73.
[51] Niessel, *L'évacuation*, p. 22.
[52] Woodward and Butler (eds.), *British Foreign Policy*, First Series, I, 792. On the drawing of the line, see Komarnick, *Rebirth of the Polish Republic*, pp. 459-60.

with the assurance that this line would not prejudice any future negotiations in regard to this frontier after the reestablishment of Russia or the obtaining of satisfactory information in regard to the desires of the people to the East of this frontier.[53]

The American delegate continually showed a desire to avoid conflict between the Lithuanians and the Poles. Polk had strongly opposed the idea of using Polish troops to force the withdrawal of the Germans, both for fear of antagonizing the Germans and for fear of conflicts with the Lithuanians, and he had been a strong supporter of the use of indirect pressures rather than direct force.[54]

As the time came for action rather than just words on the question of the relations between the Poles and the Lithuanians, the Western powers remained as divided as ever.[55] The French continued to support Poland as the most reliable element in Eastern Europe: "Although one may hesitate to reestablish Russian power in the Baltic, one can hasten to revive Polish power."[56] Poland was called the "principal champion of the Allies on the shores of the Baltic."[57] *Le Temps* continued to rely on Polish sources and to represent the Kaunas government as a tool which the Germans were using against the Poles, although it did publish Lithuanian denials of all these charges which in turn laid on the Poles the blame for the Polish-Lithuanian dispute.[58] Polish and French sources tended to view the inclination of the Baltic governments toward peace as being German-inspired.[59] *Le Temps* warned, "These small lands will not consolidate their liberties which they have acquired if they negotiate with the Russian Bolsheviks."[60] Despite the attacks on the character of the Kaunas government, the French govern-

---

[53] *Ibid.*, I, 785.   [54] *Ibid.*, I, 712, 698, 720.

[55] See Karel Pusta's complaint about the obscurity of Entente policy toward the Baltic states, in his letter to Clemenceau, September 29, 1919, United States, *Foreign Relations: 1919, Russia*, p. 718.

[56] *Le Temps*, October 4, 1919.   [57] *Ibid.*

[58] See *ibid.*, September 15, 1919, October 3 and 7, 1919.

[59] *Ibid.*, October 3, 1919.

[60] *Ibid.*, September 29, 1919. The Soviet press reported that the French threatened to cut off all aid to the Baltic states if they made peace with the Bolsheviks.

ment did not refuse the Lithuanians aid, sending some infantry instructors and, under the aegis of the peace conference, concluding an agreement for the transfer of thirty locomotives to the Lithuanian government.[61]

The Americans held to their stand for an undivided Russia, although they too sent aid to the new governments in the Baltic area. On September 15 the first shipload of American military materiel for Lithuania arrived in Liepaja.[62] A few days later the arrival of the first volunteer American officers was announced.[63] There seems, however, to have been nothing which could be called "official" aid. Officially the American government held consistently to its stand in favor of Russian territorial unity. The Russian representative in Washington, D. C., Bakhmetev, reported on September 19:

Every day I receive confirmation that in the question of the Baltic Provinces, Lithuania, and other nationalities, the American government is standing firmly on the position taken by it after the exchange by the Powers with Admiral Kolchak.[64]

British policy was not generally understood. Actually it was moving toward a recognition of the Baltic states and at the same time leaving them a free hand in their foreign relations. The British suggested to Kolchak that the peace moves of the Bolsheviks had now made it necessary to reevaluate the stand taken by his government toward the Baltic governments, possibly even to the point of recognizing the new governments.[65] The Russian representative in London, Sablin, reported on September 18 that the British military experts favored the policy of recognizing the Baltic governments as an expedient, believing that the independence would be no more than a passing phase, and that

---

[61] *Neue Zürcher Zeitung*, No. 1415 (September 18, 1919); United States, *Foreign Relations: Paris Peace Conference*, X, 640.

[62] *Monitor Polski*, No. 208 (September 16, 1919). This was the equipment bought in Paris in the summer of 1919.

[63] *Neue Zürcher Zeitung*, No. 1488 (September 30, 1919).

[64] Bakhmetev (Washington, D. C.) to Sazonov (Paris), telegram. September 19, 1919, Maklakov Archives, B, II, 2.

[65] Woodward and Butler (eds.), *British Foreign Policy*, First Series, III, 619.

eventually the economic facts of life would force the states to rejoin Russia. While he went on to note that the American and the French representatives in the Baltic states were opposed to the British encouragement of separation, Sablin concluded, "But we must reckon with the fact of intoxication with freedom."[66]

At first, the British had taken a stand against the proposed negotiations between the Baltic republics and the Bolsheviks, expressing the hope that the Baltic states would conduct their foreign policy "only as part of a concerted plan with the Allied Governments."[67] They gradually came to dissociate themselves from the responsibility for the course chosen by the Baltic states. On September 23, Curzon wired Tallents that the British government was ready to recognize Lithuania *de facto* on the same footing as Estonia and Latvia, and he asked Tallents to relay that message to Kaunas.[68] This news was received with great joy in Lithuania, where pro-British demonstrations took place.[69] On September 25, Curzon sent out a circular telegram formally explaining British policy in the Baltic. Noting the forthcoming conference of the Baltic states, he asserted that the British government had no right to anticipate the decisions of that conference. As Great Britain was no longer able to continue its policy of sending supplies to the Baltic, or to extend loans or credits, therefore it could not demand the taking of any particular action by the Baltic governments.[70] The British had now granted *de facto* recognition to all three Baltic states; *de jure* recognition was to be the job of only the peace conference or the League of Nations. On October 2, Tallents reported that this declaration had had a healthy effect at the Tartu conference by

[66] Sablin (London) to Sazonov (Paris), telegram, September 18, 1919, Maklakov Archives, B, II, 2.

[67] Curzon (London) to Tallents (Riga), telegram, September 6, 1919, Woodward and Butler (eds.), *British Foreign Policy*, First Series, III, 554.

[68] *Ibid.*, III, 567.

[69] *Ibid.*, III, 567n. See also *Neue Zürcher Zeitung*, No. 1479 (September 29, 1919).

[70] Woodward and Butler (eds.), *British Foreign Policy*, First Series, III, 569-70. The cutting off of supplies affected only Latvia and Estonia, since Lithuania had not been getting material aid from the British.

clearing up the doubts that existed with regard to British policy.[71]

Despite this formal withdrawal from the active guidance of Baltic politics, the British continued to give strong moral support to the Lithuanians against the Poles and to all three Baltic states against the Germans. One observer reported that anti-Polish posters were to be seen on the walls of the British consulate in Kaunas.[72] Another observer, strongly pro-Polish, called the British "unreasonably biased in favor of all that is Lithuanian."[73]

The White Russians vehemently opposed the peace negotiations between the Baltic governments and the Bolsheviks, asserting that the Baltic governments were not acting in accordance with the wishes of their peoples. In Paris, Sazonov expressed the belief that the more reasonable Baltic nationalists did not themselves believe in the possibility of maintaining their independence.[74] Sablin in London did not believe that the common people in the Baltic area hated Russia as much as the propagandists claimed. He thought the hatred was carried by the Russian-educated intelligentsia, and that "between it and the people there exists a great abyss."[75] In answer to the British suggestion that Kolchak adjust his Baltic policy to the fact that negotiations were being opened by the Baltic governments with the Bolsheviks, the Omsk government pointed to the terms of Kolchak's letter of June 4 and emphasized that peace with the Baltic states would offer the Bolsheviks a channel of entry to the West and would free troops for transfer to other fronts:

The very fact of the readiness to talk about peace testifies, in our opinion, to the extreme demoralization of the parties of these self-

[71] *Ibid.*, III, 570n.

[72] Ruhl, *New Masters of the Baltic*, p. 216.

[73] Report of the U. S. Military Attaché in Warsaw, October 16, 1919, United States, National Archives, 861L.00/127.

[74] Sazonov (Paris) to Neratov (Taganrog), telegram, September 23, 1919, Maklakov Archives, B, II, 2.

[75] Sablin (London) to Sazonov (Paris), telegram, September 15, 1919, Maklakov Archives, B, II, 2.

governing units which cannot alone defend themselves from the infiltration of aggressive Bolshevism.[76]

This reply ended with a demand that the Allies cease their aid to the Baltic governments unless the latter continued the struggle against the Bolsheviks.

Some White Russian spokesmen, Gulkevich in Stockholm for example, maintained that the British were behind the Baltic governments' apparent inclination to make peace. Gulkevich called it a well-thought-out plan by the British "to hinder the resurrection of our homeland in its erst-while importance and greatness."[77]

In the midst of all this furor the Lithuanians continued to build up their army. On September 27 the classes of 1896, 1899, and 1900 were mobilized, and on October 2 the classes of 1894, 1895, and 1901, thus raising to eight the number of age groups called to the colors.[78] By the end of the year the army numbered some 25,000. The Lithuanian government also sent a three-man military mission, headed by Colonel Gedgaudas, to Paris to investigate the possibility of recruiting a Lithuanian force from members of the Allied armies. Gedgaudas in turn appointed an American, Colonel Swarthout, to proceed to America to aid in the organization of an American Lithuanian brigade.[79] In Paris the mission succeeded in persuading a group of demobi-

[76] Sukin (Omsk) to Sazonov (Paris), telegram, October 9, 1919, Maklakov Archives, B, II, 2. See also Woodward and Butler (eds.), *British Foreign Policy*, First Series, III, 619.

[77] Gulkevich (Stockholm) to Sazonov (Paris), telegram, September 22, 1919, Maklakov Archives, B, II, 2. Sablin, in a telegram to Sazonov on September 30, thought the British were against the peace move. Maklakov Archives, B, II, 2. In a message to Bermondt on September 14, 1919, Niedra, on the other hand, called the British the force behind the peace moves, while he saw the Lithuanians as the greatest block to such a peace. Woodward and Butler (eds.), *British Foreign Policy*, First Series, III, 292-93. In a telegram of October 13 to Omsk, Sazonov characterized the Tartu conference as a "failure" for British efforts to organize an anti-Bolshevik front in the Baltic. Maklakov Archives, B, II, 2.

[78] See Poland, General Staff, *Wojsko litewskie*, p. 33.

[79] See Šarmaitis, "Interventsiia anglo-amerikanskikh imperialistov," *Istoricheskie Zapiski*, No. 45 (1954), p. 275; Jurgela, "Lithuania and the United States," p. 266; *Kurjer Polski*, No. 243 (September 18, 1919). Swarthout was renamed "Juododis," which corresponds to the German "Schwarzhaut."

lized British officers to go to Lithuania to help in the organization of the Lithuanian army.[80]

The Lithuanian treasury, however, was now showing even more alarming signs of depletion. Vileišis again went to Berlin to seek a loan, but without success.[81] Lithuanian hopes that England would grant them either credits or a loan after extending recognition were also disappointed, and the economic situation of the country continued to deteriorate rapidly.

Polish attitudes toward Lithuania were as mixed as ever. There was, of course, continued resentment against the arrests of Poles in Kaunas: "The Lithuanian government is conducting a planned action of suppressing the Polish nationality [polskość], an action aimed at making impossible the conditions of life for the Poles."[82] At the same time, the Polish federalists still kept alive their hopes of reaching some agreement with the Lithuanians: "The only course for Lithuania lies in union with Poland and in some agreement with Latvia and Estonia."[83] However, the Poles now felt that the initiative for such an agreement must come from the Lithuanians.

At the end of September the Lithuanian government sent Mykolas Biržiška to Warsaw to speak with Piłsudski, but those Poles who thought that this mission meant the opening of new talks were wide of the mark.[84] The mission was more a final spasm of the earlier, futile negotiations than an effort at new talks. In early August, Piłsudski had visited Vilna briefly and had then returned to Warsaw without any clear explanation for his visit. A few days later the Lithuanian writer Juozas Albinas Herbačiauskas, a supporter of the federalist idea, visited Biržiška in Vilna and reported that Piłsudski had come to Vilna in the

---

[80] Among the British officers, who arrived in Kaunas in October, was retired Brigadier General Frank Percy Crozier, who became a member of the Lithuanian General Staff. See his *Impressions and Recollections*, p. 244.

[81] *Kurjer Polski*, Nos. 230 (September 4, 1919), and 241 (September 16, 1919).

[82] *Ibid.*, No. 243 (September 18, 1919).

[83] *Ibid.*, No. 262 (October 7, 1919).

[84] The substance of Biržiška's talks with Piłsudski was not revealed at the time. See *ibid.*, No. 261 (October 6, 1919). This account is based chiefly on the information given the author by Professor Biržiška in an interview on August 14, 1956.

belief that Voldemaras wanted to speak with him. When Voldemaras failed to appear, Piłsudski returned to Warsaw. The
Polish government now wanted Herbačiauskas to go to Kaunas
and learn what had happened.[85] Biržiška decided to accompany
him, and the two men received travel permits almost immediately from the Polish authorities.[86]

In Kaunas they explained the matter to Sleževičius, who
decided that some sort of explanation was owed the Polish Chief
of State.[87] He felt that Lithuanian-Polish relations were bad
enough without allowing such needless incidents to complicate
them further, and therefore he commissioned Biržiška and
Herbačiauskas to go to Warsaw to speak with Piłsudski. The
two thereupon returned to Vilna, and at the end of September
they went to Warsaw, where Piłsudski received them hopefully.
Although he was disappointed that the mission had no more
substantive a purpose than to present an apology, nevertheless
he voiced his continued hope for some future agreement with the
Lithuanians, and the mission took its leave.

Despite the failure to reach any understanding with the Poles,
the Lithuanians made great progress in the month of September.
The peace proposal advanced by the Bolshevik government was
in effect a *de facto* recognition, and the British, although foreswearing a guiding role in Baltic politics, had bolstered the
Lithuanian government by extending it official recognition.
Furthermore, because of the need of a common policy toward
the Bolsheviks, the chances of making an alliance with Latvia
and Estonia seemed good.

On September 29 representatives of Finland, Estonia, Latvia,
and Lithuania gathered in Tartu for the long anticipated con-

---

[85] Biržiška later found out that Voldemaras actually had agreed to talk with
Piłsudski, but then had changed his mind without notifying the Poles.

[86] Previously the Lithuanians in Vilna had found it almost impossible to obtain
travel permits to go to Kaunas. See *Nepriklausomoji Lietuva*, No. 16 (May 8, 1919).

[87] In his memoirs of the mission, Herbačiauskas claimed that he had tried to
win Sleževičius over to the idea of federation, but that the latter would have none
of it, distrusting the Polish offers. Herbačiauskas, *Litwa a Polska*, p. 22. Herbačiauskas
mentions neither Biržiška nor the subsequent trip to Warsaw, but this can be considered characteristic of him.

ference on working out a common policy toward the Bolshevik regime. The Lithuanian government had sent its representatives to the conference with two definite points in its program. First of all, Sleževičius had made clear that the Lithuanian government stood against making a "separate peace" and wanted "a common policy" against the Bolsheviks.[88] Second, the Lithuanians were advocating "the strongest possible alliance" between the Baltic states, [89] possibly even confederation.[90]

The other participants at the conference agreed with the Lithuanian stand in favor of a common front, but the question of future ties was left undecided. After the conference ended on October 1, a telegram was sent to the Soviet government over the signatures of the Foreign Ministers of Latvia, Lithuania, and Estonia, offering to attend a general conference to open by October 25 at Tartu.[91] The three governments agreed among themselves to uphold their "common policy" at least until the conclusion of the peace conference with the Bolsheviks. If the conference failed, the various governments would no longer be bound by this agreement, but each promised not to enter into a separate peace with Moscow if the others decided to continue fighting.[92] Although not expressly stated in the note to the Russians, the conditions which the Baltic states demanded for peace were recognition of their independence and guarantees that the Bolsheviks would not interfere in any way in their internal affairs.[93]

[88] *Le Temps*, September 25, 1919.
[89] *Neue Zürcher Zeitung*, No. 1455 (September 25, 1919); *Le Temps*, September 25, 1919.
[90] *Le Temps*, October 25, 1919. Cf. Dziewanowski, "Piłsudski's Federal Policy, 1919-1921," *Journal of Central European Affairs*, X (1950), 120.
[91] Text of the note, dated October 4, 1919, in *Izvestiia*, No. 222 (October 5, 1919). See also *Le Temps*, October 5 and 9, 1919; Shtein, *Russkii vopros*, p. 272. Finland withheld its decision on whether to participate in the negotiations. See United States, *Foreign Relations: 1919, Russia*, p. 721; Woodward and Butler (eds.), *British Foreign Policy*, First Series, III, 570n.
[92] Haynes, (Helsinki) to American Mission in Paris, telegram, October 4, 1919, United States, National Archives, 861E.00/183.
[93] *Le Temps*, October 9, 1919; *Izvestiia*, No. 226 (October 10, 1919); *Revue Baltique*, II (1919), 52.

The Soviet government was still dissatisfied with the prospect of facing a common front and continued to see England's hand behind the maneuver. On October 7, *Pravda* published an article entitled "A Lesson for Estonia, Lithuania, and Latvia," in which the withdrawal by the British of support from the White Government in Archangel was pointed out as an example of what the Baltic governments could expect from Great Britain. Maintaining that the people of the Baltic states wanted peace, *Pravda* claimed that the governments there could not continue the war, but that at the same time they feared the wrath of the Entente, especially England, if they made peace. "Let the Mejerovič'es consider the sad fate of Mr. Chaikovskii," the article declaimed, warning the Baltic governments not to expect much useful aid from the British.[94] On the same day *Izvestiia* reported that the "rejection by the Lithuanian government of the peace proposals of the Bolsheviks" was contrary to the "mood of the Lithuanian popular masses."[95] The Communist newspapers also stressed the opposition of the French to an early conclusion of peace between Russia and its Baltic neighbors, charging that the French were even supporting Von der Goltz in the hope of preventing a settlement.[96]

On October 8 the Russians answered the message from the Tartu conference, suggesting October 12 as the date for opening talks on condition that an answer be given within three days.[97] That answer was not forthcoming, and as each of the Baltic states became increasingly involved in internal issues and in the Bermondt affair, the plan for holding talks with Soviet Russia faded into the background for a while.

In the middle of September a new cabinet crisis had arisen in Lithuania. The chief issue generally reported at the time was the inclination of the Sleževičius cabinet to negotiate for peace with the Communists.[98] In general the Left was in favor of

[94] *Pravda*, No. 223 (October 7, 1919).   [95] *Izvestiia*, No. 223 (October 7, 1919).
[96] *Ibid.*, No. 229 (October 14, 1919).
[97] *Ibid.*, No. 225 (October 9, 1919); Shtein, *Russkii vopros*, p. 272.
[98] Būtėnas and Mackevičius, "Gyvenimas ir darbai," in *Mykolas Sleževičius*, pp. 126-27. See also *Neue Zürcher Zeitung*, No. 1477 (September 28, 1919).

seeking a peace settlement. In mid-September a conference of Social Democratic parties of the Baltic states, noting the co-operation of the Germans and the Russian followers of Kolchak, declared that the Baltic peoples renounced any idea of armed intervention in Russian affairs and demanded that their governments enter into peace negotiations with Soviet Russia, seeking guarantees of peace, independence, and peaceful development.[99] According to *Izvestiia*, the Lithuanian Social Democratic Party claimed that the peace proposals of Soviet Russia offered the "only means to gain a respite" and must be "seriously considered."[100] On the other hand, the Lithuanian right opposed the opening negotiations with the Bolsheviks, claiming that the foreign missions in Kaunas were against making peace at that time.[101]

Although the debate on negotiating a peace settlement with the Bolsheviks was a major issue in the cabinet crisis, the chief cause was the desire of the members of the delegation to the peace conference, now returned to Kaunas, to have a greater voice in the government. Sleževičius had been ruling without consulting the Taryba, and the new arrivals opposed this concentration of power, seeking a share in the government for themselves. That this was the fundamental issue can be discerned in statements made by both sides. Yčas later recounted,

> M. Sleževičius had established a condition under which the State Council would not meet, would not discuss any question, and would give him a free hand to act. Professor Voldemaras and I, as members of the Taryba, delivered a sharp protest to the Chairman of the Taryba, S. Šilingas, against such a passive position. We pointed out that the functions of the Taryba were clearly laid out in the provisional constitution and that it could not dissolve itself or suspend its activity

---

[99] Sablin (London) to Sazonov (Paris), telegram, September 30, 1919, Maklakov Archives, B, II, 2. *Izvestiia*, No. 218 (October 1, 1919), reported that the declaration of the conference contained a clause charging that Russia had started the war.

[100] *Izvestiia*, No. 220 (October 3, 1919).

[101] See the estimate of Lithuanian policy in United States, *Foreign Relations: 1919, Russia*, p. 713. Cf. the reports by returning members of the delegation to the peace conference, reported in *Kurjer Polski*, No. 264 (October 9, 1919).

until the meeting of the Constituent Assembly. Šilingas could not but agree with the protest and, having convoked the Presidium, recommended the calling of a meeting of the Taryba. Prime Minister Sleževičius declared he would resign if the Taryba were convoked against his wish.

The Taryba did not concede this, and Sleževičius's cabinet fell. The President invited the engineer Galvanauskas, former secretary of the Lithuanian Peace Delegation, who had just returned from abroad, to form a new cabinet.[102]

Sleževičius's account, set forth in a letter to Šaulys, was as follows:

You see, the Paris delegation (Yčas, Voldemaras, and later Galvanauskas), having returned to Kaunas, decided to take the government into its own hands. Intrigues began. Smetona, as you know, lends himself easily to just such things. So they finally forced the cabinet to resign.[103]

On October 2, Sleževičius resigned, and Galvanauskas was invited to form a new cabinet.[104]

Sleževičius now retired from the political scene, going to Bad Nauheim in Germany to recover from the strain of overwork. He had little desire to return to the government. He wrote from Berlin in late November, "I will soon return to Kaunas and I plan to concern myself *only* with my [law] practice."[105]

Sleževičius's services to the Lithuanian state as head of the government would be difficult to overestimate. As a member of a minority party, he had found great difficulties in gaining support for his plans—hence his disputes with the Taryba. His unwavering courage, as displayed in the great crisis of January, 1919, must be admired, and he must be given much credit in stemming

[102] M. Yčas, "Lietuvos vyriausybės sudarymo etapai," in *Pirmasis dešimtmetis,* I, 124.

[103] Sleževičius (Berlin) to Šaulys (Bern), letter, November 23, 1919, Šaulys Archives, f. 76.

[104] Būtėnas and Mackevičius, "Gyvenimas ir darbai," in *Mykolas Sleževičius,* p. 126. Von der Goltz's claims that the Entente forced the change cannot be proven. See Von der Goltz, *Meine Sendung,* p. 254.

[105] Sleževičius (Berlin) to Šaulys (Bern), letter, November 23, 1919, Šaulys Archives, f. 76.

the retreat before the Bolsheviks. He seems always to have had the best interests of his country at heart. While his dictatorial policies might have become harmful, in 1919 they were the only way in which he could act with any responsibility for the government. The short-lived Dovydaitis cabinet pointed up the importance of Sleževičius's abilities. The Christian Democrats, who agreed with the policies of the Liaudininkai on the land question but not on the church question, lacked effective leadership. It is doubtful whether the Pažanga party could have provided anything so dynamic and popular as Sleževičius's programs, since the "cream" of the party was abroad. Sleževičius cannot be blamed for the loss of Vilna, as some had tried to do. That was a matter completely out of his hands. His strong support of a Baltic alliance in September shows that he was not entering into talks with the Bolsheviks blindly. The failure to secure full recognition by the Entente also cannot be blamed on Sleževičius, since the delegation to the peace conference, which was in a position to do far more than he, also had failed in this aim.

The new cabinet under Ernestas Galvanauskas took office on October 7. Galvanauskas held the posts of Prime Minister and Finance Minister. Voldemaras was again appointed Foreign Minister, a post he had held, at least formally, continuously from the organization of the first cabinet in November, 1918. Galvanauskas was a fortunate choice to head the government for several reasons. As a Lithuanian of the emigration, he drew support from all the Lithuanians abroad, regardless of party.[106] As a man with many contacts in France, he could make a greater appeal there; as a man of Western culture, he would find his relations with Entente representatives smoother than had the Russian-educated Lithuanians.

The new government, pledged to follow a tougher policy toward the Bolsheviks, at the same time was still faced with serious financial troubles. The country was also in disorder as a

---

[106] *Vienybė Lietuvninkų*, No. 42 (October 15, 1919), called him a great partisan of the Entente. Even Gabrys approved his selection (*Vers l'indépéndance*, pp. 273-74).

result of the presence of Bermondt's forces in the north and west. Continued struggle against the Bolsheviks or against the Russo-German forces of Bermondt could only be carried on with outside aid, and even then a retrenchment would be essential. It was with these prospects that the Galvanauskas cabinet, the fifth in the brief history of the young Lithuanian state, turned to its task.

VIII

"Splendid Isolation"

OCTOBER, 1919–JANUARY, 1920

On october 15 the Taryba met to hear the program of the new cabinet. Galvanauskas stated that the first task of the government was to set the country in order. This meant calling the Constituent Assembly, long postponed because of the Polish occupation of Vilna, and also bringing about the final withdrawal from Lithuania of all foreign troops, German, Russian, and Polish. Asserting that the Poles, as a group, were not being persecuted, he continued,

The government, will, however, defend the state against all traitorous maneuvers, from wherever they may come. The Lithuanian government will try to reach a good understanding with the Polish government. It will, however, not yield in matters of the interests of the Lithuanian nation and state. The government will wage a war of independence against the enemies of the Lithuanian state so long as they threaten the freedom of the Lithuanian state.[1]

Galvanauskas apparently did not discuss the Lithuanian financial crisis, since, despite the wide coverage of his speech in foreign newspapers, the financial straits of the Lithuanian government were not generally known.[2]

---

[1] *Neue Zürcher Zeitung*, No. 1620 (October 21, 1919). See also Chambon, *La Lithuanie pendant la Conférence de la Paix*, p. 161; *Kurjer Polski*, No. 284 (October 29, 1919).

[2] One visitor to Lithuania stated that there was no economic problem there. Report of U. S. Military Attaché in Warsaw, October 16, 1919, United States, National Archives, 861L.00/127. Another observer reported that Galvanauskas had refused to discuss financial matters with him. Report by Father Edmund A. Walsh, Commissioner of the National Catholic War Council in Washington, November 19, 1919, United States, National Archives, 861L.00/131. A third visitor claimed that Galvanauskas had made himself popular by paying government officials one month's back salary. Report of Captain Leach, quoted in Gibson (Warsaw) to American Mission to Paris, telegram, November 15, 1919, United States, National Archives, 861E.001/226½.

From September on, government officials were paid in goods instead of money.[3] In explaining its problem to the American Lithuanians, the government claimed that the country itself was not poor, but that the government lacked the means of mobilizing its resources because of administrative disorder and the presence of foreign troops.[4] The Lithuanians needed outside help, but none was to be found immediately. The Lithuanians turned to the British, only to learn that official loans could be made only to governments which had been recognized *de jure*.

In a dispatch to Curzon on October 20, Tallents claimed that the refusal to grant *de jure* recognition to the Baltic states was driving them into bankruptcy since they could not get the loans or credits necessary for economic reconstruction. Therefore, he suggested, "as a means of avoiding full recognition without destroying the possibilities of internal reconstruction," the Baltic governments be allowed to grant concessions for certain raw materials with an Allied guarantee that any future Russian government which might take over this area would honor these agreements.[5] Sir Eyre Crowe, the British Ambassador to Paris, suggested that rather than require Allied supervision, the British government consider acting alone to guarantee such agreements with the understanding that a future Russian government could be induced to accept them.[6] He revived the idea of a special conference on Russia with the suggestion that such a meeting could consider this question.[7] The meeting was planned for London in January, 1920, but it was abandoned as British policy changed its course.

In November, Lloyd George decided to end British aid to Kolchak and Denikin on the ground that he saw no use in continued shipments,[8] and in December the Lithuanians finally

---

[3] M. Yčas, "Lietuvos vyriausybės sudarymo etapai," in *Pirmasis dešimtmetis*, I, 125; Voldemaras (Paris) to Šaulys (Bern), letter, November 21, 1919, Šaulys Archives, f. 35.

[4] *Vienybė Lietuvninkų*, No. 49 (December 3, 1919).

[5] Woodward and Butler (eds.), *British Foreign Policy*, First Series, III, 604-5.

[6] *Ibid.*, III, 622-23.　　　[7] *Ibid.*, III, 654.

[8] United States, *Foreign Relations: 1919, Russia*, p. 126.

met with success. Martynas Yčas came to an agreement with British representatives in Paris on the granting of a concession for the sale of Lithuanian flax. By the terms of the agreement, a group of English banks, including Lloyd's, the Westminster Bank, and the National Chemical and Metal Bank, received the exclusive right of export of the 1919 flax crop at a 5 percent commission. The Lithuanian government received an immediate advance of £100,000 sterling.[9]

The agreement saved the government from bankruptcy, but the Lithuanian economy was still in a delicate condition. In the last months of 1919 the government found it necessary to cut down its expenses so severely that its power to act became very restricted, and it was difficult to attract capable men into government work.

The retrenchment in government expenditures had a great impact on the Lithuanian representation abroad. Voldemaras, the Foreign Minister, sought to effect a reorientation of foreign policy more in keeping with the economic resources of the government. In line with the promise to work in closer cooperation with the Entente, he planned to concentrate diplomatic missions in the capitals of the Great Powers and to reduce to a bare minimum the Lithuanian representation in smaller countries: "Now the positive work begins. Our ministry is looking more toward opening and extending commercial ties with foreign countries, first of all with the great states, whence stems our political future."[10] He himself set out again for Paris in order to be at the center of all activity, leaving Petras Klimas as Acting Minister of Foreign Affairs in Kaunas.

The personnel of the missions abroad underwent great changes. In September, Sleževičius had named Šaulys to replace Daumantas in Switzerland. Dissatisfied with the reduced

---

[9] See the report by John Gade, December 6, 1919, Annex A, United States, National Archives, 861.00/6169; *Manchester Guardian*, January 17, 1920; M. Yčas, "Lietuvos vyriausybės sudarymo etapai," in *Pirmasis dešimtmetis*, I, 123-26; *Times* (London), January 6, 1920; *Vienybė Lietuvninkų*, No. 2 (January 14, 1920).

[10] Voldemaras, (Paris) to Šaulys (Bern), letter, November 14, 1919, Šaulys Archives, f. 35.

budget now assigned his mission, Šaulys resigned in December, after a furious exchange of letters with Voldemaras.[11] In London, Count Alfred Tyszkiewicz, one of the few members of the Polonized nobility to remain in Lithuania, replaced Čepinskis.[12] Juozas Puryckis, who had succeeded Šaulys as Minister to Berlin in June, remained on at that post. When Voldemaras left Paris in December to return to Kaunas, the delegation to the peace conference was broken up. Milosz remained in Paris as Lithuania's diplomatic representative, even though France still did not recognize the Kaunas government. Several American Lithuanians, including Naruševičius and Kazys Balutis, went to Kaunas to work in the Foreign Ministry.

A pattern had evolved in the Lithuanian foreign service of recruiting representatives from Lithuanians already established abroad. Milosz was a long-time resident of Paris. Tyszkiewicz had formerly been a secretary in the Tsarist Russian Embassy in London. The Lithuanian Executive Committee was the official agent of the Kaunas government in the United States. Puryckis was well known in Berlin. The representative in Helsinki, Gylys, had formerly been Governor General of Finland. The Lithuanians even had a representative in Azerbaijan, where Vincas Krėvė lived from 1918 to 1920.

Though Voldemaras was now planning to concentrate on the Entente states, he found Great Britain the only Western power which openly took a favorable attitude toward the Lithuanians. Noting the differences between the Baltic governments and Kolchak, a British Foreign Office memorandum of November 15 questioned,

---

[11] See the correspondence in Šaulys Archives, f. 35. In a letter of November 19 to Smetona, Šaulys recommended that the missions abroad be financed by the American Lithuanians (Šaulys Archives, f. 35). In a letter to Šaulys on February 10, 1920, Puryckis, the Lithuanian Minister to Berlin, reported that a number of other Lithuanian diplomatic representatives also felt that their budgets had been cut too much by Kaunas. Šaulys Archives, f. 77.

[12] Čepinskis was reported to be in disagreement with the policies of the new cabinet and to have refused to be sent to the United States. *Vienybė Lietuvninkų*, No. 3 (January 21, 1920).

Have the Baltic States definitely decided that their fate depends on the defeat of the anti-Soviet forces—that it is now a matter of life and death for them? They are working in increasingly close conjunction with Finland and Poland. Will they succeed in bringing about a combination of Border States—the *cordon sanitaire* at last? If so, this *cordon sanitaire* will now be not against Bolshevik Russia, but against anti-Bolshevik Russia, for peace between the States and the Soviet is almost a foregone conclusion. In this case will it eventually involve a German orientation in the policy of these States? It is largely up to us to prevent it. The Baltic States, having finally cast the die, will need at least moral protection against an unfavorable turn in the wheel of fortune. If they fail to get it from us, they are bound to turn some day to Germany, and the foundations that Germany is laying now will then stand her in good stead.[13]

With this in mind, the British were leaning more and more toward support of Baltic independence, although they still reserved the fading possibility of a reestablished Great Russia. On the other hand, they were definitely set against Polish expansion, so much so that Clemenceau criticized their "unjust" attitude.[14] While Clemenceau called the Poles a "strong bulwark against Germany," Lloyd George called them "troublemakers."[15] When the British decision finally came in November to end aid to the White Russians and in December to back a private loan to the Lithuanian government, they had gained a strong foothold in the Baltic area.

The idea of Russian unity was also fading in France, but there Lithuania did not profit from this trend as it did in England. France was still supporting a greater Poland and so was very vague in its attitude toward Lithuania. The French favored military aid to the Baltic states against the Bolsheviks, in order to form a *cordon sanitaire* against the Communists and between Germany and Russia, but the French were hesitant about supporting political independence for these governments.[16] They still could not resign themselves to the failure of the idea of

[13] Woodward and Butler (eds.), *British Foreign Policy,* First Series, III, 229.
[14] *Ibid.,* II, 736.   [15] *Ibid.,* II, 737.
[16] See Dziewanowski, "Pilsudski's Federal Policy," *Journal of Central European Affairs,* X, 117; United States, *Foreign Relations: Paris Peace Conference,* IX, 851, 898.

federation between Poland and Lithuania, although now their attitude was more one of regret than one of hope. General A. Niessel recorded that when he left Lithuania in December, 1919, "I carried to my great regret the very clear impression that the Entente had definitely missed the opportunity to renew the union between Poland and Lithuania which had been so profitable to both."[17] With all this, the relations between France and Lithuania remained undefined.

The United States government continued to hold tightly to the idea of Russian unity and tried to pacify the Baltic governments by informal concessions. The Americans were anxiously watching Japanese actions in Siberia, and they feared that recognition of the separation from Russia of the Baltic states would create a precedent for Japanese annexation of sections of Siberia. Commenting on the British recognition of Lithuania, Polk declared on October 8, "I am in doubt whether this is an opportune moment for us to consider such recognition, involving as it does the question of the partitioning of Russia."[18] When the State Department appointed John Gade Commissioner of the United States for the Baltic Provinces of Russia in October, it specifically stated that he was not accredited to any government but was just "an observer with no power to commit or represent the Government in any diplomatic capacity."[19] The State Department assured Bakhmetev that Gade had been instructed to give no unfounded "hope of recognition of separatist tendencies beyond autonomy," but on the contrary was to encourage the acceptance of Kolchak's terms of June 4.[20]

On October 15, 1919, Lansing defined United States policy toward Lithuania in two separate notes, one to Polk and the other to the Lithuanian National Council in New York. Lansing

[17] Niessel, *L'évacuation*, p. 217.
[18] Polk to Secretary of State (Washington, D. C.), October 8, 1919, United States, *Foreign Relations: 1919, Russia*, p. 723n., 57.
[19] Lansing to Davis (London, October 14, 1919, *ibid.*, p. 722.
[20] Bakhmetev (Washington, D. C.) to Sazonov (Paris), telegram, October 11, 1919, Maklakov Archives, B, II, 2. Gade was appointed to replace Greene, but the support of his mission was undertaken by the State Department, whereas Greene had been supported by the American mission in Paris.

informed Polk that President Wilson favored "a maximum of autonomy and self-government for the Baltic Provinces" but refused to make any commitment prejudicial to Russian sovereignty there. He noted that Bakhmetev opposed the British policy in the Baltic states on the ground that those governments could hardly offer an effective barrier against the Bolsheviks.[21] In his letter to the Lithuanian National Council, Lansing repeated the views of the President, but not those of Bakhmetev, assuring the Lithuanians that they would not be deserted to the Russians without any safeguards. The right of intervention by the League of Nations was reserved for the eventuality of a failure by the Russians and the Lithuanians to come to a direct agreement:

It is believed that this arrangement assures the autonomous development of Lithuania, together with the other nationalities comprised within the former Russian Empire, and wisely leaves to a future adjustment the determination of the relations which shall exist between them and the new Russian Government.[22]

Parallel to this policy the American government made informal concessions to the Lithuanians. Although the United States refused to recognize the Taryba or the independent existence of Lithuania, the State Department declared that Affidavits of Identification and Nationality, drawn up by the Lithuanian Executive Committee, were acceptable in lieu of Russian passports in the event Lithuanians could not receive visas from Russian consuls.[23] On November 25, Voldemaras sent a message to the American mission in Paris, asking for recognition, asserting that the uncertain political status of Lithuania was causing untold troubles for American Lithuanians in passport problems, in questions of inheritance, and in similar matters. Complaining that the American Lithuanians

---

[21] United States, *Foreign Relations: 1919, Russia,* pp. 723-24.

[22] United States, Department of State, *Russian Series,* No. 5.

[23] Passport Division of State Department to Lithuanian National Council, letter, October 13, 1919, and Lansing to Lithuanian National Council, October 28, 1919, MSS in Documents Relating to the Lithuanian National Movement (Lithuanian National Council).

were accusing the Lithuanian government of negligence, he asked for visas for a Lithuanian mission to America and for *de facto* recognition.[24]

The recognition was not granted, but the mission was allowed to enter the United States. The chief of the mission, Jonas Vileišis, upon his arrival in mid-December, proceeded immediately to Washington, where he established contact with the Lithuanian Executive Committee. There seems to have been some debate as to the relationship of Vileišis and the Executive Committee, but on January 15, 1920, it was announced that Vileišis would take over the official representation of the Kaunas government, while working in close cooperation with the Lithuanian Executive Committee.[25]

On December 30, 1919, the Lithuanian Executive Committee had notified the State Department that it was the official diplomatic representative of the Lithuanian government in America.[26] This declaration was voided of course by the establishment of Vileišis's mission, but it did serve to evoke another policy declaration by Secretary of State Lansing, on January 7, 1920. Declaring that, since the United States government did not recognize the Kaunas government, the committee could not be granted any diplomatic character, Lansing went on to say,

The Department is glad to deal informally with individuals and groups of individuals which are acting disinterestedly in behalf of the Lithuanian people or any portion of them. Your committee, in common with other representative Lithuanian bodies, may therefore count upon the consideration of the Department in all matters which it may have occasion to take up with it, within the limitations set forth above.[27]

Despite the continued support of the United States the White Russian political groups were most disappointed over the political setbacks which followed the military failures of Iudenich in

[24] United States National Archives, 861L.01/15.
[25] *Vienybė Lietuvninkų*, No. 4 (January 28, 1920). See Jurgela, Lithuania and the United States, pp. 272-78.
[26] United States, *Foreign Relations: 1920*, III, 640-41.
[27] *Ibid.*, III, 642-43.

October and of Denikin in November. Kolchak continued to refuse recognition to the Baltic governments on the grounds that he "could not outbid the Bolsheviki who had nothing to lose."[28] In November, as England and France turned to a reevaluation of their respective Baltic policies, the Russians came to believe that a reevaluation was also necessary on their own part. Sablin, from London, called the Russian Political Conference's declaration of March 6 on the nationality question outdated and claimed that something new was now needed. He doubted that the English had yet settled on a concrete plan, and he expressed the belief that Churchill, for one, was against the independence of the Baltic states. Therefore, he argued, a new declaration should be made definitely promising autonomy, especially in the face of the possibility that a bloc of the border states might force through their claim to recognition. As for the Russian Constituent Assembly, Sablin opined that since it would probably be more liberal than the views of the present emigration, it would offer little objection to a previous guarantee of autonomy.[29] On December 23, Boris Savinkov submitted a memorandum to the Russian Political Council in Paris wherein he suggested treating with each nation separately in order to undercut the formation of a bloc against the Russians. He recommended the immediate recognition of Poland and Finland, which would ease the way for talks with the Ukraine and the Baltic states. He considered Latvia and Lithuania amenable to the acceptance of a status of broad autonomy, "if only for economic considerations," and so Estonia, considered the most outspoken for independence, would no longer be able to stand alone. He emphasized that the Russians had to win the sympathy and trust of these nationalities.[30]

In December, Denikin announced his readiness to treat with all the border governments on the basis of the *status quo* for the

---

[28] Lansing to Davis (London), October 23, 1919, *ibid.: 1919, Russia*, p. 727.

[29] Sablin (London) to Sazonov (Paris), telegram, November 22, 1919, Maklakov Archives, B, II, 2.

[30] Maklakov Archives, B, II, 2.

sake of common action against the Bolsheviks.[31] But despite this move, the course of events had left the Russians far behind. Short of a tremendous military victory within Russia, which was not forthcoming, the diplomatic ground now lost could not be regained.

The political eclipse of the White Russians somewhat eased the position of the Lithuanians, but the continued presence of Bermondt's forces in the northwestern part of the country still posed a great threat to Lithuania's very existence. Although his own future was doubtful, Bermondt was successful in preventing the Lithuanian government from establishing its control in over one half of the country. The Entente, too, was alarmed at the presence of the German forces in the Baltic area, fearing the establishment of German power there. They were mainly concerned with forcing the Germans to evacuate the Baltic states, a step which would leave Bermondt to his own devices and without German support, on which he depended despite his claims of being a Russian.[32] As a result, the Lithuanians found the Entente a most welcome ally in this issue, although their respective policies were parallel rather than coordinated.

The idea of an inter-Allied commission to supervise the evacuation, proposed by the Germans, was accepted by the Supreme Council on October 10, and on October 28, Clemenceau sent instructions to the man chosen to head the commission, the French General Albert Niessel.[33] The commission was to have no political dealings; its task was solely to effect the evacua-

[31] *Kurjer Polski*, No. 338 (December 24, 1919).

[32] See United States, *Foreign Relations: 1919, Russia*, pp. 736-37. Even in its correspondence with its own agents, the German government denied any official or unofficial connections with Bermondt. See Foreign Office to Zimmerle, October 20, 1919, Germany, Foreign Office, *Hauptarchiv: Litauen*, Reel 432, frame 336.

[33] See Niessel, *L'évacuation*, pp. 26-32; Woodward and Butler (eds.), *British Foreign Policy*, First Series, II, 94-97. Independently of the Supreme Council, the British Foreign Office had apparently sought to organize a unified army of Latvians, Lithuanians, and Poles, under General Crozier's command, to drive out the Germans. This project failed, however, because of the Lithuanians' opposition to the introduction of Polish troops into the area held by the Kaunas government. Crozier, *Impressions and Recollections*, p. 244.

tion of all German forces from the Baltic area. The Allied military missions in the Baltic were all subordinated to it, and direct contact with the Baltic governments and the German government was assured. The intention of the Entente not to allow this mission to be construed as a recognition of the Baltic governments was expressly stated: "It will be the task of the League of Nations to use its good offices to fix definitely the relations between the Baltic states and the future government of Russia if a direct agreement is not made.[34] On November 5, Niessel left Paris for Berlin, planning to go on from there to the Baltic area.[35]

The situation in that area had meanwhile taken a catastrophic turn, however. On October 8, Bermondt attacked the Latvians, claiming that he was trying to reach the Bolshevik front.[36] On October 10, Riga was being evacuated by the Latvians, and the Latvian General Ballod withdrew his troops from the Bolshevik front to face the new threat in the west.

In Lithuania, on October 9, the Russo-German forces in Siauliai declared that the territories they occupied were Russian and they proceeded to disarm Lithuanian forces stationed there.[37] On October 18, Galvanauskas and Bermondt exchanged telegrams, Galvanauskas demanding complete evacuation of all German and Russian forces from Lithuania, and Bermondt, in turn, demanding passage to the Bolshevik front.[38] Armed conflicts between Lithuanian forces and Bermondt's troops were reported from October 15 on.[39] On October 21, Colonel Rowan

[34] Niessel, *L'évacuation*, p. 32.

[35] The British considered it a blow to their prestige that a French general should in effect replace Gough, but Niessel's tact in his relations with British officials helped smoothe the matter over. See Woodward and Butler (eds.), *British Foreign Policy*, First Series, III, 223-24.

[36] Bermondt-Avalov, *Im Kampf*, p. 208.

[37] Report of the German Diplomatic Representative in Siauliai (Knoepfel) to Zimmerle, October 9, 1919, Germany, Foreign Office, *Hauptarchiv: Litauen*, Reel 432, frame 229. Zimmerle characterized Bermondt's policies as "politically imprudent." Zimmerle to Foreign Office, October 16, 1919, *ibid.*, Reel 432, frame 325.

[38] Bermondt-Avalov, *Im Kampf*, pp. 212-13. See *Le Temps*, October 21, 1919; *Neue Zürcher Zeitung*, No. 1620 (October 21, 1919).

[39] Woodward and Butler (eds.), *British Foreign Policy*, First Series, III, 193; *Neue Zürcher Zeitung*, No. 1620 (October 21, 1919).

Robinson, a British military representative in the Baltic area, reported that General Eberhardt, Von der Goltz's replacement, had demanded that the Lithuanians free 20 kilometers on either side of the Tilsit-Siauliai railroad, while the Lithuanians would agree only to a 10-kilometer zone. Robinson expressed the fear that this dispute might be seized upon by the Germans as an excuse to delay the evacuation.[40] On October 28, Robinson reported that the Lithuanians were threatening to blow up the railroad bridges on November 10 if the German evacuation had not been completed by that time.[41] Niessel directed Robinson to urge the Lithuanians not to carry out this threat lest the Germans use it as a pretext for further delay.[42]

On October 30, at Radviliskis, representatives of the Lithuanian government reached an agreement with Eberhardt, effective November 2, providing for a neutral zone between the Lithuanian and the German forces, an exchange of prisoners, noninterference by the Germans in Lithuanian civil affairs, and a mixed commission to handle disputes.[43] The agreement, however, set no date for the completion of the German evacuation.[44]

Arriving in Berlin on November 7, Niessel found that there were many complications to be ironed out. The German representative on the commission, General Hopmann, claimed that the German evacuation would be ended by November 14. When the surprised Allied officers asked how this was possible, he explained that Bermondt's men were Russians and so were not included in the German forces.[45] Niessel considered this view unacceptable and demanded the complete evacuation of all German soldiers.[46] While in Berlin, Niessel assured the representatives of the Baltic states that the commission would demand

[40] Woodward and Butler (eds.), *British Foreign Policy*, First Series, III, 189.
[41] *Ibid.*, III, 199.
[42] *Ibid.*, III, 210. See also Ruseckas, *Savanorių Žygiai*, pp. 32 ff.
[43] *Europäischer Geschichtskalendar, 1919* (Munich, 1923), II, 343; *Pravda*, No. 247 (November 4, 1919). See also *Neue Zürcher Zeitung*, Nos. 1649 (October 26, 1919), 1659 (October 28, 1919), and 1685 (November 1, 1919).
[44] See Woodward and Butler (eds.), *British Foreign Policy*, First Series, III, 220.
[45] Vanlande, *Avec le Général Niessel*, p. 29.
[46] Niessel, *L'évacuation*, p. 39.

complete evacuation, but in return, he stated, the Baltic governments must restrain their people so as not to hinder the course of the evacuation. The Lithuanian representative, Puryckis, pointed out the necessity of controlling the frontier in order to stop the Germans from carrying off large amounts of booty with them.[47]

At Tilsit on November 13, Eberhardt announced to Niessel that no German troops obedient to Berlin were left in the Baltic states. The soldiers still there had renounced their German citizenship and had adopted Russian citizenship. Eberhardt also produced a letter from Bermondt wherein the latter avowed his loyalty to Russia. Niessel, however, refused to recognize the independent existence of Bermondt's forces and would not enter into any relations with him.[48]

On November 14, Niessel arrived in Kaunas, where he sought the agreement of the Lithuanian government to his stipulation that the Germans not be attacked. He came away from the talks with the impression that the leaders of the government would try to cooperate with him, but that the junior army officers and the population of the country, spurred on by their hatred of the German soldiers, were liable to attack anyway.[49] While the mission was in Kaunas, news arrived which simplified somewhat the problem of Bermondt. The Latvians had put Bermondt's army to rout, and on November 15 Bermondt announced that he was placing himself under General Eberhardt's command.[50] The Germans now pleaded with the mission to arrange an armistice.[51]

At Niessel's urging the Lithuanian government demanded that Berlin recall Zimmerle and reduce the German diplomatic staff in Kaunas, which numbered some forty-seven persons. Niessel later recounted that the Lithuanians had feared to make this move before, but now with Entente backing they were

[47] *Ibid.*, pp. 45-47. The commission had only moral pressures at its command and therefore could not set up such a border control.
[48] *Ibid.*, pp. 71-72, 76.   [49] *Ibid.*, p. 80.
[50] Zimmerle (Kaunas) to Galvanauskas (Kaunas), letter, November 15, 1919, Šaulys Archives, f. 30.
[51] Niessel, *L'évacuation*, pp. 87, 96.

successful in both demands. Piłsudski sent Niessel a personal letter of thanks for his part in the recall of Zimmerle.[52]

Despite Niessel's plea to refrain from attacking the Germans during the withdrawal, the Lithuanians, anxious to stop the German removal of railroad and military materials, which was continuing unabated despite the protests of the commission, advanced on Radviliskis on November 21, and took that railroad center the next day, capturing a great deal of equipment as the Germans retreated to Siauliai.[53] The Allied mission acted quickly to force the Lithuanians to withdraw from the railroad to the line set up by the agreement of October 30.[54] The Lithuanians were very unhappy about this demand, but they complied on November 24.[55] Niessel announced on November 26 that Eberhardt had agreed to complete the evacuation of Bermondt's forces by December 13 and that all materiel not essential to the troops would be left for the Lithuanians.[56] Niessel was using the threat of urging on the Lithuanians and the Latvians unless Eberhardt yielded. As he later reported,

If the Germans have acquiesced, it is entirely due to the fear of the use of the armed forces of Latvia and Lithuania and the consequences which might have accrued to Germany from nonexecution of its promises to the Entente.[57]

[52] *Ibid.*, pp. 82-83. Cf. Gade (Tallinn) to Secretary of State, telegram, November 29, 1919, United States, National Archives, 861.00/5968; Woodward and Butler (eds.), *British Foreign Policy*, First Series, II, 89. Zimmerle did not immediately leave Lithuania as one might think from reading Niessel's account. His title was changed from Plenipotentiary to Diplomatic Representative (Diplomatischer Vertreter). He was replaced only in January, 1920.

[53] Ruseckas, *Savanoriu̜ Żygiai*, p. 33; *Le Temps*, December 6, 1919. The victory seems to have been largely due to the Latvian successes farther north. Crozier was shocked by the outmoded tactics and bad discipline in the Lithuanian army. He declared, however, that he found "no bad soldiers, only bad colonels" (*Impressions and Recollections*, pp. 244-45).

[54] Niessel, *L'évacuation*, pp. 114-15, 121-22; Woodward and Butler (eds.), *British Foreign Policy*, First Series, II, 403. Niessel feared that the Germans would send reenforcements from East Prussia.

[55] Ruseckas, *Savanoriu̜ Żygiai*, p. 35; *Neue Zürcher Zeitung*, No. 1816 (November 26, 1919).

[56] Niessel, *L'évacuation*, pp. 118-19, 128.

[57] Conference of Ambassadors, Notes of a Meeting Held at Quai d'Orsay, Paris, No. 4 (February 13, 1920), p. 10.

The threat of further fighting had not been removed by the agreement of November 26, however. The Iron Division was slow to leave Latvia, and the commission feared that a joint Lithuanian-Latvian maneuver would result if there was too great a delay.[58] The Germans were organizing armed forces in East Prussia, but their purpose was not clear.[59] Furthermore, the Germans did not live up to their promise to refrain from plundering and to leave their equipment behind. On December 6 the Iron Division began to march toward Memel, instead of Tilsit, touching off another crisis.[60] But the evacuation was completed almost on schedule as the last troops left Lithuania on December 14.[61] In January the German government agreed to turn over to the Baltic governments the war materiel and the railroad equipment left in the Baltic area by the evacuated troops.[62]

Niessel believed that the evacuation constituted a triumph for the Entente,[63] but the British member of the commission, Major General Turner, looked rather at the tremendous amount of materiel the Germans had taken with them and took a much less glowing view of the accomplishments of the commission.[64] The Lithuanians were dissatisfied with the work of the commission, feeling that it had restrained them without adequate reason and so had needlessly permitted the removal of much valuable materiel by the Germans.[65] While at Kaunas in November, Turner had reported finding a dissatisfaction with the politics of the Entente because the Poles had not been re-

[58] Woodward and Butler (eds.), *British Foreign Policy*, First Series, III, 243.

[59] See *ibid.*; United States, *Foreign Relations: Paris Peace Conference*, IX, 250-51; Vanlande, *Avec le Général Niessel*, p. 153.

[60] Woodward and Butler (eds.), *British Foreign Policy*, First Series, III, 248.

[61] *Ibid.*, III, 258n.

[62] Niessel, *L'évacuation*, pp. 226ff.; Conférence de la Paix, *Recueil*, IV, C, (7) Commission des Affaires Baltiques, pp. 263-66.

[63] "Un des rares succès positifs et durables obtenus par les vainqueurs" (*L'évacuation*, p. 5).

[64] "To say that the mission has been a success would deceive no one" (Woodward and Butler (eds.), *British Foreign Policy*, First Series, III, 252).

[65] Ruseckas, *Savanorių žygiai*, pp. 35-36.

strained from violating the lines of demarcation.[66] The Lithuanians regarded the procedure in the evacuation of the Germans
in the same way. There were also criticisms raised that Niessel
had consorted with Gabrys and Baron von der Ropp while in
Berlin.[67] The Lithuanians were thankful that the Germans had
been forced to leave, but they felt that the job could have been
done better. Furthermore, the continued presence of the evacuated troops in East Prussia, especially that of the Iron Division in
Memel, aroused anxiety about the fate of the Prussian Lithuanians.[68]

In the conflict between the Lithuanians and Bermondt, the
Poles had been ostentatiously neutral. On October 13 the Polish
Deputy Foreign Minister W. Skrzynski announced that Lithua-
nia could concentrate its forces against the Russo-German forces
without any fear of trouble with Poland. As a reminder of the
Polish attitude toward the Lithuanian government, he added,

There will come a time when the real endeavor of the Lithuanian nation will find expression in the formation of a government, which will
be an expression of the opinion of the majority of the nation and will
not, as it has up to now, have anti-Polish agitation as its only foundation.[69]

In November, *Izvestiia* reported that according to the Latvian
Foreign Minister, Mejerovič, Poland had refused an offer from
Bermondt of southern Lithuania if it would cooperate against
the Lithuanians.[70]

There were, as ever, a multitude of opinions voiced about
Lithuania among the Poles. Some still held out for the idea of
federation, some supported sponsorship of a Baltic union such as

[66] Woodward and Butler (eds.), *British Foreign Policy*, First Series, III, 232.
[67] See Woodward and Butler (eds.), *British Foreign Policy*, First Series, III, 241;
Vanlande, *Avec le Général Niessel*, pp. 18-19, 25.
[68] Woodward and Butler (eds.), *British Foreign Policy*, First Series, III, 663-64;
United States, *Foreign Relations: Paris Peace Conference*, IX, 750-51. The Iron Division left Memel on January 8, 1920, two days before the peace treaty became
effective. Woodward and Butler (eds.), *British Foreign Policy*, First Series, III, 258n.
[69] *Monitor Polski*, No. 223 (October 15, 1919); Poland, Ministry of Foreign
Affairs, *Documents diplomatiques*, I, 33; Woodward and Butler (eds.), *British Foreign
Policy*, First Series, III, 153-54; *Kurjer Polski*, No. 270 (October 15, 1919).
[70] *Izvestiia*, No. 251 (November 9, 1919).

England was thought to be effecting, and, of course, many were stronger than ever in their support of Dmowski's annexationist policy.[71] The policy of the government itself toward Lithuania was settling down along the Dmowski line, since no acceptable agreement could be reached with the Lithuanians. The voices against the alienation of Vilna were too strong to be denied. One deputy in the Constituent Assembly proclaimed, to the accompaniment of loud cheers, "There is no Poland without Vilna!"[72] The intention of the Polish government to retain Vilna was demonstrated by the opening of a Polish university there, named for Stefan Batory, in October.[73] The Lithuanians objected to the university's refusal to organize the student body by nations, but as Piłsudski told Biržiška in early October, the Poles wanted to avoid a repetition of student troubles such as had occurred at the Polish university of Lvov.[74]

On December 8 the Supreme Council approved an eastern frontier for Poland as the minimum line behind which the Poles were to be permitted to organize a civil administration.[75] The line was approximately the same as the one established between Poland and the USSR after the Second World War (with the exception, of course, of the division of East Prussia), giving the Poles Sejny and Suwalki, but leaving Vilna undecided. The drawing of the line did not expressly preclude expansion farther eastward, but the Poles nevertheless were not pleased with it. Dmowski called it "an altogether unnecessary attempt, having no possible meaning,"[76] while Aleksander Skrzynski, later the Polish Foreign Minister, felt it was "so prejudicial to Poland that under no considerations could he accept it, so much the less so as the Polish war front at that period happened to be

[71] See the reports on the Polish press in *Polnische Pressestimmen*, Nos. 25 and 27 (November 1 and 6, 1919).

[72] Sejda, November 21, 1919, *Monitor Polski*, No. 256 (November 24, 1919).

[73] See Poland, Ministry of Foreign Affairs, *Documents diplomatiques*, I, 32-33.

[74] Biržiška, interview, August 14, 1956. See *Neue Zürcher Zeitung*, No. 1569 (October 13, 1919).

[75] Wielhorski, *Polska a Litwa*, p. 320; Kutrzeba, "The Struggle for Frontiers," in *Cambridge History of Poland*, p. 522.

[76] Dmowski, *Polityka polska*, p. 478.

about 250 kilometers further East."[77] And Piłsudski had already declared that the Poles would not withdraw their forces from territory they had occupied.[78]

The Poles made no new efforts at this time to negotiate a state agreement or an agreement of union with the Lithuanians. In November a group of Vilna Polish Democrats traveled to Kaunas to seek an amelioration of the position of the Poles in Kaunas. Nothing of substance came from the talks, as each side presented a list of demands which the other was not ready to meet. The Lithuanians rejected the Polish demand for a special Ministry of Polish Affairs, claiming that if the Polish government would but recognize Lithuania, a diplomatic representative could handle the matter. The Poles wanted to discuss the internal situation within Lithuania, while the Lithuanians wanted only to discuss diplomatic relations with Warsaw. No common ground could be found, and the talks came to nought.[79]

The Polish policy of seeking an entente with Latvia and Estonia, thereby putting pressure on Lithuania, was contributing to a growing rift between the Baltic states. When Mejerovič requested that the Lithuanians permit Polish troops to pass through their country to aid the Latvians against the Germans, the Lithuanians bluntly refused.[80] The Latvians, in turn, were angered by the slowness of the Lithuanians to attack Bermondt and especially by the agreement of October 30 with Eberhardt.[81]

[77] Skrzynski, *Poland and the Peace*, p. 36.

[78] Rumbold (Warsaw) to Curzon (London), telegram, November 7, 1919, Woodward and Butler (eds.), *British Foreign Policy*, First Series, III, 633-36. In contrast to the Polish condemnations of the line, see James T. Shotwell, *Poland and Russia, 1919-1945* (New York, 1945), p. 7. Professor Shotwell called the line "an honest effort to establish an ethnographic frontier between that part of Poland which has a decided Polish majority and those parts later called Eastern Poland in which the White Russians and Ukrainians form a majority." The Lithuanian claims that the line left Vilna to Lithuania are unfounded, since the line was meant only to be the provisional eastern boundary of Poland, not a western boundary of any other state.

[79] A full account of the mission can be found in *Kurjer Polski*, No. 314 (November 29, 1919). See also *Monitor Polski*, No. 280 (November 17, 1919); *Le Temps*, December 3, 1919.

[80] See Henrys (Warsaw) to peace conference, telegram, October 16, 1919, United States, National Archives, 184.611/1264; *Izvestiia*, No. 251 (November 9, 1919).

[81] See Woodward and Butler (eds.), *British Foreign Policy*, First Series, III, 214.

The Bermondt episode resulted in the abandonment of the conference with the Bolsheviks planned for October. On October 25 the Estonian Foreign Minister notified Chicherin that Latvia and Lithuania had indicated that they could not attend the conference, but he assured the Russians that Estonia still wanted peace.[82] On October 26, Chicherin answered this message, offering to resume bilateral talks with the Estonians.[83] In a note of the same day to the Russians, the Estonians denied that they had invited the resumption of bilateral talks and indicated that the three Baltic states would soon hold another meeting, to which a Soviet delegation would be invited.[84]

The new conference assembled at Tartu on November 9. Present were delegates from Estonia, Latvia, and Lithuania, and unofficial observers from Poland, Belorussia, and the U-kraine.[85] The first job of the conference, of course, was the question of peace with Soviet Russia, and the Russians were immediately invited to send a delegate.[86] The Baltic states were prepared to demand recognition of their independence, but they would not make any agreement on exchanging diplomatic representatives or on opening trade.[87]

In an article in *Izvestiia* in mid-November, Steklov again discussed the problem of making peace with the Baltic states, asserting that Soviet Russia, as ever, wanted peace, whereas the Baltic states were moving toward a conclusion of peace only under great pressure from their peoples and against the express wishes of the Entente. He claimed that the Baltic governments were acting of their own will only in their "hatred of the proletariat and of Communism."[88] It would seem, however, that the Soviet Communists were not at all united in the desire to make peace with the Baltic governments. In January, 1920,

[82] *Izvestiia*, No. 240 (October 26, 1919).   [83] *Ibid.*, No. 242 (October 28, 1919).
[84] Copy of the note in United States, National Archives, 184.01502/107.
[85] *Izvestiia*, No. 256 (November 15, 1919).
[86] *Ibid.*; *Revue baltique*, II (1919), 52.
[87] See the report of John Gade, November 13, 1919, United States, National Archives, 861.00/5956; interview with Galvanauskas in *Manchester Guardian*, February 11, 1920.
[88] *Izvestiia*, No. 255 (November 14, 1919).

a debate was revealed in *Izvestiia* which must have been in progress ever since the Communists had first indicated their willingness to make peace. K. Danishevskii condemned the proposal to make peace with Latvia as constituting treason against the proletariat of that country. Steklov answered this argument in an article almost four times as long, criticizing Danishevskii as being too idealistic. After agreeing with Danishevskii that the small states could be a danger to Russia, he asserted that it was necessary to make peace with them in order to open a way to split the enemies of the Bolsheviks. He claimed that to go to war with the Baltic states would be suicidal, since the Entente had indicated its deep concern for their continued existence.[89] Thus it is clear that in seeking peace the Soviet government bore no special love for the Baltic governments. The move was a tactical maneuver. Rather than force a united front by appearing as an aggressor, the Soviet government wanted to retreat into the background so that the opposition might divide over other issues.

On November 17, Maxim Litvinov arrived in Tartu on his way to Copenhagen for talks with the British, and on November 18 he offered the Baltic governments recognition of their independence, withdrawal of the Red Army from eastern Latvia, and reparations for damages caused by the Bolsheviks.[90] The Baltic governments hoped to establish a neutral zone between themselves and the Russians, but when the Estonians asked the Entente to supervise the proposed zone, they were turned down. The Western powers refused to give such a direct sanction to the negotiations, and in addition they had no wish to be put in such an "unenviable position."[91] Litvinov left Tartu on the eighteenth, having made an agreement for the opening of negotiations on the question of the exchange of prisoners.[92]

---

[89] Both articles in *ibid.*, No. 12 (January 18, 1920).

[90] See Woodward and Butler (eds.), *British Foreign Policy*, First Series, III, 652-53.

[91] United States, *Foreign Relations: 1919, Russia*, p. 744.

[92] Litvinov promised that all talks would include a declaration by the Soviet government that it would conduct no propaganda in peacetime in the Baltic states. See the report by John Gade, November 2., 1919, United States, National Archives, 861.00/6008.

Despite the fact that all the Baltic states had participated in the Tartu conference, the unity of the Baltic governments was being impaired by the friction between Latvia and Lithuania, and by the dispute between Estonia and Latvia over the Valga area. In accordance with the decisions of the September conference at Tartu, the Estonians were now free to resume separate negotiations with the Russians. On November 23 they notified the Bolsheviks that they were willing to start talks on December 1. Due to delays, the talks did not begin until December 5, when the Bolshevik delegation, headed by Krassin and Joffe, arrived in Tartu.[93]

Elsewhere, the month of December, 1919, marks the first time that the Lithuanian government could really call the country its own. The German threat had been relieved by the completion of the evacuation, and with the Germans went the legitimate doubts in the West, fostered by Polish propaganda, as to the genuinely representative character of the Lithuanian government and of the Lithuanian national movement. Meanwhile, in the east the direct Bolshevik menace all but vanished at the turn of the new year, as a joint Polish-Latvian offensive took Daugavpils, thus cutting off the Bolshevik army from direct contact with Lithuania. The Lithuanians were extremely angered by the cooperation between the Poles and the Latvians, especially since they had had their own eyes on Daugavpils since the summer of 1919.[94] But they did find the new situation a boon in easing the way for undisturbed internal reorganization.

The military respite was seized upon to reduce the size of the army. This was later called a foolish move on the grounds that the army should rather have been enlarged in order to press the Poles into yielding Vilna.[95] But such a view must be considered unwarranted by the facts and even ridiculous. The financial

[93] See Woodward and Butler (eds.), *British Foreign Policy*, First Series, III, 656-57; *Izvestiia*, No. 276 (December 9, 1919).

[94] In his memoirs Crozier stated that the Poles and the Latvians did not trust the Lithuanians, suspecting them of secretly trading with the Bolsheviks, "an occurrence which was unfortunately not open to doubt" (*Impressions and Recollections*, p. 245).

[95] Ruseckas, *Savanorių Žygiai*, pp. 38-39.

crisis had been by no means solved. The economies in administration, the German evacuation, and the British loan all helped to ease the pressure, but the situation was still delicate. Ruseckas claimed that in their nationalistic ardor the army volunteers would have served for nothing,[96] but pay to the soldiers is not the only expense in maintaining an army. Furthermore, the troubles in February, 1920, to be described below, indicate that even a reduced army was a tremendous burden on the treasury, and they also raise some doubts about the morale of the troops in case they had been requested to serve for nothing.

A more detrimental blow to the national movement was the failure to realize the plans for organizing an American Lithuanian brigade. A variety of reasons have been given for this failure, including poor organizational work on the part of the American Lithuanians, the refusal of the American government to give the idea its unreserved backing, and a refusal by the American people to allow such an interference in Russian affairs.[97] But the Inspector General of the brigade, Julius J. Bielskis, places the blame elsewhere, on the Lithuanian government in Kaunas and especially on Voldemaras, the Minister of Foreign Affairs.[98]

Colonel Swarthout-Juododis had come to the United States in November to aid in organizing the brigade. It was claimed that 10,000 men were ready to go to Lithuania. The United States government would not allow the brigade to go abroad as such, because Lithuania had not been recognized, and so a plan was devised whereby the members of the brigade were to go to Canada as laborers and from there were to proceed to Lithua-

---

[96] *Ibid.*

[97] Jurgela, "Amerikos lietuvių legionas," in Ruseckas (ed.), *Pasaulio lietuviai,* p. 57; Pakštas, "Lietuvių amerikiečių kovos," *Židinys,* XXVII (1938), 643; Sarmaitis, "Interventsiia anglo-amerikanskikh imperialistov," *Istoricheskie Zapiski,* No. 45 (1954), p. 275.

[98] Dr. Bielskis related his views in an interview granted to the author in Los Angeles on August 15, 1956. His views of the causes of the failure were substantially those of Colonel Swarthout. Swarthout, however, saw German influences behind Voldemaras's attitudes, while Bielskis attributed them to purely personal political reasons. See Swarthout's report to Gade, February 11, 1920, United States, National Archives, 860M.00/19.

ia. In late November a group of officers, including Bielskis, left America for Lithuania, with the intention of preparing the way for the arrival of the troops.

Having arrived in Kaunas shortly after New Year's Day, 1920, Bielskis made the rounds of the government offices, paying his respects. When he spoke with Voldemaras, a sharp difference of opinion was revealed. Voldemaras welcomed the idea of troops coming to Lithuania, but he wanted to break them up among already existing military units. Bielskis, on the other hand, demanded that the Americans be kept together, since they were different in background from the native Lithuanians and since they were also more uniformly equipped. Voldemaras refused to allow the existence of such a distinct unit, and the interview ended in disagreement. Although Lithuanian military leaders such as Žukauskas and Liatukas favored the idea of the brigade, Voldemaras's opposition represented an insuperable barrier. With the support of the Lithuanian government, the plan for bringing over the brigade might have been feasible; without it, the project fell apart.

As the new year began in Lithuania, the prospects for the future were still forbidding. Although the British loan had provided some financial relief, the government was not out of danger. Externally, the German and the Russian threats had been dissolved for the time being, but new problems stood in their place. An Entente occupation force was to take over Memel after the Peace Treaty had taken effect, and there was the distinct possibility that the Memelland would not go to Lithuania after all. Border disputes over Palanga and Ilukste were arising with Latvia. The Vilna dispute and the arrests of Poles in Kaunas, however justified, had poisoned relations with Poland. And Lithuania still had not gained *de jure* recognition from the Entente, or even *de facto* recognition from France, the United States, and Poland. Writing to Šaulys on January 12, 1920, Smetona sarcastically declared that Lithuania's position "among the newly established states can be called 'splendid isolation.'"[99]

[99] Šaulys Archives, f. 77.

Yet the government faced serious internal troubles. The paralysis of the administration by the financial crisis created a new abyss between the people and the government. Capable Lithuanians refused to enter the poorly paid government service, with the result that many former Russian officials were holding posts in the new government, further alienating the mass of the population from the government. [100] With the foreign threat to Lithuania's state existence diminished, the time had come for the Lithuanians to prove that they could organize and administer their own independent political establishment.

[100] See the letters from Lithuania published in *Vienybė Lietuvninkų*, No. 2 (January 14, 1920).

IX

"The Independent Lithuanian State"

JANUARY–MAY, 1920

DURING THE month of January, 1920, the Lithuanian government was able to improve its financial situation considerably, but political apathy continued. Some hope was seen in the growing interest in the forthcoming elections to the Constituent Assembly, called for April 14 and 15.[1] In late January, Vaclovas Sidzikauskas, the Lithuanian representative in Switzerland, called the elections the main hope for establishing political order.[2] On February 10, Puryckis, the Minister to Berlin, in a letter to Šaulys, observed,

The financial crisis which troubled us has more or less passed; several millions have been received for the railways, the income has been somewhat reorganized since the German evacuation, and finally, very great savings—in some cases I feel even too great—have been made.

After pointing out that there was discontent in the army over the fact that the soldiers had not been given the right to vote in the forthcoming elections, Puryckis turned to foreign affairs, complaining that the Lithuanians may have delayed too long in making peace with the Bolsheviks: "There was a time when we could have made an agreement with them and won much politically and economically, but I fear that opportunity has passed unexploited."[3]

Affairs continued to deteriorate in February as Bolshevik agitation gained ground among the discontented segments of the population, while the government still found itself unable to

---

[1] Smetona announced the dates on January 12. The election law had been approved by the cabinet on October 30, 1919.

[2] Sidzikauskas (Bern) to Šaulys (Bad Nauheim), letter, January 28, 1920, Šaulys Archives, f. 77.

[3] Šaulys Archives, f. 77.

act effectively. Rumors that voting restrictions might be imposed in the forthcoming elections stirred up even more trouble.[4] Writing to Šaulys on February 23, Sidzikauskas declared, "Generally a revolutionary spirit is growing in Lithuania, and the people there openly discuss and await revolution."[5]

On February 22 a military revolt broke out in Kaunas. For several days previously unrest had been growing, and on February 21 a soldiers' council was formed which demanded the right to vote, back pay, and better living conditions, and openly expressed its desire for a change in the government, although, apparently, not specifying what sort of new government was wanted.[6] On February 22 several government buildings were attacked with artillery fire, and some Lithuanian officers were arrested, but the uprising was quickly put down, chiefly through the aid of the Entente officers in Kaunas and other parts of Lithuania.[7] The only casualty among the officers was Captain Samuel Harris, an American member of the proposed American Lithuanian brigade, who was killed.[8] The rising was generally attributed to Bolshevik agitation which had exploited the discontent of the soldiers with their living conditions.[9] Once the revolt was put down, the government moved quickly to punish the leaders,[10] but at the same time it made concessions to better the lot of the average soldier. The right to vote was extended to the soldiers and channels were opened up for the receipt of complaints.[11] As Puryckis commented, "This event seems to have had some good consequences since it has opened the eyes of the govern-

---

[4] See the report in *Kurjer Polski*, No. 54 (February 24, 1920).

[5] Sidzikauskas (Bern) to Šaulys (Bad Nauheim), February 23, 1920, Šaulys Archives, f. 77.

[6] See the statement by Voldemaras, quoted in *Pravda*, No. 59 (March 17, 1920).

[7] The official account of the revolt can be found in *Vienybė Lietuvninkų*, No. 12 (March 24, 1920). See also *Monitor Polski*, No. 47 (February 27, 1920); *Times* (London), March, 1920; Sarmaitis, "Interventsiia anglo-amerikanskikh imperialistov," *Istoricheskie Zapiski*, No. 45 (1954), pp. 275-76.

[8] His mother in America received a decoration in his name and a pension from the Lithuanian government.

[9] Letter from Crozier, *Times* (London), March 12, 1920.

[10] See *Neue Zürcher Zeitung*, No. 702 (April 20, 1920).

[11] *Ibid.*, No. 554 (April 3, 1920).

ment to the conditions in the army."[12] In another move at this time, the Lithuanian government lifted the political censorship, although it kept the military censorship.[13] Martial law, instituted in February, 1919, was ended on March 1.[14]

After the revolt a change took place in the army high command, but it was not directly connected with the revolt. General Crozier resigned from his post on the General Staff and was replaced by Žukauskas, who now became Chief of Staff.[15] The initiative for the resignation seems to have been Crozier's, and Žukauskas expressed his regret at Crozier's departure, which was said to have been over a "matter of principle."[16] There had been a strong feeling building up for several months among Lithuanians against what was considered the unwarrantedly privileged position in the Lithuanian army of foreign officers, whose countries had not yet even recognized Lithuania.[17] Crozier left Kaunas in March, still on the best of terms with the Lithuanian government, and once back in England he actively supported the Lithuanian cause, especially against the Poles.[18] About his replacement he stated only that the English and the French missions had long been trying to bring Žukauskas back into favor, and that now they had finally succeeded.[19]

In the first months of 1920 Lithuanian foreign relations did not show any significant improvement, and in some respects they deteriorated considerably. At a conference held in Helsinki, January 20 to 23, and attended by representatives of Finland, Estonia, Latvia, Lithuania, and Poland, the idea of a

[12] Puryckis (Berlin) to Šaulys (Bad Nauheim), letter, March 6, 1920, Šaulys Archives, f. 77.

[13] *Waldibas Wehstnesis*, No. 54 (March 6, 1920).

[14] *Vienybė Lietuvninkų*, No. 14 (April 7, 1920).

[15] Liatukas had been the formal head of the General Staff, but it would seem that Crozier was the real power.

[16] *Times* (London), March 9, 1920.

[17] *Vienybė Lietuvninkų*, No. 10 (March 10, 1920). Cf. the report on agitation against Crozier in *Times* (London), February 28, 1920.

[18] See his letter to *Times* (London), May 13, 1920.

[19] Letter to *Times* (London), March 12, 1920. Cf. the report by General Niessel to the French War Ministry, November 21, 1919, United States, National Archives, FW.861L.20/1.

Baltic alliance proved to be unrealizable. As in the former conferences the question of the relations of the Baltic republics with Soviet Russia occupied first place in the talks, although separate discussions were also held on means of strengthening economic relations between the attending states.[20] Estonia was already conducting peace talks with the Soviet government, and *Pravda* claimed that the conference was nothing but a maneuver by Mejerovič, the Latvian Foreign Minister, to sabotage these talks.[21] An American observer, however, believed that the Estonians had inspired the talks in order to wring more concessions from the Russians at Tartu.[22]

Various conflicting reports about the proceedings were broadcast during the conference, some glowing, some gloomy, but, in all, the conference seems to have produced no positive results. A number of resolutions were passed, but they were emasculated by divisions among the participating nations. There was a resolution against the separate conclusion of peace with Russia, but Estonia voted against it and Lithuania abstained.[23] The Estonians continued their talks with the Soviet delegation at Tartu. Plans were put forward and approved for a military convention among Finland, Estonia, Latvia, and Poland. Lithuania abstained, claiming that the Poles must evacuate all the territory claimed by Lithuania before any such convention could be concluded.[24] Poland agreed that the Western powers should grant the Baltic states *de jure* recognition, but itself refused to grant Lithuania any recognition until it received "satisfactory" guarantees for Poles living in Lithuania.[25] The conference

[20] See Tarnowski, *Two Polish Attempts to Bring About a Central-East European Organization*, pp. 3-4.

[21] *Pravda*, No. 292 (December 27, 1919).

[22] Haynes (Helsinki) to Secretary of State, telegram, January 23, 1920, United States, National Archives, 861.00/6212.

[23] *Neue Zürcher Zeitung*, No. 139 (January 26, 1920).

[24] Klimas, "L'entente baltique," in *Problèmes de la Baltique*, p. 732 (92).

[25] Poland, Ministry of Foreign Affairs, *Documents diplomatiques*, I, 37. It was falsely believed by some that Poland had recognized Lithuania. See Haynes to Secretary of State, telegram, January 23, 1920, United States, National Archives, 861.11/6212.

voted to establish a commission to arbitrate the Polish-Lithuanian dispute over Vilna; the Lithuanians abstained in the absence of instructions from Kaunas, [26] and nothing came of the resolution. Second only to the Polish-Lithuanian dispute as a major obstacle to unity was the Estonian-Latvian dispute over Valga, which prevented those two nations from acting in accord on matters of mutual interest. [27]

As a result of these many conflicts, the conference could accomplish little. Leon Wasilewski, the Polish delegate, later complained that the "anti-democratic, extremely imperialistic stand of the Lithuanian delegation" had destroyed the chances for constructive action. [28] The Lithuanians were still upset by the Polish-Latvian capture of Daugavpils, and they were greatly disappointed when the Estonians and Latvians refused to back them against the Poles at the conference. [29]

After the conference Baltic unity all but collapsed. On February 2, Estonia signed a peace treaty with Soviet Russia on very favorable terms. [30] A joint Latvian-Lithuanian commission to settle the border between the two countries disbanded in March after failing to reach an agreement. [31] A new Baltic conference was held at Warsaw in March with the hope of reestablishing some sort of common action against Russia, but it seems that the Lithuanians were not even formally invited. In a note to the Finnish Foreign Ministry, Voldemaras claimed that Kaunas had learned of the proposed conference only accidentally at the end of February. Since the Lithuanians considered the holding of the conference a violation of a resolution of the Helsinki conference in January for common action against the Soviet government, Voldemaras maintained that the Lithu-

[26] Poland, Ministry of Foreign Affairs, *Documents diplomatiques*, I, 36.
[27] See *Waldibas Wehstnesis*, No. 22 (January 28, 1920).
[28] *Kurjer Polski*, No. 41 (February 11, 1920).
[29] *Waldibas Wehstnesis*, No. 29 (February 5, 1920); Klimas, "L'entente baltique," in *Problèmes de la Baltique*, p. 732 (92).
[30] See *Neue Zürcher Zeitung*, No. 184 (February 2, 1920).
[31] The dispute was settled by arbitration in 1921. See Šapoka (ed.), *Lietuvo istorija*, pp. 577-78.

anian government was now no longer bound by that resolution.[32] Sleževičius was quoted by *Kurjer Polski* as asserting that Lithuania had nothing to gain in the future by seeking to cooperate with its neighbors against the Russians and must now conduct its relations with Russia directly and alone.[33]

The participation of the Estonians and Latvians in the Warsaw talks served to deepen the breach between Lithuania and its two northern neighbors.[34] Preparations were made for another conference of the Baltic states, to be held at Riga on May 15, but mainly through Lithuanian opposition it was postponed until August. On May 11 the Lithuanian government accused the Poles of seeking to aggrandize themselves and at the same time to establish a hegemony over their neighbors, thereby making a Baltic alliance impossible.[35]

Of the Entente powers during this period, only Great Britain gave the Lithuanians direct aid, but the British government still refused *de jure* recognition, maintaining that such action could be taken only in concert with France and the United States.[36] Nevertheless, the British gave the Lithuanians extremely important help. During a visit to London in February, 1920, Galvanauskas concluded a financial agreement whereby British financiers were to aid in the establishment of a banking system in Lithuania.[37] Toward the end of March another agreement with the National Metal and Chemical Bank, London, was concluded on the exploitation of the Lithuanian state forests,

[32] *Kurjer Polski*, No. 79 (March 20, 1920). Cf. the report on the conference by Mejerovič, quoted in *Kurjer Polski*, No. 87 (March 28, 1920). Polish writers tend to regard Lithuania's war with Russia as having ended with the fall of Daugavpils, and so they even dispute the accuracy of calling the July, 1920, treaty between Lithuania and Soviet Russia a "peace treaty."

[33] *Kurjer Polski*, No. 79 (March 20, 1920).

[34] Klimas, "L'entente baltique," in *Problèmes de la Baltique*, p. 735 (95)..See also United States, *Foreign Relations: 1920*, III, 648.

[35] Klimas, "L'entente baltique," in *Problèmes de la Baltique*, p. 736 (96). Cf. *Pravda*, No. 90 (April 28, 1920).

[36] *Parliamentary Debates: Commons* (London, 1920), CXXVII, 41; CXXIX, 240.

[37] *Monitor Polski*, No. 39 (February 18, 1920); *Neue Zürcher Zeitung*, No. 267 (February 16, 1920).

according to which Lithuania was also to obtain a gold loan.[38] The emergence of the Baltic states with relatively stable foundations in early 1920 must be credited to the British, who thus gained a strong foothold in these states.[39]

The French continued to support Poland and ignore Lithuania, although some French commentators expressed dismay at the strong position the British had gained and criticized their own government for its failure to act along similar lines. In an article in *Le Temps*, Charles Rivet complained that the French government had missed its opportunity to bring about a Polish-Lithuanian union and that the consequences could now be plainly seen. He declared that even the French military mission in Kaunas was distrusted, some calling it too pro-Polish, others too pro-Lithuanian.[40] In March a member of the French Chamber of Deputies criticized the government sharply for having stood aside and allowed British interests to establish themselves firmly in Lithuania. The deputy called the policy of supporting a single large state in Eastern Europe a mistaken one.[41] Despite these occasional voices, however, the French government continued to back the Poles as the chief link in the *cordon sanitaire*, in which Lithuania was to find its own place after Poland had been satisfied.[42] In return, France continued to reap a harvest of Lithuanian ill will.[43]

The United States persevered in its policy of nonrecognition,

---

[38] *Times* (London), April 19, 1920; *Neue Zürcher Zeitung*, No. 654 (April 20, 1920). The agreement, to last fifteen years, gave the British concern the exclusive right to fell, transport, work, ship, and sell timber from the state forests. See the report of John Gade, April 3, 1920, United States, National Archives, 860M.61721.

[39] See the editorial in *Neue Zürcher Zeitung*, No. 234 (February 11, 1920). When the concessions were first being discussed toward the end of 1919, one American observer foresaw that such agreements on flax and timber would give England "complete control over all foreign trade" of Lithuania. Report of John A. Lehrs, November 10, 1919, United States, National Archives, 861.00/6167.

[40] *Le Temps*, January 25, 1920. Birontas criticized the mission as being too pro-Russian (*Bermontininkams Lietuvą užpuolus*, pp. 34-35).

[41] Gaihard-Bancel, March 27, 1920, as quoted in Chambon, *La Lithuanie pendant la Conférence de la Paix*, pp. 162-66.

[42] See Milosz's report on France in *Vienybė Lietuninkų*, No. 5 (February 3, 1920).

[43] See the statement on Lithuanian foreign relations made by Galvanauskas, quoted in *Izvestiia*, No. 100 (May 11, 1920).

seeking mainly to protect the concept of Russia's territorial integrity as a barrier to Japanese designs on large parts of Siberia. On January 17, Vileišis wrote to Lansing requesting recognition, pointing out that plans had already been completed for the calling of the Constituent Assembly,[44] but the United States government refused to act and stood by the position taken in Secretary Lansing's letters of October 15, 1919, and January 7, 1920.[45] On March 24, Vileišis reported to Kaunas that he expected recognition to be forthcoming soon, but he seems to have relied too much on the fact that a resolution favoring recognition of Lithuanian independence would soon be introduced before the United States Senate. The opinions of the other members of his mission, appended to the same report, were not so optimistic.[46] The American government made another concession to Lithuanian national feeling in March by ending the practice of stamping visas "Russia (Lithuania only)" and substituting instead just "Lithuania." But in its letter of March 8 announcing this move, the State Department hastily added, "In taking this step you will, of course, understand that the Department is no wise, either directly or indirectly, passing upon any question involving the recognition of Lithuania as a sovereign state."[47]

Although its diplomatic activities had met with but little success, the Lithuanian mission to America was extremely important for its financial activities. One of its main purposes was to collect money for the Kaunas government. To this end, three ways were offered the American Lithuanians to aid their native land: direct purchase of Lithuanian government bonds, exchange of United States Liberty Bonds for Lithuanian government bonds, and purchase of stamps which could be sent to

[44] MS in Documents Relating to the Lithuanian National Movement (Joseph Hertmanowicz).

[45] *Waldibas Wehstnesis*, No. 41 (February 19, 1920).

[46] MS Documents Relating to the Lithuanian National Movement (Lithuanian National Council).

[47] MS in Documents Relating to the Lithuanian National Movement (Lithuanian National Council).

relatives or friends in Lithuania, who could there exchange them for Lithuanian currency.[48] The response of the American Lithuanians was most encouraging, even though the Socialists seem to have opposed the loan drive because they were dissatisfied with the make-up of the Galvanauskas cabinet.[49] The American Lithuanians bought some $1,800,000 worth of Lithuanian bonds; and even though some embezzlement cropped up,[50] it was later said that "without American aid, it would have been very difficult for our government to get started in the beginning—it would have been mired in debts up to its ears."[51] The American Lithuanians were also urged to make themselves heard in Washington with the demand that the American government refuse any loans to Poland until the latter had withdrawn from all of Lithuania.[52]

Many of the émigrés had wanted to return to Lithuania to take part in the building of the new state, but most of these hopes were destined to be disappointed. The financial crisis in Lithuania had made jobs scarce, and the government was forced to take measures restricting the flow of foreign currency into Lithuania. In March, 1920, Naruševičius reported from Lithuania that just 40,000 American Lithuanians, with just $1,000 apiece, could buy up almost all of Lithuania.[53] The government was therefore compelled to restrict land purchases by persons coming from abroad, with the result that some ill will arose between the Kaunas government and the emigration.[54]

Relations continued to be bad with the Poles, who still saw the ogre of Germany behind every move the Lithuanians made.[55] Although the Poles continually hoped that the Lithuanians were becoming more amenable to making an agreement on

[48] *Vienybė Lietuvninkų*, No. 49 (December 3, 1919).
[49] *Ibid.*, No. 2 (January 14, 1920).
[50] Kemešis, "Amerikos lietuvių kova," in *Pirmasis dešimtmetis*, I, 61.
[51] Šapoka (ed.), *Lietuvos istorija*, p. 657.
[52] *Vienybė Lietuvninkų*, No. 4 (January 28, 1920).
[53] *Ibid.*, No. 12 (March 24, 1920).
[54] See Kemešis, "Amerikos lietuvių kova," in *Pirmasis dešimtmetis*, I, 61-62.
[55] See *Kurjer Polski*, No. 45 (February 15, 1920).

Polish terms,[56] these hopes were unfounded. In February, 1920, a group of Kaunas Poles declared that they recognized Lithuania's independence and that Vilna should belong to the Lithuanian state.[57] This announcement was met with surprise in the Warsaw press, which wanted to reserve judgment until it could ascertain whether the Kaunas Poles (sometimes called *żubry* or "buffaloes") had made this declaration under pressure. Something of a paranoic strain could occasionally be noted in the Polish press, as, for instance, when the claim was raised that a Czech scientific mission visiting Kaunas was really there only to plan a common action against Poland.[58]

The Polish press sought to picture Lithuania in the darkest tones possible.[59] Throughout the entire term of office of the Galvanauskas cabinet, reports were published in Poland presenting Lithuania as a land of political anarchy. In November, 1919, the report was that Sleževičius had succeeded in overthrowing Galvanauskas.[60] In December, 1919, Sleževičius was said just to be plotting Galvanauskas's overthrow.[61] In January, 1920, Polish newspapers claimed that Yčas had replaced Galvanauskas.[62] In February, 1920, it was reported that "anti-government" elements were raising their heads in Lithuania and that Sleževičius was agitating against the Constituent Assembly.[63] In April, just before the scheduled elections to the Constituent Assembly, one Warsaw newspaper predicted that the Christian Democrats would fail to win a majority of the

[56] See *Monitor Polski*, No. 47 (February 27, 1920).

[57] *Kurjer Polski*, No. 48 (February 18, 1920). Cf. *Neue Zürcher Zeitung*, No. 1285 August 26, 1929).

[58] *Kurjer Polski*, No. 51 (February 21, 1920).

[59] See *ibid.*, No. 54 (February 24, 1920); *Pravda*, No. 61 (March 20, 1920). The reports on Lithuania in the Polish press were similar to those on Poland in German newspapers, such as *Die Post*.

[60] *Kurjer Polski*, No. 304 (November 19, 1919). Sleževičius was still in Germany at this time.

[61] *Monitor Polski*, No. 282 (December 27, 1919).

[62] *Waldibas Wehstnesis*, No. 23 (January 29, 1920).

[63] *Kurjer Polski*, No. 54 (February 24, 1920). Sleževičius had long before been chosen as the symbol of anti-Polonism in Lithuania. See *Monitor Polski*, No. 47 (February 27, 1920).

seats and that therefore the elections would be broken up by the army.[64]

Although talks were held in January between the Polish and the Lithuanian governments on the exchange of prisoners,[65] there were no new attempts to bring about a political settlement between the two states, beyond what had been done at the Helsinki conference in January. In March, fighting broke out in the region of Antakol. Each side claimed that the other had begun the hostilities. The Poles attacked on March 14, claiming that the Lithuanians had violated the neutral zone by attacking Polish outposts.[66] Fighting lasted for about a week. The Lithuanians claimed that their first advance had been legitimate and that the Polish action was not a retaliation but a premeditated attack in order to advance the line of demarcation another 4 kilometers to the west.[67] On March 31 the British Ambassador to Paris, Lord Derby, brought the matter before the Conference of Ambassadors at the urging of the British Foreign Office, with the suggestion that Poland be warned against further advances into Lithuania.[68] On April 1 it was decided to notify the Poles, through the French mission at Warsaw, that the Allied and Associated Powers would tolerate no violation of the lines of demarcation by the Poles.[69] The message was given to the Polish government on April 3, and the Polish Foreign Minister, S. Pasek, visibly upset by the condemnation, persuaded the French representative that the Lithuanians and not the Poles were at fault for the flare-up.[70]

The relations between Lithuania and Germany were now being adjusted to the new situation brought about by the evacuation of the German troops and the expulsion of Zimmerle. The

---

[64] *Naród*, No. 14 (April 16, 1920).

[65] *Vienybė Lietuvninkų*, No. 6 (February 11, 1920).

[66] See Poland, Ministry of Foreign Affairs, *Documents diplomatiques*, I, 37-38.

[67] Voldemaras, *Les relations russo-polono-lituaniennes*, (Paris: Demineaux et Brisset, p. 32.

[68] Conference of Ambassadors, Notes of a Meeting Held at Quai d'Orsay, Paris, No. 27 (March 31, 1920).

[69] Text in American Embassy, E.S.H. Bulletins, No. 325 (April 7, 1920).

[70] *Ibid,*, No. 341 (April 13, 1920).

Poles maintained that the Germans were still the evil genius behind the Lithuanian government, as did the Bolsheviks, when they were not busy gleefully pointing out that Lithuania could serve as a bridge from Germany to Russia.[71] Actually it would appear that the English had now completely supplanted the Germans in Lithuania, although, because of the disorderly internal conditions, there seems to have been considerable activity by German spies.[72] The direct relations between Germany and Lithuania apparently were restricted to attempts at trade, and even these were under close supervision by the Allies. The Lithuanians furthermore openly demonstrated their independence of the Germans by coopting four representatives from the Memelland to the Taryba on March 20 and by exerting an economic blockade on the region with the aim of bringing it under Lithuanian domination.[73]

Throughout the early months of 1920 the inclination in Lithuania toward seeking peace with Soviet Russia was growing. The settlement between Estonia and Russia showed that an agreement would not necessarily bring down the wrath of the West on the head of the signer.[74] On February 17 a Lithuanian Red Cross mission under Juozas Alekna set out for Russia by way of Latvia in order to open negotiations for an exchange of prisoners.[75] The Russians, for their part, were showing an inclination to regard the revolution in Lithuania as having failed because the Lithuanian people did not want it. In March, Kapsukas, who had been in Russia since the fall of Vilna to the Poles in April, 1919, delivered a speech in Moscow in which he

[71] See *Kurjer Polski*, No. 45 (February 15, 1920); *Pravda*, No. 62 (March 21, 1920).

[72] See the report by John Gade, March 16, 1920, United States, National Archives, 860N.00/1.

[73] See American Embassy, E.S.H. Bulletins, No. 780 (July 23, 1920). See also *Vienybè Lietuvninkų*, No. 17 (April 28, 1920); Kellor and Hatvany, *Security against War*, I, 265.

[74] See Sleževičius's interpretation of the signing of peace, quoted in *Kurjer Polski*, No. 62 (March 3, 1920).

[75] *Kurjer Polski*, No. 65 (March 6, 1920); *Vienybè Lietuvninkų*, No. 13 (March 31, 1920).

claimed that the bourgeoisie had proved stronger in Lithuania than in Russia because it had allied itself with the landholding peasants. Asserting that it might be some time before Lithuania would be ripe for soviet rule, he advised his fellow Communists to concentrate on strengthening the party organization rather than on attempting "action which can be easily suppressed."[76] Although Kapsukas did not renounce revolution entirely, his intention to present a softer line is clear. The Russians wanted to persuade the Baltic states that they had nothing to expect from the West. As proof of this contention, *Izvestiia*, in February, published documents captured from the White Russians which pointed out the desire of the American government to uphold Russia's territorial integrity.[77]

In March, *Laisvė*, a newspaper published by the Christian Democrats, reportedly criticized Voldemaras as an "idealist with closed eyes."

We are fighting with Russia. And when all nations are trying to make peace with the Bolsheviks, what is Voldemaras doing? . . . Voldemaras must finally realize that the interests of the Entente are different from those of Lithuania and that their policy does not correspond with that of Lithuania.[78]

A memorandum originating in late March from the Lithuanian mission at Berlin also stressed the need to make peace, but approached the problem from a different viewpoint. Asserting that the Russian Bolsheviks were not a passing phenomenon, it claimed that Lloyd George was now definitely inclined toward making peace with the Communists. When that peace was concluded, the English would probably recognize Lithuania and its northern neighbors. Since "England was the only world power factor, on which the fate of Lithuania depends," Lithuanian policy must be set on the same lines as English policy. The Lithuanians had already fallen behind in seeing the trends in British policy, since Lloyd George had apparently become

[76] *Pravda*, No. 55 (March 11, 1920).
[77] *Izvestiia*, No. 24 (February 4, 1920).
[78] *Laisvė*, No. 169 (March 29, 1920), as quoted in *Naród*, No. 15 (April 7, 1920).

more favorable toward peace, Churchill's policy had apparently been abandoned, and Asquith would be the quickest of all to conclude peace. Soviet Russia was presumably seeking to make peace with the Baltic states as a stepping stone to reaching a settlement with Great Britain. Therefore, Lithuania, in order to get the best possible terms, should act quickly and make peace lest a direct British-Russian agreement came first, in which case the Russians would be less generous with the Lithuanians, having nothing more to gain by it. Estonia had already acted without any unfavorable consequences for its relations with the West. Lithuania, having delayed so long, should now act immediately, before it was too late.[79]

On March 31 Voldemaras acted, sending a dispatch to Moscow through Zaunius in Riga. Whether the note was prompted by an earlier Russian communication cannot be determined from the sources available. In his message Voldemaras asserted that the Lithuanians had been fighting only in self-defense, and that since there were no longer any Russian soldiers on Lithuanian territory, the Lithuanian government was ready to make peace:

The major condition of peace is the recognition of the complete independence of Lithuania in its ethnographic boundaries, i.e., including parts of the former guberniyas of Vilna, Kaunas, Suwalki, and Grodno, with Vilna as its capital. If the Russian Government is agreeable to our offer, we will send our delegates to work out details and to sign a peace agreement. The time and place of the meeting will be decided by mutual agreement.[80]

On April 2, Chicherin answered this offer:

The Russian Soviet Government, always unalterably true to the principles of self-determination of nations, has never made nor will it make any exception toward Lithuania, and it accepts your offer to enter into talks to work out and conclude an agreement, which should establish peaceful relations between Russia and Lithuania, and one of the conditions for which is the recognition of the independence of the latter. The Russian Soviet Government agrees to apply the ethno-

[79] Anonymous manuscript, Šaulys Archives, f. 23.
[80] *Pravda*, No. 73 (April 3, 1920).

graphic principle as the basis for determining the borders of the Lithuanian state, leaving the discussion of details and the question of the national character of this or that city to the proposed conference of representatives of both governments. We propose the opening of the the conference at Moscow on April 15.[81]

On April 4, Voldemaras demanded a clear answer as to whether Vilna and Grodno were recognized as Lithuanian territory, claiming that recognition must be granted before the talks could begin.[82] On April 8, Chicherin expressed "surprise" that the Lithuanians found his earlier declaration "insufficiently exact." He asserted that *de jure* recognition could only be granted in a treaty and that the boundaries could be decided only after the Lithuanians had presented proof of their claims.[83] The Lithuanians finally accepted this stand, and after a Lithuanian proposal that the talks be held at Tallinn was rejected, they agreed to Moscow as the site of the negotiations. The Lithuanians announced that they were sending a delegation of thirty, headed by Naruševičius, which left Kaunas on April 30.[84]

On April 28 the Poles had opened an attack on the Bolsheviks, and so, when the Russian-Lithuanian talks finally started in Moscow on May 7, the Bolsheviks were probably more eager than ever to make some sort of agreement with Poland's northern neighbor. At the opening session, Joffe, the chairman of the Russian delegation, declared that since fighting was not at the moment being conducted between Lithuania and Soviet Russia, the talks could concern themselves with the establishment of relations rather than with terms of peace. He further stressed the common dislike of Polish ambitions and expressed the hope that Lithuania would be a corridor to the West for Russia.[85]

At this time the Communists in Russia were publicly washing their hands of Lithuanian internal affairs. *Komunistas*, the organ

[81] *Ibid.*   [82] *Ibid.*, No. 79 (April 14, 1920).
[83] *Ibid.* See also *Monitor Polski*, No. 88 (April 17, 1920).
[84] *Neue Zürcher Zeitung*, Nos. 755 (May 6, 1920) and 757 (May 7, 1920).
[85] *Izvestiia*, No. 99 (May 9, 1920). The Poles viewed the talks as an anti-Polish forum. See *Neue Zürcher Zeitung*, No. 858 (May 23, 1920).

of the Lithuanian Communist Party, declared that the Lithuanian workers should not expect intervention from Russia on their behalf. In explanation of the Moscow government's negotiations with the nationalist government, the paper stated, "Since the Lithuanian workers have failed to throw the bourgeoisie off their shoulders, it is necessary for the sake of peace to open diplomatic relations with the old regime and to negotiate with it."[86] At the same time, however, the Lithuanian Communists declared that they could not make a *Burgfriede* with the existing Lithuanian government, since its "bourgeois" leaders were only British "tools."[87] Thus, although the Russian government disavowed any intentions of intervening in Lithuanian affairs, the Russian Communist Party, which directed the government, still considered itself free to help the Lithuanian Communists, who formed an integral part of the Russian Communist Party.

Actual negotiations between the Russians and the Lithuanians began on May 8, and the Russians again refused to make a special declaration recognizing Lithuania's independence. A clash immediately arose as the Bolsheviks rejected the Lithuanians' historical claims to such non-Lithuanian areas as Grodno.[88] The Lithuanian delegation included Rosenbaum and Semashko, but these two seemed unable to convince the Russians that they were representative of the Jewish and Belorussian populations, respectively, in the territory claimed by the Lithuanian government.[89] The Lithuanian argument that Grodno in Lithuanian hands would be a buffer zone between Russia and Poland was rejected by Joffe, who claimed that if Grodno did not go to Lithuania, it should belong to Russia, not to Poland. The territorial claims were referred to a special commission, and the talks had to be recessed in mid-May while the Lithuanian dele-

[86] *Komunistas*, No. 125 (May 26, 1920).
[87] *Ibid.*   [88] *Izvestiia*, No. 102 (May 13, 1920).
[89] The Russians rejected the idea that a region or a "part" of a nationality could determine itself. They argued that all members of a particular nationality had to belong to one political entity. See the discussion of May 9, in *Izvestiia*, No. 108 (May 20, 1920).

gation returned to Kaunas for further instructions.[90] Resumption of the negotiations was then delayed by the slow transfer of power from the Lithuanian Provisional Government to the newly elected Constituent Assembly.

The elections for the assembly had been held as scheduled on April 14 and 15, with some 90 percent of the electorate turning out to vote. The results were a victory for the Christian Democrats, just as had been the case in the elections to the State Conference held at Kaunas in January, 1919. Of the 112 seats, the Christian Democrats held 59, the Liaudininkai 29, the Social Democrats 13, and the various minorities 11.[91] The Communists had boycotted the elections.[92]

The assembly met on May 15. In his welcoming speech, Smetona, after praising the struggle of the Lithuanian people for independence, declared:

Working against Lithuanian independence, our enemies up to now have tried to tell the world that the Lithuanian nation does not want to become an independent state, that the aim of independence was an effort of only a small group of persons who were in opposition to the national will.

He claimed that the elections had proved the reality of the national desire for independence and went on to proclaim the end of the Provisional Government:

The task of the Provisional Government is ended. The State Council, the State President, the Cabinet of Ministers, the State Control, the General Staff, having brought Lithuania to the point of the Constituent Assembly, now withdraw and turn over to that body all the authority of the country. The Provisional Government leaves an established state apparatus, with all its branch organs, armed military forces, organized national finances, established political and economic

[90] See *Kurjer Polski*, No. 154 (June 8, 1920).

[91] Lithuania, Constituent Assembly, *Steigiamojo Seimo darbai*, p. 1. See also *Neue Zürcher Zeitung*, No. 741 (May 4, 1920).

[92] Kapsukas later called the boycott a mistake: "Our party stands for exploitation of the parliaments for the ends of Communist revolution. Therefore we should have entered even the Constituent Assembly." He claimed that the boycott had aided only the Social Democrats, and had not served any useful purpose for the Communists. *Komunistas*, No. 124 (May 9, 1920).

relations with foreign states—in a word, the established fact of an independent government.

He expressed his regrets that Vilna and Klaipeda were not represented in the assembly, but he declared that the achievement of the national aims was now the task of the Constituent Assembly.[93]

After Smetona's speech the assembly expressed its thanks to the British by a standing ovation for the British observers in the hall.[94] Alexandras Stulginskis was then elected president of the Constituent Assembly. In his acceptance speech, he expressed the indebtedness of the country to the Taryba, saying that through it the Constituent Assembly had been made possible: "Although it did not have a formal mandate, still it functioned more through divining the national will."[95]

Stulginskis thereupon declared that a formal declaration of independence had to be made:

With all authority we must declare to the world that Lithuania has broken all state ties which ever bound it to other states! The Constituent Assembly declares Lithuania to be reestablished as an independent state! (Enthusiastic agreement.)[96]

All the members of the Constituent Assembly rose to agree with the declaration:

The Constituent Assembly of Lithuania, expressing the will of the Lithuanian people, proclaims that the independent Lithuanian State is reestablished as a democratic republic with ethnic frontiers and free of all state ties which had existed with other states.[97]

The Galvanauskas cabinet was requested to remain in office until a new one could be organized, but the Provisional Government as such had yielded its place.[98]

----

[93] Lithuania, Constituent Assembly, *Steigiamojo Seimo darbai*, pp. 1-2. There were unofficial representatives from both Vilna and Klaipeda present at this opening session.

[94] *Ibid.*, p. 3. It is recorded in the proceedings of the assembly that the Social Democrats refused to take part in this action, remaining seated.

[95] *Ibid.*, p. 4.   [96] *Ibid.*   [97] *Ibid.*, p. 5.

[98] The new cabinet, under Kazys Grinius, was formally installed on June 11, 1920, and the word "provisional" was then dropped from all official documents.

On the heels of the meeting of the Constituent Assembly came long-sought and long-awaited recognition. France, actually anticipating the meeting, granted *de facto* recognition on May 11. On July 4 came *de facto* recognition from Poland.[99] Only the American government of the Big Three in the West still refused to act. On August 10 the United States Secretary of State, Bainbridge Colby, made clear the American stand in a note to the Italian Ambassador to Washington, Avezzana. Since "no final decision should or can be made without the consent of Russia," the United States, in "loyal friendship," to Russia, would withhold any recognition of the border governments. It could recognize only Poland, Armenia, and Finland.[100]

To the east the Lithuanians' negotiations with Soviet Russia had yet to be completed, and as matters developed, they turned out to be inextricably bound up with the renewed Polish-Russian war. A new memorandum from the Lithuanian mission at Berlin, dated May 21, 1920, but anonymous, suggested that the Lithuanians exploit the situation to seize Vilna by force, but that this action be taken independently of Russia in order to avoid any indebtedness to the Bolsheviks. When the Polish offensive had weakened, Kaunas should make a demand for Vilna. If the Poles refused, the Lithuanians should attack.[101]

The Lithuanians had no need to issue an ultimatum to the Poles since they found support from the British for their claims to Vilna.[102] In early July, when the Polish representative at Spa, Grabski, sought aid against the Bolsheviks, who had now assumed the offensive, the British demanded the withdrawal of Polish forces from all territory east of the Bug River, the line of demarcation of December 8, in favor of the Russians, with the exception of Vilna, which was to be turned over to the

---

[99] See Poland, Ministry of Foreign Affairs, *Documents diplomatiques*, I, 40-41.
[100] United States, *Foreign Relations: 1920*, III, 465.
[101] Šaulys Archives, f. 23.
[102] Western diplomats actually feared that the Lithuanians would join the Russians in attacking the Poles if Vilna were not yielded. See United States, *Foreign Relations: 1920* III, 650-51.

Lithuanians.[103] With this "knife at his throat," the condition for Entente aid to Poland, Grabski agreed on July 10.[104] On July 12, closely following this turn of events, Russia and Lithuania signed a peace treaty. By the treaty Vilna was ceded to Lithuania, while the border in Suwalki between Poland and Lithuania was to be set by mutual agreement between those two parties.[105]

Polish partisans and regular troops resisted the advance of the Lithuanians into Vilna, with the result that the Russians occupied the city first, taking it from the Poles on July 14.[106] Lithuanian troops arrived in Vilna a few days later, but the Russians refused to yield the city to them, and a sort of condominium was set up, with the Russians holding final authority. Subsequently the Lithuanians also advanced into Suwalki, crossing the line of December 8 to occupy Sejny.[107]

The actions of the Bolsheviks and the Lithuanians in Vilna gave rise to charges that there was a secret protocol to the treaty between them whereby the Lithuanians would grant the Bolsheviks access to the Polish front. Voldemaras later admitted this contention in a letter to the League of Nations, in which he asserted that the Bolsheviks had offered a choice: either the Lithuanians were to attack the Poles or they were to grant passage to Bolshevik troops. The Lithuanians had chosen the latter course, since, as Voldemaras explained, the Poles, by occupying Vilna in April, 1919, had already arrogated to themselves the right of passage through the region.[108]

---

[103] United States, National Archives, 184.612/838; Zoltowski, *Border of Europe*, p 204.

[104] Budecki, *Stosunki polsko-litewskie*, p. 27.

[105] *Izvestiia*, No. 154 (July 15, 1920).

[106] See Poland, Ministry of Foreign Affairs, *Documents diplomatiques*, I, 42; Lithuania, Constituent Assembly, *Steigiamojo Seimo darbai*, p. 238; Arenz, *Polen und Russland*, p. 89.

[107] Chase claims that the advance was made at the request of the inhabitants of the area (*Lithuania*, p. 277). Budecki considers it an act of unprovoked aggression (*Stosunki polsko-litewskie*, pp. 28-29).

[108] Voldemaras, *Les relations russo-polono-lituaniennes*, p. 709. Text of protocol in *Times* (London), August 5, 1920.

It would seem that the Lithuanians had little choice, for the Bolsheviks could easily have marched on Kaunas had they so wished. The Lithuanians sought to get as much as they could for themselves without worrying about how much they might be aiding the Soviet propaganda machine or even about what might be the consequences to them of a Russian victory over the Poles. They wanted Vilna regardless of other considerations. They believed that the Russians were yielding Vilna as a "beau geste," "to inspire confidence in their good faith among the Western nations."[109]

Despite their promises, the Bolsheviks did not immediately relinquish control of the city of Vilna. This led to unexpected opposition in the Lithuanian Constituent Assembly when the peace treaty was brought up on August 8 for ratification. The Social Democrats opposed ratification on the grounds that Vilna had not been clearly ceded. Kairys demanded that the Bolsheviks evacuate Vilna before the treaty was ratified.[110] Sleževičius, agreeing in principle with Kairys, backed the government, saying that ratification would strengthen its hand in pressing its demands for the city.[111] Other supporters of ratification claimed the *de jure* recognition in Article 1 was the most important part of the treaty, since it confirmed the "act of separation of Lithuania from Russia."[112] Grinius noted that the Bolsheviks were not giving Vilna to the Lithuanians "for our beautiful eyes or from good will," but to protect their right wing.[113] Puryckis argued that only if the treaty were ratified could the Lithuanians claim that Vilna was indisputably theirs.[114] Three Social Democrats were the only opponents of ratification at the third and final reading when the treaty was formally accepted.[115]

---

[109] Voldemaras, *Les relations russo-polono-lituaniennes*, p. 9. On July 16, Puryckis claimed that Tallents had stated that the Lithuanians had made a wise move in concluding peace. Lithuania, Constituent Assembly, *Steigiamojo Seimo darbai*, p. 238. Whether Tallents knew of the secret protocol is not clear.

[110] Lithuania, Constituent Assembly, *Steigiamojo Seimo darbai*, pp. 301-2.

[111] *Ibid.*, p. 302. [112] *Ibid.*, p. 304. [113] *Ibid.*, p. 305.

[114] *Ibid.*, p. 311. [115] *Ibid.*, p. 312.

Over the years, the Lithuanians have pointed to the peace treaty with Russia as the culmination of the national movement, since through it Lithuania's independence was recognized by the Russians themselves. In 1920, however, it might well have been only the preface to the collapse of that movement. Outside events made it what it came to be. The "miracle of the Vistula" in August, 1920, when the Russian advance westward was stopped and the Poles again resumed the attack, is even more a turning point in the affirmation of Lithuanian independence. While the subsequent events, including the Vilna affair, are outside the province of this study, it must be pointed out that had the Poles not stopped the Bolshevik advance, Lithuania might well have fallen under Soviet control in spite of the peace treaty. The Bolsheviks had signed a treaty with an independent Georgia at about the same time, but that state, lacking outside help, was unable to resist Bolshevik infiltration and invasion. Lithuania might well have met with a similar fate. Vilna would have served as an entering wedge for the Bolsheviks to conquer Lithuania. In fact, Kapsukas had come there in July with the Red Army, and under its protection he might have established a firm basis for a coup.[116] It is true that the Polish victory over the Russians in August, 1920, cost the Lithuanians possession of Vilna, but it may well have saved them Lithuania.

[116] The Red Army finally turned over the city to the Lithuanians at the end of August, and Kapsukas, who had been working openly up to that time, then went into underground work. See Šarmaitis, "V. Mickevičius-Kapsukas," in Būtėnas and Sprindis (eds.), *Lietuvių literatūra*, II, 41. Cf. the report by Evans E. Young, August 6, 1920, United States, National Archives, 860N.00/6.

X

Lithuania as a National State

A NUMBER of theories have been offered to explain how the Lithuanian national state came into being. These theories range from claims that the Lithuanians, fighting off all enemies by themselves, erected the state almost without any outside aid, to violent attacks on Germany or on the Western powers as having invented the state, if not the nation, for sinister purposes of their own. Actually there can be no one-sentence "explanation." The establishment of Lithuania was an outgrowth of the Russian revolutions, a by-product of the First World War, and a reflection of the twentieth century *Zeitgeist* of democracy and national self-determination. At the same time it was the culmination of a particular national movement. Any theory purporting to explain Lithuania's emergence as a national state must consider all these aspects. Furthermore, internal and external events were inseparably connected; neither can be understood in isolation from the other.

In the period from 1918 to 1920 the Lithuanian national state evolved from a council of twenty-two men with no definite authority into a regularly constituted and elected government. Although the initiative for organizing the state came from the Lithuanians themselves, they were dependent on a succession of outside aid to protect them from other outside threats. This aid came in various forms. In November, 1918, the German army, which had established its own order, began to disintegrate, and into its place swept the Russian Red Army, bringing with it a Communist government for Lithuania. The obligation to hold Lithuania against the Bolsheviks had been thrust upon the Germans by the terms of the armistice, but it was more in defense of their own borders than in discharge of a duty that they finally undertook the task of defending Kaunas, in January, 1919. With the stiffening of the German lines, the Bolshevik advance came quickly to a halt.

Largely because of its agrarian program, the Communist regime in Vilna alienated the greater part of the population of Lithuania, and when the German-Lithuanian forces and the Polish army assumed the offensive in the late winter of 1919, the Communists were unable to withstand them. The fall of Vilna to the Poles in April, 1919, marked the virtual elimination of the Communist threat to Lithuania, and the importance of the German forces stationed in Lithuania was sharply reduced. From the spring of 1919 on, the Entente, and especially the British, gradually displaced the German influences, and by December, 1919, German power in Lithuania was almost non-existent.[1]

Having failed to take and hold Lithuania and the other western border regions by force of arms, the Bolsheviks sought to split their opponents by diplomacy, and in September, 1919, they proposed the opening of peace talks with the various Baltic governments. In 1920 the Russians signed treaties with each of the new states, recognizing their independence. The Bolshevik counteroffensive into Poland in the summer of 1920 could conceivably have brought Lithuania to the same fate as Georgia, but the "miracle of the Vistula" ratified the Treaty of Moscow, although at the same time it radically rewrote the territorial settlement.

As neighbors between the great powers of Russia and Germany, Lithuania and Poland have always found their fortunes closely linked. The failure of the Polish ambition to revive the historical union between the Poles and the Lithuanians came

---

[1] Because the Bolshevik threat had been practically eliminated by the time the Entente representatives established themselves in the Baltic area, the Allies tended to underestimate the contribution made to the Baltic governments by the German forces. In February, 1920, General Gough declared that the Bolsheviks had never been a threat to the Baltic nations, and so the Germans should never have been allowed to remain there after November, 1918. *Manchester Guardian*, February 7, 1920.

as a disappointment, even a surprise, to many. Because the Lithuanian nobility had long before accepted Polish language and culture, it was thought that the Lithuanian people would now welcome a renewal of the old ties. But the very success of the earlier Polish expansion now prevented the reestablishment of the union because of the conflicts which it introduced into Lithuania. The problems of landownership and of language, arising separately, fused, and "a joint territorial nationality [of Poles and Lithuanians] became utterly impossible. Poland . . . could claim [its] historical frontiers only so long as the peasant masses did not count politically."[2] Because of the territorial intermingling of the two nationalities, the Lithuanians could not cooperate unreservedly with the Poles until all the sources of conflict were removed, and these sources could not be eradicated so long as Warsaw was free to interfere in favor of the privileged minority.

The idea has been broached that had the Lithuanians not had the Vilna question as a rallying point for anti-Polish feeling, they would have found some other excuse for throwing up a wall against the Poles.[3] This view can claim a great deal of support, since the Vilna question itself was not so much an original cause of conflict as it was a manifestation of the problems arising when two nationalities, which had formerly freely cooperated, each developed its own political ambitions. But at the same time it must be asserted that without the Vilna question, the conflicts would have been much less violent. Even before 1918, Vilna seemed to the Lithuanians to be life itself, however weak their ethnic claims to it were. Once assured of Vilna, they might well have had more confidence and been less suspicious in dealing with the Poles.

Of the alternative Polish policies toward Lithuania, the annexationist variant seemed almost destined to emerge triumphant. The federalist idea had several vital weaknesses: it assumed the guise of a territorial nationalism, or superanational

[2] L. B. Namier, *Avenues of History* (London, 1952), p. 42.
[3] Pobóg-Malinowski, *Najnowsza Historia*, II, Part 1, 186.

patriotism, whereas it was really the extension of an ethnic nationalism; it could not succeed by itself since it was based on the principle of agreement between nations; and it assumed that the other nationalities involved would be willing to follow Polish leadership without offering any forceful opposition.[4] From the beginning the federalists were hamstrung by the aims and actions of the annexationists, who were in the majority and who aroused distrust toward the Poles among other nationalities. The annexationists then used that same distrust to discredit the federalists' "idealism" in Polish circles.

Although the Entente powers repeatedly declared that the military occupation of various areas such as Vilna would not prejudice future political decisions, the new national states were not convinced:

The contrast . . . between the claims of the Conference to determine the boundaries and to impose minority treaties, on the one hand, and, on the other, its obvious impotence to deal with Bolshevism and with accomplished facts could not fail to impress the newer states.[5]

As one Polish writer put it, "Poland will have those lands in the east which it occupies."[6] This proved to be the principle on which the Polish-Lithuanian dispute was "settled" in 1920-23.

Although the federalist sympathies were dominant in the Polish executive into 1920, the annexationists, who controlled the Constituent Assembly, won out because they were the more self-reliant and "practical."[7] Their program could be realized by Poland acting alone, and since Lithuania refused to accept the terms of the federalists, Poland had no choice but to act alone. The federalists, for example, took the great step of recognizing Lithuania's historic claim to Vilna on condition that the Lithuanians unite with the Poles, but they would not recognize

[4] See Skrzynski, *Poland and the Peace*, pp. 36-37.

[5] Reddaway, "The Peace Conference," in *Cambridge History of Poland*, p. 509. If criticism is to be leveled at the Entente for its shortcomings in the problem of Poland's eastern frontier, it should not be for the conference's failure to draw a frontier, but rather for its insistence that it would do so.

[6] Studnicki, *W sprawie stosunku politycznego Polski do iej ziem wschodnich*, p. 9

[7] See Skrzynski, *Poland and the Peace*, p. 46.

the validity of this claim for an independent Lithuania. The Lithuanians saw the shadow of the National Democrats everywhere and therefore distrusted all Polish offers.

Influenced by their disappointment with the Lithuanian refusal to accept Polish leadership and by the violent and unabating reaction of the Lithuanians to Żeligowski's seizure of Vilna in October, 1920, many Polish writers have tended to picture Lithuanian "separatism" as a product of outside intervention. They see the Lithuanian state as having been based solely on anti-Polish fanaticism rather than on a coherent national idea of its own.[8] Russia has generally been condemned for the conflicts before 1914, while Germany has been blamed for the troubles during and after the First World War. This interpretation of Lithuanian nationalism, based on the prima facie evidence of Lithuanian attitudes toward Polish ambitions, was the cause of much of the bad feeling between Poland and Lithuania in 1919 and also of the subsequent failure of the Poles after 1920 to understand the Lithuanian position. The refusal to recognize Lithuanian nationalism as a genuine force was, of course, reflected back in an even stronger resentment against the Poles on the part of the Lithuanians.

It might be said that Germany was the only state which consistently supported Lithuanian independence from November, 1918, on, but this statement should by no means be construed as an acceptance of Polish claims that Lithuania was a German invention. The efforts of 1917 and 1918 to bring Lithuania into the fold of the empire having failed,[9] the new German government after October and November, 1918, wanted Lithuania as an ally against Poland and a buffer against Bolshevik Russia. It is unlikely that the Germans hoped, despite their own military defeat, to keep Lithuania as a client state. It is clear that the Lithuanians had no intention of accepting that role.

[8] Poland, General Staff, *Wojsko litewskie*, p. 26; Budecki, *Stosunki polsko-litewskie*, p. 3.

[9] Germany originally supported Lithuanian separatism as an anti-Russian, and not just an anti-Polish, stratagem.

In the autumn of 1918 the new Lithuanian government was
still very dependent on the Germans. When the German forces
retreated, Lithuania was on the verge of extinction, and, had
the volunteers not come in January, 1919, the Lithuanian
state might have been wiped out. The result would probably
have been a Polish occupation of all of Lithuania, and, although
the Poles might have considered that solution the best, the en-
suing conflicts between the Polish administration and the Lithuanian peasantry would probably have been more bitter than
that which actually came about between the Polish and the
Lithuanian states.

The Western Allies followed essentially a course of adapting
their policies to the changing conditions in Lithuania. They
were at first cold and even unfriendly toward the German-
supported government, but once they saw that this was a
genuinely national organization, wherever its aid came from, the
Western powers undertook, in the spring of 1919, to eradicate
the remaining German footholds in Lithuania. By the end of
1919, with the forced evacuation of the German troops which
had by now become a threat to Lithuania's existence, this task
was completed. The British loan in December, 1919, was perhaps the mark of its completion.

In 1918 none of the three major Western powers expected
Lithuania to become independent. It was generally expected
that the Lithuanians would either unite with Poland or else
accept an autonomous position within a democratic Russia.
The Lithuanians found this attitude hard to overcome, especially
since the Taryba was generally considered a German creation,
and this attitude, in turn, hindered the organization of the
Lithuanian state by making it extremely difficult to obtain aid
abroad. Because of the general refusal to recognize Lithuania
as an entity, even the Lithuanian emigration found it difficult
to send help.

England was the only Western power which even gave *de
facto* recognition in the difficult days of 1918-1919, and that came
only in September, 1919, after peace seemed sure between the

Bolshevik regime and the Baltic states. France withheld recognition until the meeting of the Constituent Assembly, as did Poland. The United States refused to grant recognition until 1922, even though in 1918, in the official commentary to the Fourteen Points, the *de facto* recognition of the border states had been anticipated,[10] and even though the Russian Political Conference in Paris had suggested it.

Despite these refusals to grant recognition, the Allies helped the Lithuanians by supplying aid against the Bolsheviks and by imposing restraints on the Germans and the Poles. The direct aid in 1918 and 1919 was mainly in the form of missions. Very little material aid, other than what the Lithuanians purchased for themselves, was sent.

The Entente may well be said to have come around to supporting Lithuania through the dual fear of the Bolsheviks and the Germans. Even the English, who were the most outspoken in favoring the independence of the Baltic states, had serious reservations about the possibility of their securing a complete and lasting independence. The picture which Lithuania presented to the West was at best a confusing one, since the Poles, who were probably the most well informed of the non-Lithuanian sources, did their utmost to discredit the Lithuanian government. A group of Polish landowners from Lithuania, testifying to an American commission at Warsaw in February, 1919, claimed "that there are too few real Lithuanians and that the average intelligence among the Lithuanians is too low to warrant the formation of an independent Lithuanian state."[11] Another visitor to Lithuania in the fall of 1919 regarded "the separate entity of Lithuania as a farce."[12] The Poles usually argued that the Lithuanians were only demanding independence at German urging. If German "control" were removed, the Lithuanians

[10] Seymour (ed.), *The Intimate Papers of Colonel House*, IV, 195-96.
[11] Report of Coolidge commission, United States, National Archives, 184.-01101/96.
[12] Report of Captain Leach, summarized in Gibson (Warsaw) to American Mission to Paris, telegram, November 15, 1919, United States, National Archives, 861E.00/226½.

would voluntarily unite with Poland. Experience proved that the Lithuanians did not need German guidance to dislike the idea of Polish preponderance. On the other hand, it must be admitted that the backing of the Germans strengthened the determination of the Lithuanians to oppose the Poles.[13]

The reports of the Entente missions stationed in Lithuania were probably the most important factor in the recognition of Lithuania by the Western powers. The sympathetic communications of the American, French, and British teams undoubtedly did much to wipe out the bad impressions received by other visitors such as Hollister and Ross in March, 1919. The Lithuanian delegation to the peace conference also played an important role in this matter, but, without the favorable reports of the Allied missions, the delegation would probably have had a much more difficult time establishing its case.

The chief direct threat to the existence of the Lithuanian government came from the east. The Russian Bolsheviks at first sought to take over the country by direct occupation. Profiting by the disorder in the country, they found the initial advance in December, 1918, relatively easy. When the German retreat halted, the situation changed. The Communist regime moved too quickly in its policies of trying to "remold" society, before it was completely in control of the country, with the result that when the differences between the intentions of the Soviet government and the desires of the Lithuanian people became clear, the Bolshevik forces were not yet strong enough to override their opposition. Wracked by internal disorder, the Soviet Lithuanian regime, even with the aid it got from Moscow and despite its merger with Belorussia, could not withstand the pressure from the newly organized Polish forces.[14]

[13] It is interesting to speculate as to whether the Polish charges of German domination in Lithuania did not backfire in so far as they served to convince the British that Lithuania had to be aided.

[14] The Soviet Lithuanian state was for all intents and purposes destroyed in April, 1919, when Vilna fell. It lived on in name only until July 31, 1920, when the Lithuanian-Belorussian Republic was renamed the Belorussian Soviet Socialist Republic.

At first the failure of the Communist state was attributed by Soviet writers to the faulty agrarian and nationality policies of the Lithuanian Communists and to "unripe" conditions for revolution in Lithuania. But in 1931, Kapsukas declared that Lithuania could not be viewed separately from the rest of Russia, and so, despite certain shortcomings in party policy, Communist rule would have survived but for the foreign intervention.[15] The question whether the Lithuanian Communist state collapsed for internal or external reasons is a rather sterile one. To be sure, it might not have fallen apart had not the Poles and the Lithuanian-German forces moved against it, but it almost certainly could not have stood without aid from Moscow. Therefore the picture is one of "outside intervention" on both sides, with the intervention from Moscow coming first.

It is clear that no new state as small as Lithuania could have arisen without help from abroad, particularly since there were three large neighbors each with its own ideas about Lithuania's future. The collapse of Russia, the defeat of Germany, and the exercise by the Entente of restraint on Poland were essential factors in Lithuania's birth. But the contributions of the Lithuanians themselves must be neither overlooked nor overemphasized.

Because no power had directly supported Lithuanian demands as such, the Lithuanians have tended to minimize the importance of outside help:

We owe no debt of gratitude to any nation or country in the world. In our darkest days, we received no sympathy from any nation; we received no foreign aid in anything. . . . We were surrounded on all sides by uncompromising enemies and treated by the entire civilized world with prejudice, neglect and cold indifference. . . . You are, no doubt, proud of these achievements of your kin, proud of the fact that no nation in the world can come and say, "Lithuania is my work."[16]

[15] See Mickevičius-Kapsukas, "Bor'ba za sovetskuiu vlast'," *Proletarskaia Revoliutsiia*, No. 108 (1931), 65-107.

[16] Povylas Žadeikis to an assembly of Lithuanians in Chicago, February 19, 1920, as quoted in Joseph Hertmanowicz, The Resurrection of Lithuania, MS in Documents Relating to the Lithuanian National Movement.

Lithuania did not singlehandedly fend off Poland, Russia, and Germany, as some writers would have their readers believe, but neither did the outside intervention by itself create the Lithuanian state, as other writers, especially Poles and Russians, would have their readers believe.

The Lithuanian national consciousness had been growing rapidly before 1914, and the First World War offered the Lithuanians an unexpected opportunity. The Russians refused to yield to their demands for autonomy, and when the Germans proved willing to offer aid, the Lithuanians reached out for it. After the collapse of Germany, the Lithuanians rejected Polish aid, which carried the string of federation, and sought Entente support instead. German, and subsequently Entente, aid did not create the national goals of the Lithuanians; it simply aided in their realization.

The Lithuanians showed a strong sense of national unity in seeking to keep their political quarrels strictly a domestic matter. Even now, almost forty years later, very little of the internal political competition for power has been revealed in languages other than Lithuanian. The press releases in the period from 1918 to 1920 gave almost no indication of serious internal disagreements. This may be partly due to the fact that the Lithuanian politicians had no foreign public from which they could seek support. Gabrys was perhaps the only Lithuanian nationalist who was internationally known before 1919, and it is significant that he was the only one to publish his complaints in a Western language.

The Lithuanian state as it finally emerged was essentially a creation of the Russian Lithuanians, who had been educated at Russian universities and who had played leading roles in the rapid development of a Lithuanian national culture in the years before the First World War. Individual members of the emigration were brought into the government, but the Russian Lithuanians kept a tight control on the reins of government. This caused considerable discontent in émigré circles, and differences on this score continued throughout Lithuania's period of independence. Again, however, the national idea surmounted these conflicts, and on the whole, the emigration supported the government in 1918-20, even though it felt that it should be given a bigger voice in the policies of that government. The fact that the Russian Lithuanians, who were closest to all the national problems, also controlled the government was probably the major factor in Lithuania's becoming independent as a national unit rather than entering into some sort of union with any of its neighbors.

Although there were several important Jewish and Belorussian members of the Lithuanian government, Lithuanian nationalists were in complete control. The other nationalities as such had little say in political affairs in general. They each had only one representative in the cabinet, which held the real power of government. But at the same time the Lithuanians did not try to dominate the Belorussians and the Jews by force, instead making extensive cultural and linguistic concessions to them in order to gain their voluntary support. The Poles were the only nationality with whom the Lithuanians could not reach a direct agreement. In November, 1918, the Poles in Lithuania, wanting to be part of Poland rather than just a minority in Lithuania, refused to join the Taryba. In November, 1919, the Lithuanians, now fearful of Polish plots against Lithuania's independence, refused the Poles a place in the government, because of their continued opposition to the separate existence of the new state.

In the final analysis, the decisive factor in the establishment of the Lithuanian national state was the existence of a titanic power struggle in Eastern Europe in 1918-20. In seeking their place in that struggle, the Lithuanians gained first the aid of the Germans and then that of the British. They could not have stood without external aid, but the establishment of the state can be attributed to "foreign intervention" only if the reservation is made that had Lithuania collapsed in 1919, that collapse too would have been largely due to "foreign intervention." Although the Lithuanian government had won the support of the people, mainly through advocating a vigorous program of land reform, it probably would never have had the chance to try to rule had the international situation not been so favorable for such an effort. As Voldemaras learned in 1918, the fate of Lithuania was not simply an internal problem.

Chronology

November 11	Armistice signed in West.
	Installation of First Cabinet of Ministers, headed by Voldemaras.
December 16	Lithuanian Communist government proclaimed in Vilna, although Germans still in occupation.
December 26	Installation of Second Cabinet of Ministers, headed by Sleževičius.

1919

January 2	Lithuanian government withdraws from Vilna, going to Kaunas.
January 4-5	Bolsheviks occupy Vilna.
January 17-23	State Conference in Kaunas (conflict between Taryba and Cabinet of Ministers still unresolved).
January 18	Peace Conference opens in Paris; Lithuanian delegation not admitted.
March 12	Installation of Third Cabinet of Ministers, headed by Dovydaitis.
March 19	French military mission arrives in Kaunas.
April 6	Smetona elected President of Lithuania.
	First English representative, Grant-Watson, arrives in Kaunas.
April 12	Installation of Fourth Cabinet of Ministers, headed by Sleževičius.
April 20	Poles occupy Vilna.
April and May	Šaulys in Warsaw conducting first official talks between Poland and Lithuania.
June 26	Line of demarcation drawn by Entente between Poles and Lithuanians.
July 11	Germans evacuate Kaunas.
July 26	New line of demarcation drawn by Entente between Poles and Lithuanians ("Foch line").
August 26	Polish plot uncovered in Kaunas.
September 11	Soviet Russia suggests to Lithuanians opening of peace talks.
September 23	England grants Lithuania *de facto* recognition.
October 7	Installation of Fifth Cabinet of Ministers, headed by Galvanauskas.
December 8	Peace Conference establishes eastern boundary for Polish administration ("Curzon line").
December 15	Final evacuation of all German troops from Lithuania, effected through General Niessel.

1920

January 17-23	Helsinki conference of Baltic states.
February 21-22	Military revolt in Kaunas.
March 20	Co-option of representatives of Lithuania Minor (Memelland) into Taryba.
April 14-15	Elections to Lithuanian Constituent Assembly.
May 7	Peace talks begun with Soviet Russia.
May 15	Opening of Constituent Assembly.
July 12	Peace treaty signed in Moscow between Soviet Russia and Lithuania; Russia recognizes Lithuania's independence.
October 10	Żeligowski seizes Vilna from Lithuanians.

Personnel of the Lithuanian Nationalist and Communist Governments, 1917–1920

MEMBERS OF THE TARYBA, 1917–1920

Elected, September, 1917

Saliamonas Banaitis, Jonas Basanavičius, Mykolas Biržiška (resigned July, 1918, rejoined November, 1918), Kazimieras Bizauskas, Pranas Dovydaitis, Steponas Kairys (resigned July, 1918), Petras Klimas, Donatas Malinauskas, Vladas Mironas, Stasys Narutavičius (resigned July, 1918), Alfonsas Petrulis, Jurgis Šaulys, Kazys Šaulys, Jokubas Šernas, Antanas Smetona (chairman, September, 1917, to April, 1919, resigned April, 1919, to become State President), Jonas Smilgevičius, Justinas Staugaitis, Aleksandras Stulginskis, Jonas Vailokaitis, Jonas Vileišis (resigned July, 1918, rejoined November, 1918, resigned January, 1919).

Co-opted, July, 1918

Jurgis Alekna, Elizajus Draugelis, Juozas Puryckis, Stasys Šilingas (chairman, April, 1919, to May, 1920), Augustinas Voldemaras, Martynas Yčas

Co-opted, November, 1918

Danielius Alseika (resigned January, 1919), Valdemaras Čarneckis, Liudas Noreika, Vytautas Petrulis

Jewish representatives: Nochman Rachmilevich, Simon Rosenbaum, Jacob Vygodski

Belorussian representatives: Ivan Falkevich, Vaclav Lastauski, Lutskevich (resigned January, 1919), Domonik Semashko, Stankevich (resigned January, 1919), Vladislav Tolocko

Elected, January, 1919

Liudas Brokas, Juozas Ivanauskas, Jonas Jakimavičius, Juozas Kavoliunas, Jonas Šatas

Belorussian representatives: Korchinski, Voronko, Bielecki

Co-opted, March, 1920

Vilius Gaigalaitis, Martynas Jankus, Kristupas Lekšas, Jurgis Strekys

CABINETS OF THE LITHUANIAN GOVERNMENT, 1918–1920

First, November 11, 1918

Prime Minister, Minister of Foreign Affairs, Minister of Defense: Voldemaras
Minister of Internal Affairs: Stašinskis
Minister of Finance: M. Yčas
Minister of Justice: Leonas
Minister of Agriculture: Tubelis
Minister without Portfolio for Belorussian Affairs: Voronko
Minister without Portfolio for Jewis Affairs: Vygodski
Acting Minister of Education: J. Yčas

Second, December 26, 1918

Prime Minister: Sleževičius
Minister of Foreign Affairs: Voldemaras
Minister of Internal Affairs: Vileišis
Minister of Finance: M. Yčas
Minister of Defense: Velykis
Minister of Justice: Leonas
Minister of Agriculture: Tubelis
Minister of Education: M. Biržiška
Minister of Industry and Commerce: Šimkus
Minister without Portfolio: Stulginskis
Minister without Portfolio for Belorussian Affairs: Voronko
Minister without Portfolio for Jewish Affairs: Vygodski
Acting Minister of Foreign Affairs: Janulaitis
Acting Minister of Finance: Čarneckis
Acting Minister of Communications: Šimoliunas

Third, March 12, 1919

Prime Minister: Dovydaitis
Minister of Foreign Affairs: Voldemaras
Minister of Internal Affairs, Minister of Information and Provisions: Stulginskis
Minister of Finance: M. Yčas
Minister of Defense: Merkys
Minister of Justice: Noreika
Minister of Agriculture: Matulionis
Minister of Education: J. Yčas
Minister of Industry and Commerce: Šimkus
Acting Minister of Finance: Petrulis
Acting Minister of Communications: Šimoliunas

Fourth, April 12, 1919

Prime Minister, Acting Minister of Foreign Affairs: Sleževičius
Minister of Foreign Affairs: Voldemaras
Minister of Internal Affairs: Leonas
Minister of Finance: Vileišis
Minister of Defense: Merkys
Minister of Justice: Noreika
Minister of Agriculture: Stulginskis
Minister of Education: Tubelis
Minister of Industry and Commerce: Šimkus
Minister of Information: Kairys
Minister of Labor and Social Affairs: Paknys
Minister of Communications: Čarneckis
Minister without Portfolio: Šernas
Minister without Portfolio for Belorussian Affairs: Voronko
Minister without Portfolio for Jewish Affairs: Soloveichik

Fifth, October 7, 1919

Prime Minister, Minister of Finance, Industry, and Commerce: Galvanauskas
Minister of Foreign Affairs: Voldemaras
Minister of Internal Affairs: Draugelis
Minister of Justice: Noreika
Minister of Agriculture, Minister of Education: Tubelis
Minister of Communications: Čarneckis
Minister without Portfolio for Belorussian Affairs: Voronko
Minister without Portfolio for Jewish Affairs: Soloveichik
Acting Minister of Defense: Liatukas

Sixth, June 20, 1920

Prime Minister: Grinius
Minister of Foreign Affairs: Puryckis
Minister of Internal Affairs: Skipitis
Minister of Finance, Industry, and Commerce: Galvanauskas
Minister of Defense: Žukas
Minister of Justice: Karoblis
Minister of Agriculture: Aleksa
Minister of Education: Bizauskas
Minister without Portfolio for Belorussian Affairs: Semashko
Minister without Portfolio for Jewish Affairs: Soloveichik

LITHUANIAN DELEGATION TO THE PARIS PEACE CONFERENCE

Augustinas Voldemaras (chairman), Tomas Norus-Naruševičius (acting chairman), Kazys Balutis, Pijus Bielskus, Juozas Dabužis, Ernestas Galvanauskas, Petras Klimas, O. V. Lubicz-Milosz, Balys Mastauskas, Domonik Semashko (Belorussian representative), Simon Rosenbaum (Jewish representative), Martynas Yčas, Jonas Zilius

LITHUANIAN MISSIONS ABROAD, 1918–1920

Berlin: Šaulys (November, 1918), Puryckis (June, 1919)
Bern: Daumantas (December, 1918), Šaulys (October, 1919), Sidzikauskas (December, 1919)
Copenhagen: Savickis (January, 1919)
Helsinki: Gylys (February, 1919)
London: Čepinskis (March, 1919), Tyškevičius (December, 1919)
Paris: Olšauskis (January, 1919), Voldemaras (February, 1919), Milašius (December, 1919)
Riga: Šliupas (August, 1919), Zaunius (January, 1920)
Stockholm: Jurkunas (January, 1919)
Washington, D. C.: Vileišis (December, 1919)

CABINETS OF THE LITHUANIAN COMMUNIST GOVERNMENT

First, January 6, 1919

Chairman of the Council of People's Commissars and Commissar of Foreign Affairs: Mickevičius-Kapsukas
Deputy Chairman of the Council of People's Commissars and Commissar of Internal Affairs: Aleksa-Angarietis
Commissar of Food: Jakševičius
Commissar of Labor: Dimanstein
Commissar of Finance: Cichovski
Commissar of Transport: Svotelis
Commissar of Agriculture: Weinstein
Commissar of Education: V. Biržiška

Second, January 22, 1919

Chairman of the Council of People's Commissars and Commissar of Foreign Affairs: Mickevičius-Kapsukas
Commissar of Internal Affairs: Aleksa-Angarietis
Commissar of Food: Slivkin

Commissar of Labor: Dimanstein
Commissar of Finance: Cichovski
Commissar of Roads: Jakševičius
Commissar of Agriculture: Bielskis
Commissar of Education: Biržiška
Commissar of Communications: Svotelis-Proletaras
Commissar of Military Affairs: Rasitis
Commissar of the People's Economy: Branovski
State Control: Požela
Commissar of Trade and Industry: Weinstein

Third, February 27, 1919

Chairman of the Council of People's Commissars and Commissar of
   Foreign Affairs: Mickevičius-Kapsukas
Commissar of Internal Affairs: Aleksa-Angarietis
Commissar of Food: Kalmanovich
Commissar of Labor: Dimanstein
Commissar of Finance: Weinstein
Commissar of Roads: Savicki
Commissar of Agriculture: Bielskis
Commissar of Education: Leshchinski
Commissar of Communications: Rozental
Commissar of Justice: Kozlovski
Commissar of War: Unshlicht
Commissar of Health: Avižonis
Commissar of the People's Economy: Ginzburg
Commissar of Social Affairs: Oldak
State Control: Berson

Bibliography

THE FORMATION of the Lithuanian national state is one of those developments in the political history of man which has brought forth much heat but little light. Memoir material is at a minimum, and even that which exists is of erratic quality. This study has depended chiefly on public documents, archives, and newspapers. The two best repositories of these materials are the Library of the University of Pennsylvania, which, in addition to the Šaulys Archives, has an excellent collection of books on Lithuania, and the Hoover Library on War, Revolution, and Peace, Stanford University, California, which is very rich in materials on Polish affairs and also has a fine newspaper collection.

UNPUBLISHED MATERIALS

The Šaulys Archives, listed below, form the foundation of this study. Without them, the undertaking would have been almost impossible. The United States National Archives also proved to be very rich. Of the unpublished studies, that by Jurgela is perhaps the most useful, depicting as it does the work of the American Lithuanians, but it is very weak in its discussion of affairs in Lithuania.

American Embassy, Paris, E.S.H. Bulletins. Paris, 1919-1921. [Copy in Hoover Library on War, Revolution, and Peace, Stanford University, California.]

Bielskis, Julius J., see Documents Relating to the Lithuanian National Movement.

Conference of Ambassadors. Notes of a Meeting Held at Quai d'Orsay, Paris. Paris, 1920-1921. [Copy in Hoover Library on War, Revolution, and Peace, Stanford University, California.]

Documents Relating to the Lithuanian National Movement, under the names of Julius J. Bielskis, Malbone Graham, Joseph Hertmanowicz, and the Lithuanian National Council. Hoover Library on War, Revolution, and Peace, Stanford University, California. [These collections, of uneven quality, contain much valuable correspondence of the Lithuanian National Council and also many copies of newspaper articles which would be hard to find otherwise.]

Gabrys, Juozas, Archives of. In the possession of his widow, Mrs. Juozas Gabrys, Vevey, Switzerland. [This collection is useful for its information on Gabrys's activities, although it is surprisingly incomplete in many respects.]

Graham, Malbone, *see* Documents Relating to the Lithuanian National Movement.

Hertmanowicz, Joseph, *see* Documents Relating to the Lithuanian National Movement.

House, Edward, Private Papers of. Yale University Library, New Haven, Connecticut.

Jurgela, Constantine. Lithuania and the United States: The Establishment of State Relations. Ph.D. dissertation, Department of History, Fordham University, New York, 1954.

Liesyte, Julijona. Soviet-Lithuanian Relations, 1920-1939. Master's thesis, Department of History, University of California (Berkeley), 1950.

Lithuania. Delegation to the Paris Peace Conference. Official and Unofficial Propaganda of the Delegation. Hoover Library on War, Revolution, and Peace, Stanford University, California.

Lithuanian National Council, *see* Documents Relating to the Lithuanian National Movement.

Maklakov, Vasilii, Archives of. Hoover Library on War, Revolution, and Peace, Stanford University, California.

Mitkiewicz, Leon. Litwa i Polska pomiędzy dwóma wojnami światowami (Lithuania and Poland between the Two World Wars). Mid-European Studies Center, New York, 1955.

Poland. Delegation to the Paris Peace Conference. Official and Unofficial Propaganda of the Delegation. Hoover Library on War, Revolution, and Peace, Stanford University, California.

Priest, Lyman William. The *Cordon Sanitaire*, 1918-1922. Ph.D. dissertation, Department of History, Stanford University, California, 1954.

Šaulys, Jurgis, Archives of. University of Pennsylvania Library, Philadelphia, Pennsylvania. [This valuable collection contains personal and official correspondence between Šaulys and other leading Lithuanians, many Lithuaian state papers, and many documents from the files of the Soldatenrat der 10. Armee.]

United States. National Archives. Washington, D. C. [Especially valuable are the collection of reports on Lithuanian affairs in general, Paris Peace Conference file, 861L.00; and the collection of reports by the Greene Commission, Paris Peace Conference file, 184.01502.]

PUBLIC DOCUMENTS

Among the items in this list, the archives of the German Foreign Office are particularly important in that they constitute a rich and hitherto untapped source of information. Also important are the publications of the Polish and the Lithuanian delegations to the Paris Peace Conference. The documents published by the Lithuanian government are of relatively little value, while those published by the Polish Ministry of Foreign Affairs, which were much more useful, nevertheless suffer from being one-sided, having been issued originally as evidence in a dispute. The British and American documents are very important, although the British documents unfortunately have more pertinence for the evacuation of the German troops from the Baltic than for the problem of direct British-Lithuanian relations. The two collections put out by the Communists, *Lietuvos TSR istorijos šaltiniai* (in Lithuanian) and "K istorii bor'by . . . " (in Russian), are primarily compilations of material which appeared in the Communist press in 1917-20. The collection in Lithuanian is the more valuable of the two, since it includes some material—tendentiously chosen, to be sure— from non-Communist sources and also since it discusses personalities, such as Angarietis, whose names were anathema in Russia before the period of de-Stalinization. Unfortunately, the French have not yet made public their archives on this topic.

Brest-Litovsk Peace Conference, Proceedings of the. Washington, D. C., 1918.

Conférence de la Paix. *Recueil des Actes de la Conférence.* Part IV: Commissions de la Conférence, C: Questions Territoriales, (2) Commission des Affaires Polonaises, and (7) Commission des Affaires Baltiques. Paris, 1923-24. [Copy in Hoover Library on War, Revolution, and Peace, Stanford University, California.]

Dailidė, Pranas (ed.). *Lietuvos sutartys su svetimomis valstybėmis* (Lithuania's Treaties with Other States). Vol. I. Kaunas, 1930.

Germany. Foreign Office. *Hauptarchiv: Die Zukunft der baltischen Provinz Litauen, 1918-1920.* Whaddon Hall Project (microfilm), Reels 430-33. [Available from the United States National Archives, Washington, D. C.]

Great Britain. Foreign Office. *Russian Poland, Lithuania and White Russia.* Handbooks Prepared Under the Direction of the Historical Section of the Foreign Office, No. 44. London, 1930.

——Naval Staff. Naval Intelligence Division. *Lithuania: Geography.* London, 1918

Hale, Robert. *The Baltic Provinces.* U. S. Senate Document No. 105.

66th Congress, 1st Session. Washington, D. C., 1919.

"K istorii bor'by litovskogo naroda za sovetskuiu vlast', 1918-1919 gg." (On the History of the Struggle of the Lithuanian People for Soviet Rule, 1918-1919), *Krasnyi Arkhiv* (Red Archive), No. 102 (1940), pp. 3-44.

Klimas, Petras (ed.), *Le développement de l'état lituanien*. Paris, 1919.

Lietuvos TSR istorijos šaltiniai (Sources for the History of the Lithuanian SSR). Vol. III. Vilna, 1958.

Lithuania. Constituent Assembly. *Steigiamojo Seimo darbai* (Proceedings of the Constituent Assembly). Kaunas, 1920.

——Delegation to the Paris Peace Conference. *Composition de la Délégation de Lituanie à la Conférence de la Paix*. Paris, 1919.

——Ministry of Foreign Affairs. *Documents diplomatiques: Conflict polono-lituanien: Question de Vilna*. Kaunas, 1924.

——Ministry of Foreign Affairs. *Documents diplomatiques: Question de Memel*. Kaunas, 1924.

Merkys, A. (ed.). *Lietuvos įstatymai* (The Laws of Lithuania). Kaunas, 1922.

Poland. Delegation to the Paris Peace Conference. *Akty i dokumenty dotyczące sprawy granic Polski na knoferencji pokojowej w Paryżu, 1918-1919r*. (Acts and Documents Concerning the Problem of the Borders of Poland at the Conference of Peace in Paris, 1918-1919). Paris, 1920.

——General Staff. *Wojsko litewskie* (The Lithuanian Army). Warsaw, 1925.

——Ministry of Foreign Affairs. *Documents diplomatiques concernant les relations polono-lithuaniennes*. Vol. I. Warsaw, 1920.

Pomaranski, Stefan (ed.). *Pierwsza wojna polska* (The First Polish War). Warsaw, 1920.

RSFSR. People's Commissariat of Foreign Affairs. *Krasnaia kniga: Sbornik diplomaticheskikh dokumentov o russko-polskikh otnosheniiakh, 1918-1920 gg.* (The Red Book: A Collection of Diplomatic Documents on Russian-Polish Relations, 1918-1920). Moscow, 1920.

——People's Commissariat of Foreign Affairs. *Sovetskaia Rossiia i Pol'sha* (Soviet Russia and Poland). Moscow, 1921.

——People's Commissariat of Nationalities. *Politika sovetskoi vlasti po natsional'nym delam za tri goda, 1917-1920* (The Policy of Soviet Rule in National Affairs, 1917-1920). Moscow, 1920.

——People's Commissariat of Nationalities. *Spravochnik narodnogo komissariata po delam natsional'nostei* (Guide of the People's Commissariat of Nationalities). Moscow, 1921.

Russia. State Duma. *Gosudarstvennaia Duma: Stenografcheskie otchety* (State Duma: Stenographic Accounts). St. Petersburg, 1906-16.

Texts of the Russian "Peace." Washington, D. C., 1918.

United States. Department of State. *Papers Relating to the Foreign Relations of the United States.* Volumes used in this study are: *1918, Russia,* Vol. II; *Paris Peace Conference,* Vols. I-XII; *1919, Russia; 1920,* Vol. III. Washington, D. C., 1931-48.

——Department of State. *Russian Series, No. 5.* Washington, D. C., 1920.

——War Department. Military Intelligence Division. *Russia: The Baltic Entrances to Russia.* Washington, D. C., 1919.

Woodward, E. L., and Rohan Butler (eds.). *Documents on British Foreign Policy, 1919-1939.* First Series, Vols. I-III. London, 1947-49.

BOOKS AND ARTICLES

The most valuable memoir material is to be found in the works by Bartuška, Būtėnas and Mackevičius (fragments of Sleževičius's unpublished memoirs), Gabrys, Mickevičius-Kapsukas, Wasilewski, and Yčas. The best secondary account is in Pobóg-Malinowski's study, although it is incomplete in some respects. Of the Communist studies, Šarmaitis's is the most original, but even it suffers gravely from the attempt to cast Communists and anti-Communists in white and black molds. Pesikina's work offers much new material, but she seems to have given too much credit to Stalin's Commissariat of Nationalities, thereby neglecting the work of the Communist Party organizations. Andreev's book is a revised version of his article in *Voprosy Istorii* (Problems of History), and peculiarly enough most of the revisions consist of blatant falsifications, leaving the impression that the book is meant to be a propaganda piece rather than a serious study.

Abramowicz, L. *Litwa podczas wojny* (Lithuania during the War). Warsaw, 1918.

Alseika, Danielius. *Lietuvių tautinė idėja istorijos šviesoje* (The Lithuanian National Idea in the Light of History). Vilna, 1924.

Andreev, A. M. *Bor'ba litovskogo naroda za sovetskuiu vlast', 1918-1919 gg.* (The Struggle of the Lithuanian People for Soviet Rule, 1918-1919). Moscow, 1954.

——"Bor'ba litoskogo naroda za ustanovlenie sovetskoi vlasti v 1918-1919 godakh" (The Struggle of the Lithuanian People for the Establishment of Soviet Rule, 1918-1919), *Voprosy Istorii* (Problems of History), September, 1949, pp. 3-31.

Angarietis, Zigmas Aleksa-."Litva i oktiabr'skaia revoliutsiia" (Lithuania and the October Revolution), *Zhizn' Natsional'nostei* (The Life of the Nationalities), I (1923), 217-20.

Arenz, Wilhelm. *Polen und Russland, 1918-1920.* Leipzig, 1939.

Bagdonas, Juozas. *Iš mūsų kovų ir žygių* (From Our Struggles and Campaigns). Vol. I. Kaunas, 1930.

Bagiński, Henryk. *Wojsko polskie na wschodzie, 1914-1920* (The Polish Army in the East, 1914-1920). Warsaw, 1921.

Bane, Suda Lorena, and Ralph Haswell Lutz (eds.). *The Blockade of Germany after the Armistice, 1918-1919.* Stanford, Calif., 1942.

——*Organization of American Relief in Europe, 1918-1919.* Stanford, Calif., 1943.

Bartuška, V. *Lietuvos nepriklausomybės kryžiaus keliais* (On the Way of the Cross of Lithuanian Independence). Memel, 1937.

——*Les Lituaniens d'Amérique.* Lausanne, 1918.

Basanavičius, Jonas. *Dėliai vasario 16d. 1918m. Lietuvos nepriklausomybės paskelbimo* (On the Declaration of Lithuania's Independence of February 16, 1918). Vilna, 1926.

Batilliat, René. *Origine et développement des institutions politiques en Lithuanie.* Paris, 1932.

Benedictsen, Age Meyer. *Lithuania: The Awakening of a Nation.* Copenhagen, 1914.

Bermondt-Avalov, Pavel Mikhailovich. *Im Kampf gegen den Bolschewismus.* Glückstadt, 1925.

Bielskis, J. J. "Amerikos lietuviai Lietuvos laisvės kovoje" (The American Lithuanians in Lithuania's Struggle for Freedom), *Lietuvių Dienos* (Lithuanian Days), September, 1954, to May, 1955 (serialized in a monthly periodical).

Bielskis, J. J. (ed.). *Lithuania: Facts Supporting Her Claims for Reestablishment as an Independant Nation.* Washington, D. C., 1918.

Bilmanis, Alfred. *A History of Latvia.* Princeton, N. J., 1951.

——*Latvia in the Making, 1918-1928.* Riga, 1928.

Birontas, A. *Bermontininkams Lietuvą užpuolus* (After the Bermondtists Attacked Lithuania). Kaunas, 1934.

Biržiška, Mykolas. "Amerikos lietuviai" (The Lithuanians of America), in *Lietuviškoji Enciklopedija* (Lithuanian Encyclopedia), Vol. I (Kaunas, 1933), cols. 405-84.

——*Lietuvių tautos kelias* (The Path of the Lithuanian Nation). 2 vols. Los Angeles, 1952-53.

Blociszewski, J. *La restauration de la Pologne et la diplomatie européenne.* Paris, 1927.

Bonsal, Stephen. *Suitors and Suppliants*. New York, 1946.

Borch, Nicolas de. *Le principe des nationalités et la question lituanienne.* Louvain, 1925.

Braatz, Kurt von. *Fürst Anatol Pawlowitsch Lieven*. Stuttgart, 1926.

Budecki, Zdisław. *Stosunki polsko-litewskie po wojnie światowej, 1918-1928* (Polish-Lithuanian Relations after the World War, 1918-1928). Warsaw, 1928.

Bunyan, James (ed.). *Intervention, Civil War, and Communism in Russia, April–December 1918*. Baltimore, 1936.

Būtėnas, Julius, and Mečys Mackevičius. "Gyvenimas ir darbai" (Life and Work), in *Mykolas Sleževičius*. Chicago, 1954. Pages 1-150.

Butler, Ralph. *The New Eastern Europe*. New York, 1919.

Carr, E. H. *The Bolshevik Revolution, 1917-1923*. 3 vols. New York, 1951-53.

Chamberlin, William Henry. *The Russian Revolution*. 2 vols. New York, 1935.

Chambon, Henry de. *La Lithuanie moderne*. Paris, 1933.

——*La Lithuanie pendant la Conférence de la Paix (1919)*. Lille, 1931.

Chase, Thomas G. *The Story of Lithuania*. New York, 1946.

Churchill, Winston S. *The Aftermath*. New York, 1929.

Colliander, Borje. *Die Beziehungen zwischen Litauen und Deutschland während der Okkupation*. Turku, 1935.

Crozier, Frank Percy. *Impressions and Recollections*. London, 1930.

Daniszewski, Tadeusz. *Polska w okresie powojennego wzniesienia rewolucyjnego (1918-1923)* (Poland at the Time of the Postwar Revolutionary Movement, 1918-1923). Warsaw, 1953.

Denikin, A. I. *Ocherki russkoi smuty* (Notes of the Russian Turmoil). Vol. IV. Paris, 1925.

Deutscher, Isaac. *Stalin: A Political Biography*. London, 1949.

Devereux, Roy. *Poland Reborn*. London, 1922.

Dmowski, Roman. *Polityka polska i odbudowanie Państwa* (Polish Politics and the Restoration of the State). Warsaw, 1925.

Dogelis, Paulius. *Mano gyvenimo prisiminimai* (Memories of My Life). Kaunas, 1936.

Dopkewitsch, H. "Zur englischen Politik im Baltikum, 1918-1919," *Deutsches Archiv für Landes- und Volksforschung*, VI (1942), 119-47.

Dziewanowski, M. K. "Pilsudski's Federal Policy, 1919-1921," *Journal of Central European Affairs*, X (1950), 113-28, 271-87.

Ehret, Joseph. *Litauen in Vergangenheit, Gegenwart und Zukunft*. Bern, 1919.

Engelhardt, Eugen von. *Weissruthenien: Volk und Land*. Berlin, 1943.

Erzberger, Matthias. *Erlebnisse im Weltkrieg*. Stuttgart, 1920.

Etchegoyen. *Le problème lithuanien.* Alençon, n.d.

Fischer, Louis. *The Soviets in World Affairs, 1917-1929.* Princeton, N. J., 1949.

Fisher, Harold Henry. *America and the New Poland.* New York, 1928.

Frankel, Henryk. *Poland: The Struggle for Power, 1772-1939.* London, 1946.

Gabrys, Juozas. *Kodel aš nerêmiau laikinosios Lietuvos valdžios, 1918-1919m.* (Why I Did Not Support the Provisional Government of Lithuania, 1918-1919). N.p., n.d.

——(pseud. Inorodetz). *La Russie et les peuples allogènes.* Bern, 1917.

——*A Sketch of the Lithuanian Nation.* Paris, 1911.

——*Vers l'indépendance lituanienne: faits, impressions, souvenirs, 1907-1920.* Lausanne, 1920.

Gade, John. "The Memel Controversy," *Foreign Affairs,* II (1924), 410-20.

Gaigalat, W. *Litauen, das besetzte Gebiet und sein Volk.* Frankfurt, 1917.

——*Die litauisch-baltische Frage.* Berlin, 1915.

Gaillard, Gaston. *L'Allemagne et le Baltikum.* Paris, 1919.

Garfunkelis, L. *Žydų tautinė autonomija Lietuvoje* (Jewish National Autonomy in Lithuania). Kaunas, 1920.

Gečys, Kazys. *Katalikiškoji Lietuva* (Catholic Lithuania). Chicago, 1946.

Genkina, E. B. *Obrazovanie SSSR* (The Formation of the USSR). Moscow, 1943.

Gerson, Louis L. *Woodrow Wilson and the Rebirth of Poland, 1914-1920.* New Haven, Conn., 1953.

Gessen, S. Ia. *Okrainnye gosudarstva* (The Border Governments). Leningrad, 1926.

Gineitis, Kazys. Amerika ir Amerikos lietuviai (America and the Lithuanians of America). Kaunas, 1925.

Girinis, S. "*Kanun i sumerki sovetskoi vlasti na Litve*" (The Eve and the Twilight of Soviet Rule in Lithuania), *Proletarskaia Revoliutsiia* (The Proletarian Revolution), No. 8 (1922), pp. 71-92.

Glaser, Stefan. *Okupacja niemiecka na Litwie w latach 1915-1918.* (The German Occupation in Lithuania, 1915-1918). Lvov, 1929.

Gleichen, Edward (ed.). *The Baltic and Caucasian States.* London, 1923.

Goltz, Rüdiger von der. *Meine Sendung im Finnland und im Baltikum.* Leipzig, 1920.

Gorzuchowski, Xavier. *Les rapports politiques de la Pologne et de la Lithuanie.* Paris, 1927.

Grabianski, Alexandre. *La Pologne et la Lithuanie.* Paris, 1919.

Grabski, Stanisław. *Uwagi o bieżącej historycznej chwili Polski* (Notes on the Current History of Poland). Warsaw, 1922.

Graham, Malbone W. Jr. *New Governments of Eastern Europe*. New York, 1927.

Grappin, Henri. *Pologne et Lithuanie*. Paris, 1919.

Grazhdanskaia voina, 1918-1921 (The Civil War, 1918-1921). Ed. A. S. Bubnov, *et al.* 3 vols. Moscow, 1928-30.

Grinius, Kazys. *Atsiminimai ir mintys* (Memories and Thoughts). Vol. I. Tübingen, 1947.

Grosfeld, Leon. *Polskie reakcyjne formacje wojskowe w Rosji, 1917-1919* (Polish Reactionary Military Formations in Russia, 1917-1919). Warsaw, 1956.

Habdank, Adam. *Prześladowanie polaków na Litwie kowieńskiej* (Persecution of the Poles in Kaunas, Lithuania). Vilna, n.d.

Hale, Richard R. (ed.). *Letters of Warwick Greene, 1915-1928*. Boston, 1931.

Halecki, Oskar. "Poland's Eastern Frontiers, 981-1939," *Journal of Central European Affairs*, II (1941), 325-38 (Part II).

Harrison, E. J. *Lithuania Past and Present*. London, 1922.

Haumant, Emile. *Le problème de l'unité russe*. Paris, 1922.

Hehn, Jürgen von. "Die Entstehung der Staaten Lettland und Estland und der Bolschewismus und die Grossmächte," *Forschungen zur osteuropäischen Geschichte*, IV (1956), 103-218.

Hellmann, Manfred. "Die litauische Nationalbewegung im 19. und 20. Jahrhundert," *Zeitschrift für Ostforschung*, II (1953), 66-106.

Herbačiauskas, Juozas Albinas (Juozapas Herbačevskis). *Kur eini, Lietuvi?* (Where Are You Going, Lithuanian?). Vilna, 1919.

——(Józef Herbaczewski). *Litwa a Polska* (Lithuania and Poland). Vilna, 1921.

——(Józef Herbaczewski). *O Wilno i nie tylko o Wilno* (About Vilna and Not Just about Vilna). Vilna, 1922.

Howard, Esme. *Theatre of Life*. London, 1936.

Hurwicz, Elias. *Der neue Osten*. Berlin, 1927.

Iakubovskaia, S. I. *Ob"edinitel'noe dvizhenie za obrazovania SSSR* (The Unification Movement for the Formation of the USSR). Moscow, 1947.

Inorodetz, *see under* Gabrys, Juozas.

Istoriia grazhdanskoi voiny v SSSR (History of the Civil War in the USSR). Ed. M. Gorki *et al.* 2 vols. Moscow, 1936-43.

Ivanovich, V. *Sovetskii Soiuz i Angliia v Pribaltike* (The Soviet Union and England in the Baltic). Moscow, 1927.

Ivinskis, Zenonas. "Lietuvos padėtis 1917 metais ir vasario 16d. akto genezė" (The Position of Lithuania in 1917 and the Genesis of the Act of February 16), *Židinys* (The Hearth), XXVII (1938), 610-34.

Jakštas. "Saksų savanorių dalys Lietuvoje 1919m." (The Saxon Volunteer Unit in Lithuania), *Karo Archyvas* (War Archive), VI (1935), 180-206.

Jakštas, Adomas. *Głos Litwinów* (The Voice of the Lithuanians). Kaunas, 1906.

Jezierski, E. *Jak lud litewski wałczył o wolność Polski* (How the Lithuanian People Fought for the Freedom of Poland). Warsaw, 1919.

Johannet, René. *Le principe des nationalités*. 2d ed. Paris, 1923.

Jurgela, K. Rudminas. "Amerikos lietuvių legionas" (The American Lithuanian Legion), in Petras Ruseckas (ed.), *Pasaulio lietuviai* (Lithuanians of the World). Kaunas, 1935. Pages 57-71.

——*History of the Lithuanian Nation*. New York, 1948.

Jusaitis, Antanas. *The History of the Lithuanian Nation and Its Present National Aspirations*. Philadelphia, 1919.

Kalnins, Bruno. *De baltiska staternas frihetskamp*. Stockholm, 1950.

Kamieniecki, Witold. *Państwo litewskie* (The Lithuanian State). Warsaw, 1918.

Kapsukas, *see* Mickevičius-Kapsukas.

Karys, Jonas. *Nepriklausomos Lietuvos pinigai* (The Currency of Independent Lithuania). New York, 1953.

Kasakaitis, A. "Lietuviai Varšuvoj" (Lithuanians in Warsaw), in Petras Ruseckas (ed.), *Pasaulio lietuviai* (Lithuanians of the World). Kaunas, 1935.

Kellor, Frances, and Antonia Hatvany. *Security against War*. Vol. I. New York, 1924.

Kemešis, K. F. "Amerikos lietuvių kova už Lietuvos laisvę" (The Struggle of the American Lithuanians for the Freedom of Lithuania), in *Pirmasis nepriklausomos Lietuvos dešimtmetis* (The First Decade of Independent Lithuania). London, 1955. Vol. I, pp. 50-62.

Keršys, M. *Lietuvių politikos partijos* (Lithuanian Political Parties). Kaunas, 1919.

Kisinas, Izidorius. *Lietuviškų knygų sistematinis katalogas* (Systematic Catalogue of Lithuanian Books). Kaunas, 1938.

Klimas, Petras. "L'entente baltique et la Lithuanie," in *Les problèmes de la Baltique*. Paris, 1927. Pages 721-42.

——*Istorinė Lietuvos valstybės apžvalga* (Historical Survey of the Lithuanian State). Kaunas, 1922.

——"Lietuvos valstybės kurimasis 1915-1918 metais" (The Formation of the Lithuanian State, 1915-1918), in *Pirmasis nepriklausomos Lietuvos dešimtmetis* (The First Decade of Independent Lithuania). London 1955. Vol. I, pp. 1-32.

——*Les rapports des nations lituanienne et polonaise*. Paris, 1927.

Kolarz, Walter. *Myths and Realities in Eastern Europe.* London, 1946.
——*Russia and Her Colonies.* London, 1952.
Kolesinskii, B. *Nashi zapadnye sosedi* (Our Western Neighbors). Moscow, 1930.
Komarnicki, Titus. *The Rebirth of the Polish Republic.* London, 1957.
Korostowetz, W. K. *The Re-Birth of Poland.* London, 1928.
Kowalski, Józef. *Wielka Październikowa Rewolucja Socjalistyczna a wyzwolenie Polski* (The Great October Socialist Revolution and the Liberation of Poland). Warsaw, 1952.
Kozicki, Stanisław. *Sprawa granic Polski na konferencji pokojowej w Paryżu* (The Problem of the Boundaries of Poland at the Peace Conference in Paris). Warsaw, 1921.
Kučas, A. "Jungtinių Amerikos Valstybių lietuviai" (The Lithuanians of the United States of America), in *Lietuvių Enciklopedija* (Lithuanian Encyclopedia), X (Boston, 1957), 36-71.
Kumaniecki, Kazimierz (ed.). *Odbudowa państwowości polskiej: najważniejsze dokumenty, 1912–styczeń, 1924* (The Restoration of Polish Statehood: The Most Important Documents, 1912–December, 1924). Warsaw, 1924.
Kutrzeba, Stanisław. *Polska Odrodzona, 1914-1922* (Poland Reborn, 1914-1922). Cracow, 1922.
——"The Struggle for Frontiers, 1919-1923," in *The Cambridge History of Poland, 1697-1935.* Ed. by W. F. Reddaway *et al.* Cambridge, England, 1941. Pages 512-34.
Land Ober-Ost, Das. Stuttgart, 1917.
Laroix, Vincent. *Quand la lumière nous vient du nord.* Paris, 1938.
Lavinskas, Frank. *Angliakasio atsiminimai* (Memoirs of a Coal Miner). Long Island City, N. Y., 1952.
Lehnich, Oswald. *Währung und Wirtschaft in Polen, Litauen, Lettland und Estland.* Berlin, 1923.
Lietuvis, *see under* Morauskas, Alfonsas.
Linkevičius. "Lietuviai Sibire" (Lithuanians in Siberia), *Karo Archyvas* (War Archive), I (1925), 25-72.
Linksch, Erich. *Litauen und die Litauer.* Stuttgart, 1917.
Lithuanie et la Paix de Versailles. Lausanne, n.d.
Lord, Robert H. "Lithuania and Poland," *Foreign Affairs,* I (1923), 38-58.
——"Poland," Edward Mandell House and Charles Seymour (eds.), in *What Really Happened at Paris.* New York, 1921. Pages 67-86.
Luckiewicz, A. *Polska okupacja na Białorusi* (The Polish Occupation in Belorussia). Vilna, 1920.

Ludendorff, Erich von. *The General Staff and Its Problems*. 2 vols. New York, 1922.

——*Ludendorff's Own Story*. 2 vols. New York, 1919.

Lugan, M. A. *L'Europe et les problèmes de la paix*. Paris, 1919.

Lukasiewicz, Juljusz. *Polska w Europie w polityce Józefa Piłsudskiego* (Poland in Europe in the Politics of Joseph Piłsudski). London, 1944.

Machray, Robert. *Poland, 1914-1931*. London, 1932.

Maciūnas, Vincas. "Adam Mickiewicz in Lithuanian Literature," in Waclaw Lednicki (ed.), *Adam Mickiewicz in World Literature*. Berkeley, Calif., 1956. Pages 383-97.

Maciunas, Vincas, and Kostas Ostrauskas. "The Šaulys Collection," *Library Chronicle* (University of Pennsylvania Library), XX (1954), 35-46.

Mackiewicz, Stanisław. *Istorija Polski* (History of Poland). London, 1941.

Manning, Clarence. *The Forgotten Republics*. New York, 1952.

Markwardt, W. "Der Vielvölkerstaat und seine Probleme," in *Litauen und seine Deutschen*. Beiheft zum Jahrbuch der Albertus Universität, Vol. XIII. Wurzburg, 1955. Pages 49-72.

Martel, René. *Les grands problèmes*. Paris, 1931.

——*La Pologne et nous*. Paris, 1928.

Matulaitis, Jurgis. *Užrašai* (Diary). London, n.d.

Matušas, Jonas. *Lietuvių rusinimas per pradžios mokyklas* (The Russification of Lithuanians in the Elementary Schools). Kaunas, 1927.

Mauclère, Jean. *Le pays du chevalier blanc*. Paris, 1930.

——*Le rayonnement de la France en Lithuanie*. LeRaincy, 1946.

——*Sous le ciel pale de Lithuanie*. Paris, 1926.

Merkelis, A. *Juozas Tumas Vaižgantas*. Vol. I. Kaunas, 1934.

Michaelis, Paul. *Kurland und Litauen in deutscher Hand*. Berlin, 1918.

Mickevičius-Kapsukas (Russian form: Mitskevich-Kapsukas), Vincas. "Bor'ba za sovetskuiu vlast' v Litve i zapadnoi Belorussii (1918-1919)" (The Struggle for Soviet Rule in Lithuania and Western Belorussia, 1918-1919), *Proletarskaia Revoliutsiia* (The Proletarian Revolution), No. 108 (1931), pp. 65-107.

——*Caro kalejimuos* (In the Prisons of the Tsar). Brooklyn, N. Y., 1929.

——"Istoki i zarozhdenie kommunisticheskoi partii Litvy" (Sources and Birth of the Communist Party of Lithuania), *Proletarskaia Revoliutsiia* (Proletarian Revolution), No. 84 (1929), pp. 153-78.

——*Jono Biliūno biografija* (Biography of Jonas Biliunas). Philadelphia, 1917.

——"Litovtsy za 5 let Oktiabr'skoi Revoliutsii" (The Lithuanians Five Years after the October Revolution), *Zhizn' Natsional'nostei*

(The Life of the Nationalities), No. 1 (1923), pp. 220-27.

——"Revoliutsiia v Litve (1918) i sozdanie vremennogo pravitel'stva revoliutsionnogo rabochego-krestianskogo" (Revolution in Lithuania, 1918, and the Creation of the Provisional Revolutionary Workers' and Peasants' Government), *Istorik Marksist* (The Marxist Historian), No. 2-3 (1935), pp. 44-52.

Miliukov, Pavel N. *Natsional'nyi vopros* (The National Question). N.p., 1925.

Mitskevich-Kapsukas, *see* Mickevičius-Kapsukas.

Molis, P. (ed.). *The American Press on Lithuania's Freedom*. Brooklyn, N. Y., 1920.

Morauskas, Alfonsas (A. Moravskis). *Ekonomicheskoe polozhenie Litvy i Belorussii* (The Economic Situation of Lithuania and Belorussia). Moscow, 1919.

——(pseud. Lietuvis). *S Germaniei ili s Rossiei?* (With Germany or with Russia?). Petrograd, 1918.

Moresthe, Georges. *Vilna et le problème de l'est européen*. Paris, 1922.

Moriez, Stanislas de. *La question polonaise vue d'Allemagne*. Paris, 1919.

Nalecz, Jerzy. *Litwa a Polska* (Lithuania and Poland). Warsaw, 1920.

Natkevičius, Ladas. *Aspect politique et juridique du différend polono-lithuanien*. Paris, 1930.

——*Lietuvos kariuomenė* (The Army of Lithuania). Boston, 1919.

Navakas, Jonas. *Lietuvai besikeliant* (Lithuania Arising). Kaunas, 1928.

Newman, E. W. Polson. *Britain and the Baltic*. London, 1930.

Niessel, Henri Albert Vairas. *L'évacuation des pays baltiques par les allemands*. Paris, 1935. Translated into Lithuanian as *Vokiečių issikraustymas iš Baltijos kraštų* (Kaunas, 1938).

Norus, T., and J. Zilius. *Lithuania's Case for Independence*. Washington, D. C., 1918.

Noske, Gustav. *Von Kiel bis Kapp*. Berlin, 1920.

Page, Stanley W. "Lenin, the National Question and the Baltic States, 1917-1919," *American Slavic and East European Review*, VII (1948), 15-31.

Pakštas, Kazys. "Lietuvių amerikiečių kovos del Lietuvos nepriklausomybės" (The Struggles of the American Lithuanians for the Independence of Lithuania), *Židinys* (The Hearth), XXVII (1938), 635-52.

Palmer, Frederick. *Bliss, Peacemaker*. New York, 1934.

Pesikina, E. I. *Narodnyi Komissariat po Delam Natsional'nostei i ego deiatel'nost' v 1917-1918 gg.* (The People's Commissariat of Nationalities and Its Activity, 1917-1918). Moscow, 1950.

Pilsudska, Alexandra. *Pilsudski*. New York, 1942.

Piłsudski, Józef. *Pisma zbiorowe* (Selected Letters). Vol. V. Warsaw, 1937.

Pipes, Richard E. *The Formation of the Soviet Union.* Cambridge, Mass., 1954.

Pobóg-Malinowski, Władysław. *Najnowsza historia polityczna Polski* (Modern Political History of Poland). 2 vols. London and Paris, 1953-56.

Prochnik, Adam. *Powstanie państwa polskiego* (The Establishment of the Polish State). Warsaw, 1938.

Propolanis, Kazimierz. *Polskie Apostolstwo w Litwie, 1387-1912* (The Polish Apostleship in Lithuania, 1387-1912). Vilna, 1913.

Przybylski, Adam. *La Pologne en lutte pour ses frontières, 1918-1920.* Paris, 1929.

Punga, Kh. A. *Nashi pribaltiiskie sosedi* (Our Baltic Neighbors). Moscow, 1927.

Puryckis, Juozas. "Lietuvių veikimas Šveicarijoje didžiojo karo metu" (Lithuanian Activity in Switzerland during the Great War), in *Pirmasis nepriklausomos Lietuvos dešimtmetis* (The First Decade of Independent Lithuania). London, 1955. Vol. I, pp. 63-73.

——"Seimo laikai" (The Period of the Constituent Assembly), in *Pirmasis nepriklausomos Lietuvos dešimtmetis* (The First Decade of Independent Lithuania). London, 1955. Vol. I, pp. 128-73.

Rabenau, Friedrich von. *Seeckt: Aus seinem Leben, 1918-1936.* Leipzig, 1940.

Rainys, J. *POW Lietuvoje* (The POW in Lithuania). Kaunas, 1936.

Raštikis, Stasys. *Kovose del Lietuvos* (In the Struggles for Lithuania). 2 vols. Los Angeles, 1956-57.

Rauch, Georg von. *Russland: Staatliche Einheit und nationale Vielfalt.* Munich, 1953.

Reddaway, W. F. *Marshal Pilsudski.* London, 1939.

——"The Peace Conference, 1919," in *The Cambridge History of Poland, 1697-1935.* Ed. W. F. Reddaway *et al.* Cambridge, England, 1941. Pages 490-511.

Rimka, Albinas. "Lietuvių tautos atgimimo socialiniai pagrindai ir 'Auszros'-'Varpo' gadynės (1883-1893) socialekonominiai raštai" (The Social Bases of the Rebirth of the Lithuanian Nation and the Social-Economic Writings of the *Aušra-Varpas* Period, 1883-1893), in *Vytauto Didžiojo Universiteto Teisių Fakulteto Darbai* (Works of the Law Faculty of the University of Vytautas the Great), VI, Part 3 (1932), 207-337.

Rimscha, Hans. "Die Entstehung der baltischen Staaten," *Schicksalslinie,* I (1955), 12-18.

Robinson, Geroid T. *Rural Russia under the Old Regime.* New York, 1949.

Romer'is Mykolas. *Lietuvos konstitucinės teisės paskaitos* (Lectures on Lithuanian Constitutional Law). Vol. I. Kaunas, 1935.

——(Polish form: Michał Romer). *Litewskie stronnictwa polityczne* (Lithuanian Political Parties). Vilna, 1921.

——*Litwa* (Lithuania). Lvov, 1907.

——*Organizacja władzy politycznej w rozwoju konstytucyjnym respubliki litewskie* (The Organization of Political Power in the Constitutional Development of the Republic of Lithuania). Warsaw, 1939.

Rosenbaum, S. *La question polono-lituanienne.* Paris, 1919.

Royal Institute of International Affairs. Information Department. *The Baltic States.* London, 1938.

Ruhl, Arthur. *New Masters of the Baltic.* New York, 1921.

Ruseckas, Petras (ed.). *Savanorių žygiai* (Campaigns of the Volunteers). Kaunas, 1937.

Rutenberg, Gregor, *Die baltischen Staaten und das Völkerrecht.* Riga, 1928.

Šalčius, M. *Lenkų sąmokslas Lietuvoje* (The Polish Plot in Lithuania). Chicago, 1921.

Šalkauskis, Stasys. *Sur les confins de deux mondes.* Geneva, 1919.

Šapoka, Adolfas (ed.). *Lietuvos istorija* (History of Lithuania). Kaunas, 1935.

Šarmaitis, R. J. (Russian form: R. Ia. Sharmaitis). "Interventsiia anglo-amerikanskikh imperialistov v Litve v 1918-1920 gg." (The Intervention of the Anglo-American Imperialists in Lithuania, 1918-1920), *Istoricheskie Zapiski* (Historical Notes), No. 45 (1954), pp. 257-77.

——"V. Mickevičius-Kapsukas," in J. Būtėnas and A. Sprindis (eds.), *Lietuvių literatūra* (Lithuanian Literature). Vol. II. Kaunas, 1956.

Šaulys, Jurgis. "Nepriklausomybės išvakarese" (On the Eve of Independence), *Mūsų kelias* (Our Road), Vol. IV, February 12, 19, and 26, 1948.

Savickis, J. "Skandinavija" (Scandinavia), in *Pirmasis nepriklausomos Lietuvos dešimtmetis* (The First Decade of Independent Lithuania). London, 1955, Vol. I, pp. 74-77.

Schröder and Heygendorff. *Die sächsischen Freiwilligen-Truppen in Litauen, 1919.* Erinnerungsblätter deutscher Truppenverbände, No. 69. Dresden, 1933.

Senn, Alfred Erich. "Die bolschewistische Politik in Litauen, 1917-1919," *Forschungen zur osteuropäischen Geschichte,* V (1957), 93-118.

Seymour, Charles (ed.). *The Intimate Papers of Colonel House.* Vol. IV. Boston, 1928.

Sforza, Carlo. *Diplomatic Europe since the Treaty of Versailles.* New Haven, Conn., 1928.

Sharmaitis, R. Ia., *see* Šarmaitis, R. J.

Shtein, B. E. *Russkii vopros na parizhskoi mirnoi konferentsii (1919-1920gg.)* (The Russian Question at the Paris Peace Conference, 1919-1920). Moscow, 1949.

Simutis, Anicetas. *The Economic Reconstruction of Lithuania after 1918.* New York, 1942.

Širvydas, Vytautas. *Bronius Kazys Balutis.* Sodus, Mich., 1951.

Skierko, Adam. *The Jews and the Polish Question.* Paris, 1919.

Skorupskis, A. *Karas už Lietuvos laisvė, 1914-1934* (The War for Lithuania's Freedom, 1914-1934). Kaunas, 1934.

——*La Resurrection d'un peuple, 1918-1927.* Paris, 1930.

Skrzynski, Aleksander. *Poland and the Peace.* London, 1923.

Šliupas, Jonas. *Lietuvių-Latvių Respublika ir Šiaures Tautų Sajunga* (The Lithuanian-Latvian Republic and the League of Northern Nations). Stockholm, 1918.

——(John Szlupas). *Lithuania in Retrospect and Prospect.* New York, 1915.

Sobolevičius, Elias. *Les états baltes et la Russie soviétique.* Paris, 1930.

Stalin, J. V. *Sochineniia* (Works). Vols. III, IV. Moscow, 1947.

Stankevich, V. *Sud'by narodov Rossii* (Fates of the Peoples or Russia). Berlin, 1921.

Steponaitis, Vytautas. "Ginkluotų jegų klausimas Lietuvos Valstybės Taryboje" (The Armed Forces Question in the Lithuanian State Council), *Karo Archyvas* (War Archive), III (1926), 3-23.

Stöhr, Felix. *Die Wirtschaft der Republik Litauen im ersten Jahrzehnt ihres Bestehens (1918-1928).* Erlangen, 1930.

Studnicki, Władysław. *Das östliche Polen.* Kitzingen, 1953.

——*Państwo kowienskie* (The Kaunas State). Vilna, 1922.

——*Die polnische Ostmarkenfrage.* Warsaw, n.d.

——*W sprawie stosunku politycznego Polski do jej ziem wschodnich* (On the Problem of the Political Relationship of Poland to Its Eastern Lands). Warsaw, 1919.

Syrkin, Albert. *Gosudarstva pribaltiki* (States of the Baltic). Moscow, n.d.

Szlupas, John, *see under* Šliupas, Jonas.

Tallents, Stephen, *Man and Boy.* London, 1943.

Tarnowski, Adam. *Two Polish Attempts to Bring About a Central-East European Organization.* London, 1943.

Temperley, H. W. V. (ed.). *A History of the Peace Conference of Paris.* 6 vols. London, 1920-24.

Tennenbaum, H. *Les liens économiques entre la Pologne, la Lithuanie, et les provinces ruthènes.* Paris, 1919.

Tibal, A. *L'Allemagne et la Baltique orientale de 1915 à 1919.* Riga, 1932.

Totoraitis, Jonas. *Lietuvos atgijimas* (The Rebirth of Lithuania). Chicago, 1921.

Tumas-Vaižgantas, Juozas. *Vaižganto Raštai* (The Works of Vaižgantas). Vols. I, II, IV. Kaunas, 1922.

Uspenskis. "1-as gudų pulkas Gardine ir kaip jis tapo lenkų nuginkluotas" (The First Belorussian Regiment in Grodno and How It Was Disarmed by the Poles), *Karo Archyvas* (War Archive), I (1925), 161-77.

Vaičiulaitis, Antanas. *Outline History of Lithuanian Literature*. Chicago, 1942.

Vakar, Nicholas. *Belorussia: The Making of a Nation*. Cambridge, Mass., 1954.

Vanlande, René. *Avec le Général Niessel en Prusse et en Lithuanie*. Paris, 1922.

Vileišis, Petras. *Lietuvių-lenkų ginčas* (The Lithuanian-Polish Dispute). Kaunas, 1922.

——*La Lithuanie et le problème de la sécurité internationale*. Paris, 1937.

Viscont, Antoine. *La Lithuanie et la guerre*. Geneva, 1917.

Vitols, Hugo. *La mer baltique et les états baltes*. Paris, 1935.

Vladimirovas, L., *et al. Vilniaus Universitetas* (The University of Vilna). Vilna, 1956.

Voldemaras, Augustinas. *Lithuanie et Pologne*. Berlin, 1920.

——*La Lithuanie et ses problèmes*. Lille, 1933.

——*Les relations russo-polono-lituaniennes*. Paris, 1920.

Volkov, S. I., *et al.* "Ob"edinennaia nauchnaia sessiia po voprosam istorii Pribaltiki v posleoktiabr'skii period" (Joint Scientific Session on the Question of the History of the Baltic Area in the Post-October Period), *Voprosy Istorii* (Problems of History), December, 1954, pp. 159-63.

Voronko, J. J. *Gudų klausimas Versalės Taikos Konferencijos metu* (The Belorussian Question during the Versailles Peace Conference). Kaunas, 1919.

Vydūnas, W. St. *Siebenhundert Jahre deutsch-litauischer Beziehungen*. Tilsit, 1932.

Waite, Robert G. L. *Vanguard of Nazism*. Cambridge, Mass., 1952.

Waligóra, Bolesław. *Na przełomie: Zdarzenia na ziemiach Białorusi i Litwy oraz w krajach baltyckich (1918-1919)* (The Turning Point: Events in Belorussia and Lithuania and the Baltic Lands, 1918-1919). Warsaw, 1934.

Wasilewski, Leon. *Józef Piłsudski, jakim go znałem* (Joseph Piłsudski As I Knew Him). Warsaw, 1935.

——*Litwa i Białoruś* (Lithuania and Belorussia). Warsaw, 1925.

——*Les Polonais et les Lithuaniens pendant la Guerre Mondiale*. Warsaw, 1930.

Wasilewski, Leon (*Continued*)
——*Stosunki polsko-litewskie w dobie popowstaniowej* (Polish-Lithuanian Relations in the Days since the Rising). Warsaw, 1946.

Wejtko, Władysław. *Samoobrona Litwy i Białorusi* (The Self-Defense of Lithuania and Belorussia). Vilna, 1930.

Wielhorski, Władysław. *Państwowość Litwy etnograficznej wobec zagadnienia trwałego pokoju w Europie* (The Statehood of Ethnographic Lithuania and the Problem of a Lasting Peace in Europe). Warsaw, 1919.

——*Polska a Litwa: Stosunki wzajemne w biegu dziejów* (Poland and Lithuania: Their Mutual Relations in the Course of History). London, 1947.

——"Warunki rozwoju świadomości narodowej Litwinów i powstania współczesnego państwa litewskiego," (Conditions of the Development of the National Consciousness of the Lithuanians and the Establishment of the Present Lithuanian State), in *Pamiętnik VI Powszechnego Zjazdu Historyków Polskich w Wilnie 17-20 września 1935 r.* (Journal of the VI General Congress of Polish Historians in Vilna, September 17-20, 1935). Lvov, 1935.

Woroniecki, Edward. *Niemcy a powstanie samodzielnej Litwy* (The Germans and the Establishment of Independent Lithuania). Warsaw, 1920.

Yčas, Jonas. "Mažosios Lietuvos praeitis" (The Past of Lithuania Minor), in *Kovo 20 diena* (March 20). Kaunas, 1921. Pages 48-62.

Yčas, Martynas. *Atsiminimai nepriklausomybės keliais* (Memoirs Along the Path of Independence). 3 vols. Kaunas, 1935.

——"Lietuvos vyriausybės sudarymo etapai ir jos pirmieji žingsniai" (The Stages of the Formation of the Lithuanian Government and Its First Steps), in *Pirmasis nepriklausomos Lietuvos dešimtmetis* (The First Decade of Independent Lithuania). London, 1954. Vol. 1, pp. 78-127.

——"Rusijos lietuvių pastangos kovose už Lietuvos nepriklausomybę" (The Efforts of the Russian Lithuanians in the Struggle for Lithuanian Independence), in *Pirmasis nepriklausomos Lietuvos dešimtmetis* (The First Decade of Independent Lithuania). London, 1954. Vol. I, pp. 7-32.

Žadeikis, Pranas. *Didžiojo karo užrašai* (Diary of the Great War). 2 vols. Memel, 1921-24.

Žiugžda, J. "Draugas J. V. Stalinas ir lietuvių tautos kova del nacionalinės nepriklausomybės" (Comrade J. V. Stalin and the Struggle of the Lithuanian Nation for National Independence), *Lietuvos Istorijos Instituto Darbai* (Works of the Lithuanian Institute of History) (Vilna), I (1951), 5-41.

Zoltowski, Adam. *Border of Europe*. London, 1950.

NEWSPAPERS AND PERIODICALS

Baltische Blätter (Berlin), 1919.
Der Bund (Bern), 1918-19.
Darbo Balsas (The Voice of Labor) (Vilna), 1918.
Dziennik Narodowy (National Daily) (Piotrkow), 1918.
Echo Litwy (Echo of Lithuania) (Vilna), 1919.
Frankfurter Zeitung, 1918-20.
Izvestiia (News) (Moscow), 1918-20.
Journal des Débats (Paris), 1919.
Komunistas (Communist) (Vilna and Smolensk), 1918-20.
Kurjer Polski (Polish Courier) (Warsaw), 1918-20.
Laisvé (Freedom) (Kaunas), 1919.
Lietuva (Lithuania) (Kaunas), 1919.
Lietuvių Balsas (Lithuanian Voice) (Petrograd and Voronezh), 1917-
    18.
Manchester Guardian, 1918-20.
Monitor Polski (Polish Monitor) (Warsaw), 1918-20.
Nepriklausomoji Lietuva (Independent Lithuania) (Vilna), 1919.
Naród (Nation) (Warsaw), 1920.
Das Neue Litauen (Berlin), 1917-18.
Neue Zürcher Zeitung (Zurich), 1918-20.
New York Times, 1918-20.
Polnische Pressestimmen (Breslau), 1919-20.
Die Post (Berlin), 1918-19.
Pravda (Truth) (Moscow), 1918-20.
Przełom (Turning Point) (Warsaw), 1918-19.
Le Temps (Paris), 1918-20.
The Times (London), 1918-20.
Vienybė Lietuvninkų (Unity of Lithuanians) (Brooklyn, N. Y.), 1918-
    20.
Vyriausbybės Žinios (Government News) (Vilna and Kaunas), 1918-
    20.
Waldibas Wehstnesis (Government News) (Riga), 1919-20.

Index

Agrarian question in Lithuania, 5, 72, 79-82, 84, 104, 207, 222, 226, 228-29, 231-32

Alekna, Juozas, 210

Aleksa-Angarietis, Zigmas, 63, 64, 79-80

Alexander-Sinclair, Edwyn S., 59

Allied missions to Baltic area, 97-98, 228; *see also* individual missions, e.g., American Commission in the Baltic Provinces

American Commission in the Baltic Provinces, 97, 124, 180, 228

American Liquidation Commission, 135-136

American Lithuanian brigade, 127, 166, 196-97

American Lithuanians: Catholics and Tautininkai, 16; attitude toward Lithuanian question after outbreak of First World War, 22; at Lausanne conference, 38; recognition of Lithuanian independence, 56, 93; Lithuanian delegation at Paris Peace Conference and, 88, 89, 89*n*, 90; financial aid and medical supplies, 125, 136*n*, 206-7; difficulties of, derived from nonrecognition of Lithuania by United States, 181-82

American Red Cross, 97-98

Amerikos Lietuvių Tautinė Taryba, 23

Angarietis, Zigmas Aleksa-, *see* Aleksa-Angarietis, Zigmas

Annexation of Lithuania to Poland, question of; Dmowski's activities in favor of, 44; adoption of program by Polish National Committee at Paris, 94-95; debates in Polish Constituent Assembly, 101; currents for, in Poland, 111, 191, 223-24

Armistice, provision regarding withdrawal of German troops, 53

Aušra (Lithuanian newspaper), 12

Baden, Max von, 39, 40

Bakhmetev, White Russian representative in Washington, D. C., 163, 180, 181

Balfour, Arthur James, 133-34, 142-43

Baltic states: Entente attitude toward question of recognition of, 56, 140-41; political and economic relations among, 86, 192, 195, 204; program of Russian Political Conference for, 95; lifting of blockade of Baltic Sea, 97; formation and functions of Commission on Baltic Affairs, 122-23; plans for union of, 138-39, 153; favorable attitude of Western powers toward autonomous position within Russia, 140; relations with Bolshevik Russia and peace negotiations, 151, 154-57, 165, 169, 193, 202, 222; Riga conference (*1919*), 153-55; joint appeal for recognition to Paris Peace Conference, 157-58; *de facto* recognition by Great Britain, 164-65; White Russians' policy toward, 165, 183-84; Tartu conference (Nov. 9, *1919*), 193; Helsinki conference (*1920*), 201-3; Warsaw conference (*1920*), 203

Balutis, Kazys, 178

Banga (German trade organization), 77

Basanavičius, Jonas, 8, 12, 70

Bavaria, opposition to union of Lithuania with Prussia, 36

Beliny-Prazmowski, Lieut. Col., 105

Belorussia, First Congress of Soviets of, 81

Belorussians in Lithuania: participation in Lithuanian government, 26, 49,

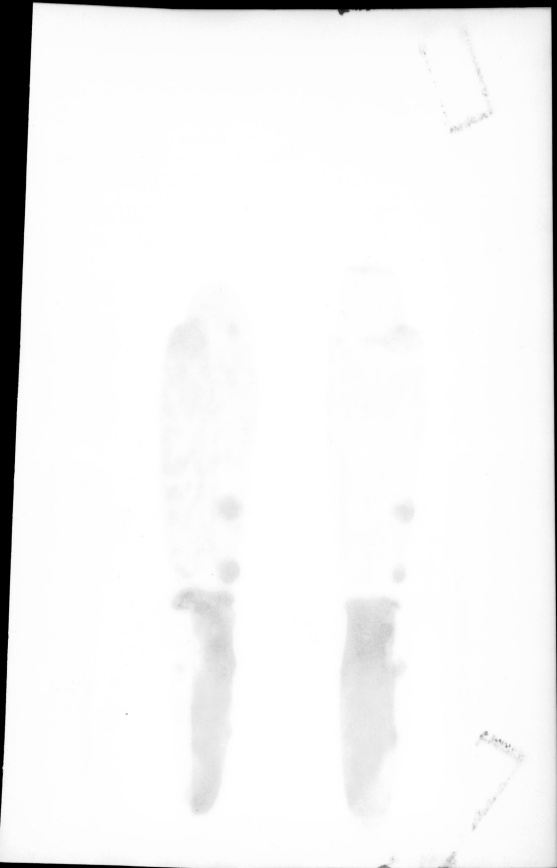

DATE DUE	

GAYLORD

PRINTED IN U.S.A.